Extravagant Strangers

Caryl Phillips was born in St Kitts, West Indies. Brought up in England, he has written for television, radio, theatre and cinema. He is the author of one book of non-fiction, *The European Tribe*, and six novels, *The Final Passage, A State of Independence, Higher Ground, Cambridge, Crossing the River* and *The Nature of Blood*. His awards include the Martin Luther King Memorial Prize, a Guggenheim Fellowship and a James Tait Black Memorial Prize. He divides his time between London and New York.

Extravagant Strangers

A Literature of Belonging

Edited by
CARYL PHILLIPS

faber and faber

First published in 1997
by Faber and Faber Limited
3 Queen Square London WC1N 3AU
This paperback edition first published in 1998

Photoset by Parker Typesetting Service, Leicester
Printed and bound in Great Britain by
Mackays of Chatham PLC, Chatham, Kent

This anthology © Caryl Phillips, 1997

Caryl Phillips is hereby identified as editor of this work
in accordance with Section 77 of the Copyright,
Designs and Patents Act 1988

A CIP record for this book
is available from the British Library

ISBN 0-571-19240-8

2 4 6 8 10 9 7 5 3 1

For Aziza and Radhiyyah

Your daughter, if you have not given her leave,
I say again, hath made a gross revolt;
Tying her duty, beauty, wit and fortunes
In an extravagant and wheeling stranger
Of here and every where.

Othello, Act 1 Scene 1

Contents

Editor's Note

This anthology would have been impossible for me to complete without the help of two remarkable people, Ming Nagel and Nalini Jones, who worked tirelessly on this project, searching libraries, following my often badly expressed hunches, deciphering my always impossible handwriting and dealing with many publishers, agents and authors. I am fortunate to have had the experience of working with two such assistants and I thank them wholeheartedly.

I have sought the advice and enlisted the help of various other people during the editing of this volume. My thanks to Helen Anglos, Fiona Carpenter, Frédéric Constant, Maura Dooley, Margaret Drabble, Georgia Garrett, Michael Gorra, Antony Harwood, Maya Jaggi, Suzannah Lucas, the librarians of Amherst College, Julian Loose, Frank Pike, Bill Pritchard, Jo Shapcott and Marina Warner.

Preface

I conceived of this anthology during a period as writer-in-residence at a university in Singapore. The head of my department asked me to give a lecture, and among the suggested topics was a familiar one. Would I be interested in addressing the phenomenon of the recent wave of writing by 'outsiders' to Britain which is 'reinvigorating' the canon? I bristled at the implication that before this 'recent wave' there was a 'pure' English literature, untainted by the influence of outsiders. To my way of thinking, English literature has, for at least 200 years, been shaped and influenced by outsiders.

As I thought more about this subject, it occurred to me that to compile and edit an anthology of writing by British writers who are outsiders in the most clear-cut way – those not born in Britain – might illustrate my point. I left Singapore and returned to Britain, whereupon I began to collect and read works by authors who fitted my brief. An organizing theme soon began to emerge around the vexing question of 'belonging'. The once great colonial power that is Britain has always sought to define her people, and by extension the nation itself, by identifying those who don't belong. As a result, Britain has developed a vision of herself as a nation that is both culturally and ethnically homogeneous, and this vision has made it difficult for some Britons to feel that they have the right to participate fully in the main narrative of British life.

The truth is, of course, that Britain has been forged in the crucible of fusion – of hybridity. Over the centuries, British life at all levels – its royal family, the nation's musical heritage, Parliament, military, sport, entertainment and the City – has been invigorated and to some extent defined by the heterogeneous nature that is the national condition. However, in the face of overwhelming evidence, the mythology of homogeneity not only exists but endures. Daniel Defoe's late-seventeenth-century poem 'The True-born Englishman' defines the mongrelized 'mixtures' that underpin the heterogeneous British tradition.

The Scot, Pict, Briton, Roman, Dane, submit,
And with the English-Saxon all unite;
And these the mixtures have so close pursued,
The very name and memory's subdued.
No Roman now, no Briton does remain . . .
Fate jumbled them together, God knows how;
Whate'er they were, they're true-born English now.

Defoe's satirical work was levelled against the English for their mistreatment of the Dutch who arrived in Britain with William III. In the 300 years since it was written, one can add to Defoe's 'mixtures' the Pole, American, Nigerian, Jamaican, Hungarian, Indian, Trinidadian, German and so on. In many ways, this anthology is an attempt to illustrate what Defoe perceived all those years ago: that British society has always been a melting pot of diverse cultural influences, and her heterogeneous condition runs very deep.

For British writers not born in Britain, the question of 'belonging' surfaces in their work in a variety of ways. Depending upon race, class and gender, the degree to which they feel alienated from British society will differ, and these variables will, of course, be further complicated by factors of time and historical circumstances. However, out of the tension between the individual and his or her society – in this case, British – the finest writing is often produced, and this would certainly seem to have been the case with reference to the work collected in this anthology. In their many different ways, all of the writers here are seeking to understand how they 'belong' to Britain.

The first group in the anthology comprises the black writers who emerged in the wake of the slave trade. Best exemplified by Olaudah Equiano, they grappled not only with the ethnic difficulties of belonging but also with linguistic problems. They were succeeded by

a group of writers who were born in British colonies and were keen,
if not altogether contented, observers of Britain. William Thackeray
stands at the head of this nineteenth- and early-twentieth-century
tradition, and to his name can be added those of Rudyard Kipling
and George Orwell. The colonial subjects among whom these writers
were born eventually began to express themselves in literature. These
'subject' writers, who betray a deep desire to 'belong' to the mother
country, are primarily represented here by Caribbean migrants to
Britain, C. L. R. James being the pre-eminent figure, along with
writers such as Samuel Selvon and V. S. Naipaul.

In the second half of the twentieth century, the legacy of empire
has produced writing by both descendants of the colonizers and
descendants of the colonized. The former are represented by writers
such as Jean Rhys, Doris Lessing, Penelope Lively and William Boyd,
and the latter by Salman Rushdie, Linton Kwesi Johnson and Ben
Okri among others. All of these, whether colonizers or colonized,
seem to be carrying a freight of expectation with regard to Britain,
and their various anxieties are reflected in the extracts here.

Standing somewhat apart from these groupings is a category that
includes writers such as T. S. Eliot, George Szirtes and Kazuo
Ishiguro, whose work exhibits an often microscopic concern with the
nature of Britishness. Although these writers' lives are unencumbered
by the trappings of empire, it is clear that the powerful traditions of
Britain exert a strong hold over their imaginations. Finally, there are
the writers who, armed with the English language, appear to have
moved to the literary centre in order to take part in a cosmopolitan
world that is free from the difficulties of either geographical
marginalization or political turbulence. Katherine Mansfield, Peter
Porter and Christopher Hope would seem to fall into this group.

For many British people, to accept the idea that their country has a
long and complex history of immigration would be to undermine
their basic understanding of what it means to be British. One of my
hopes in compiling and editing this anthology is that by engaging
with the following writers and their work, readers will come to
accept that as soon as one defines oneself as 'British' one is

participating in a centuries-old tradition of cultural exchange, of ethnic and linguistic plurality, as one might expect from a proud nation that could once boast she ruled most of the known world. The evidence collected here confirms that one of the fortuitous by-products of this heterogeneous history has been a vigorous and dynamic literature.

Caryl Phillips,
September 1996

Extravagant Strangers

Ukawsaw Gronniosaw

[1710–death unknown]

Ukawsaw Gronniosaw was born in Bornu, in the north-eastern tip of modern Nigeria. No biographical information exists on him apart from what is provided in his own *Narrative*, which was published in 1770. There we learn that he was born into an affluent family, his mother being the oldest daughter of the reigning king of Bornu; Gronniosaw was the youngest of six children. Due to his naturally inquisitive mind and his increasing dissatisfaction with family life in Bornu, Gronniosaw had decided to leave home by the time he was a teenager. He travelled with an ivory merchant to the coast of Africa but, on arrival, was betrayed. Sold into slavery, he passed into the hands of the captain of a Dutch ship bound for Barbados. In Barbados, Gronniosaw was sold on to a man from New England named Vanhorn who took him back to his home in New York as his servant. Among the visitors to his house was a minister called Mr Freelandhouse, who, taking a particular interest in Gronniosaw's growing sense of God, bought him and set about teaching him the ways of Christianity.

Upon Freelandhouse's death, Gronniosaw was granted his freedom. Inspired by an English minister, Mr Whitfield, whom he had heard preach in New York, Gronniosaw looked to England as his future home. Within days of arriving in Portsmouth, he was the victim of thieves. A disillusioned Gronniosaw headed for London, where he sought out his associate Mr Whitfield, who in turn helped him to find and pay for lodgings in Petticoat Lane, east London. Soon after, he left and spent a year in Amsterdam, but by 1763 or so Gronniosaw had returned to England to marry Betty, a weaver he had met in London. Before the wedding he was baptized by the eminent Baptist theologian Dr Andrew Gifford. Gronniosaw and Betty had three children.

The final section of Gronniosaw's *Narrative* paints a graphic picture of the family's decline into poverty in England. They were frequently near to starvation and eventually one of the children died. When a clergyman refused to bury his dead child, Gronniosaw's otherwise cautious tone of humility in the *Narrative* becomes empowered by an underlying rage.

Gronniosaw's account, although related by himself, was 'committed to paper by the elegant pen of a young lady of the town of Leominster'. The reader cannot be certain whether the tone of humility that pervades the piece comes from the writer or from Gronniosaw himself. Nevertheless, the account marks an important beginning in the genre of slave narrative, and it is likely that those who went on to develop this form – principally Olaudah Equiano – would have read Gronniosaw's story.

Gronniosaw is typical of early black writers in Britain in his somewhat naïve faith that the country will redeem him from the miseries of servitude and slavery. In the following extract from his autobiographical Narrative *(1770), we witness him passing through the uncomfortable stage in which his faith in the English is shattered, before beginning the difficult process of reconciling himself to a more realistic view of his new countrymen as individuals tainted by all the vices that are common to humanity.*

The Shortcomings of Christian England

I never knew how to set a proper value on money. If I had but a little meat and drink to supply the present necessities of life, I never wished for more; and when I had any, I always gave it where I saw an object in distress. If it was not for my dear wife and children, I should pay as little regard to money now as I did at that time. I continued some time with Mr Dunscum as his servant, and he was very kind to me. But I had a vast inclination to visit England, and wished continually that it would please Providence to make a clear way for me to see this island. I entertained a notion that if I could get to England, I should never more experience either cruelty or ingratitude; so that I was very desirous to get among Christians. I knew Mr Whitfield very well. I had often heard him preach at New York. In this disposition I enlisted in the 28th regiment of foot, who were designed for Martinico, in the late war. We went in Admiral Pocock's fleet from New York to Barbados, and from thence to Martinico. When that was taken, we proceeded to the Havannah, and took that place likewise. There I got discharged. I was at that time worth about thirty pounds, but I never regarded money in the least. I would not tarry for my prize-money, lest I should lose my chance of going to England. I went with the Spanish prisoners to Spain, and came to Old England with the English prisoners. I cannot describe my joy when we arrived within sight of Portsmouth. But I was astonished, when we landed, to hear the inhabitants of that place curse and swear, and be otherwise profane. I expected to find nothing but goodness, gentleness, and meekness in this Christian land, and I suffered great perplexity of mind at seeing so much wickedness.

I inquired if any serious Christian people resided there, and the woman I made the inquiry of answered me in the affirmative, and added that she was one of them. I was heartily glad to hear her say so. I thought I could give her my whole heart. She kept a public house. I deposited with her all the money that I had not an immediate occasion for, as I thought it would be safer with her. I gave her twenty-five guineas, six of which I desired her to lay out to the best advantage, in buying me some shirts, a hat, and some other necessaries. I made her a present of a very handsome large looking-glass that I brought with me from Martinico, in order to recompense her for the trouble I had given her. I must do this woman the justice to acknowledge that she did lay out some little for my use, but the nineteen guineas, and part of the six guineas, with my watch, she would not return, but denied that I ever gave them to her.

I soon perceived that I had got amongst bad people, who defrauded me of money and watch, and that all my promised happiness was blasted. I had no friend but God, and I prayed to him earnestly. I could scarcely believe it possible that the place where so many eminent Christians had lived and preached could abound with so much wickedness and deceit. I thought it worse than Sodom, considering the great advantage they possessed. I cried like a child, and that almost continually. At length God heard my prayers, and raised me up a friend indeed.

This publican had a brother who lived on Portsmouth Common, whose wife was a very serious, good woman. When she heard of the treatment I had met with, she came and inquired into my real situation, and was greatly troubled at the ill-usage I had received, and she took me home to her own house. I now began to rejoice, and my prayer was turned into praise. She made use of all the arguments in her power to prevail upon her who had wronged me to return my watch and money, but it was to no purpose, as she had given me no receipt, and I had nothing to show for it; so that I could not demand it. My good friend was excessively angry with her, and obliged her to give me back four guineas, which she said she gave me out of charity, though, in fact, it was my own, and a great deal more. She would have employed other means to oblige her to give up my money, but I would not suffer her. 'Let it go,' said I; 'my God is in heaven.' I did not mind my loss in the least. All that grieved me was that I had been disappointed in finding some Christian friends, with whom I hoped to enjoy a little sweet and comfortable society.

I thought the best method that I could take now was to go to London, and find out Mr Whitfield, who was the only living soul that I knew in England, and get him to direct me how to procure a living without being troublesome to any person. I took leave of my Christian friends at Portsmouth, and went in the stage to London. A creditable tradesman in the city, who went up with me in the stage, offered to show me the way to Mr Whitfield's tabernacle, knowing that I was a perfect stranger. I thought it very kind, and accepted his offer; but he obliged me to give him half-a-crown for going with me, and likewise insisted on my giving him five shillings more for conducting me to Dr Gifford's meeting.

I began now to entertain a very different idea of the inhabitants of England to what I had figured to myself before I came among them. Mr Whitfield received me very friendly, was heartily glad to see me, and directed me to a proper place to board and lodge, in Petticoat-lane, till he could think of some way to settle me in, and paid for my lodging, and all my expenses. The morning after I came to my new lodgings, as I was at breakfast with the gentlewoman of the house, I heard the noise of some looms over our heads, and upon inquiring what it was, she told me that a person was weaving silk. I expressed a great desire to see it, and asked if I might. She told me that she would go up with me, for she was sure that I should be very welcome; and she was as good as her word. As soon as we entered the room, the person that was weaving looked about and smiled upon us, and I loved her from that moment. She asked me many questions, and I, in return, talked a great deal to her. I found that she was a member of Mr Allen's meeting, and I began to entertain a good opinion of her, though I was almost afraid to indulge this inclination, lest she should prove like the rest that I had met with, at Portsmouth, &c., and which had almost given me a dislike to all white women. But after a short acquaintance, I had the happiness to find that she was very different, and quite sincere, and I was not without hopes that she entertained some esteem for me. We often went together to hear Dr Gifford. As I had always a propensity to relieve every object in distress as far as I was able, I used to give to all that complained to me, sometimes half a guinea at a time, as I did not understand the real value of it. But this good woman took great pains to correct and advise me in that and many other respects.

After I had been in London about six weeks, I was recommended to the notice of some acquaintances of my late master, Mr Freeland-house, who had heard him speak frequently of me. I was much persuaded by them to go to Holland, as my master lived there before he bought me, and he used to speak of me so respectfully among his friends there that it raised in them a curiosity to see me, particularly the gentlemen engaged in the ministry, who expressed a desire to hear my experience and to examine me. I found that it was my good old master's design that I should have gone if he had lived, for which reason I resolved upon going to Holland, and informed my dear friend Mr Whitfield of my intention. He was much averse to my going at first; but after I gave him my reasons he appeared very well satisfied. I likewise informed my Betty (the good woman that I have just named) of my determination to go to Holland, and told her I believed she was to be my wife; and if it was the Lord's will I desired it, but not else. She made me very little answer, but has since told me that she did not think it at that time.

Ignatius Sancho
[1729–80]

Ignatius Sancho was born on board a slave ship sailing from the Guinea coast to the West Indies. During the voyage, both his parents died. At the age of two he was brought to England from the West Indies and passed into the hands of three maiden sisters in Greenwich, south London. The women, as Sancho later wrote in a letter to the novelist Laurence Sterne, 'judged Ignorance the best and only security for obedience'. By chance, at the age of twenty, Sancho met the Duke of Montagu in the Greenwich area. The Duke, well known for his views against slavery and racism, was attracted to Sancho's spirit, as yet unbroken by servitude, and he decided to make him his protégé. He allowed him to borrow books and secured for him the education that Sancho's mistresses had wilfully denied him.

When the Duke died in 1749, Sancho unlawfully fled from the three sisters and took service with the Duchess of Montagu. Two years later, the Duchess died, leaving Sancho a considerable amount of money. However, this he soon squandered on gambling and women, and he returned to service with the Montagu family. During the years that Sancho served them, he gained the admiration of many people, such as Samuel Johnson, Laurence Sterne and the actor David Garrick. It was through these friendships that Sancho developed his passion for the theatre and the arts. Respected for his solid judgement in these fields, he befriended musicians, painters and sculptors, attempted acting and wrote music, some of which still survives. Gainsborough made him the subject of a portrait, and it is thought that he is depicted in one of Hogarth's paintings. Sancho married Anne, a West Indian woman, and had six children. By 1773, overweight and suffering from gout, he was no longer physically able to work as a servant and so he opened a grocery business in London's Mayfair.

Having spent most of his life in a relatively secure middle-class environment, Sancho's letters (published as *Letters of the Late Ignatius Sancho*, 1782) show him to be the most integrated of the black British writers in England at that time. His near contemporaries such as Equiano had begun their lives in Africa, but Sancho had no direct memories of his homeland, nor had he suffered to the same extent under slavery. While these writers had obtained their inspiration and unique style through personal suffering, Sancho owed much of his style to the fashion of the circles he moved in. The sentimentality of a writer such as Sterne was well suited to Sancho's favourite subject, domestic life. However, when writing on topics such as British politics and the abolition of slavery, Sancho's 'Britishness' becomes mixed with an ironic sense of his own detachment. In one instance, he describes himself as 'only a lodger [in England] – and hardly that'; clearly he is always aware of himself as an African in England. Nevertheless, Sancho remains the most urbane and mannered of those of African descent who were writing in Britain in the eighteenth century.

Sancho's letters, while never descending to protestation, are often mildy critical of his adopted country. At the same time, they exhibit a desperate need to belong. Such a need is clearly displayed in the following letter to Laurence Sterne, which, while praising Sterne as a novelist in general and as somebody who has spoken out against slavery in particular, begs him to do more to help Sancho's 'miserable black brethren'.

To Mr Sterne

July, 1776

REVEREND SIR,
It would be an insult on your humanity (or perhaps look like it) to apologize for the liberty I am taking. – I am one of those people whom the vulgar and illiberal call 'Negurs.' – The first part of my life was rather unlucky, as I was placed in a family who judged ignorance the best and only security for obedience. – A little reading and writing I got by unwearied application. – The latter part of my life has been – thro' God's blessing, truly fortunate, having spent it in the service of one of the best families in the kingdom. – My chief pleasure has been books. – Philanthropy I adore. – How very much, good Sir, am I (amongst millions) indebted to you for the character

of your amiable uncle Toby! – I declare, I would walk ten miles in the dog-days, to shake hands with the honest corporal. – Your Sermons have touch'd me to the heart, and I hope have amended it, which brings me to the point. – In your tenth discourse, page seventy-eight, in the second volume – is the very affecting passage – 'Consider how great a part of our species – in all ages down to this – have been trod under the feet of cruel and capricious tyrants, who would neither hear their cries, nor pity their distresses, – Consider slavery – what it is – how bitter a draught and how many millions are made to drink it!' – Of all my favourite authors, not one has drawn a tear in favour of my miserable black brethren – excepting yourself, and the humane author of Sir George Ellison. – I think you will forgive me; – I am sure you will applaud me for beseeching you to give one half-hour's attention to slavery, as it is at this day practised in our West Indies. – That subject, handled in your striking manner, would ease the yoke (perhaps) of many – but if only of one – Gracious God! – what a feast to a benevolent heart! – and, sure I am, you are an epicurean in acts of charity. – You, who are universally read, and as universally admired – you could not fail – Dear Sir, think in me you behold the uplifted hands of thousands of my brother Moors. – Grief you pathetically observe is eloquent; – figure to yourself their attitudes; – hear their supplicating addresses! – alas! – you cannot refuse. – Humanity must comply – in which hope I beg permission to subscribe myself,

Reverend Sir, &c.

IGN. SANCHO

Olaudah Equiano

[1745–97]

Olaudah Equiano was born in an Igbo village, Essaka, probably the present-day Iseke in Nigeria. Kidnapped at the age of eleven by Africans, he was sold to white slave traders. He travelled to Barbados, then to Virginia, where he was purchased by an English naval officer, Michael Pascal. In 1759, he was baptized and renamed Gustavus Vasa. He served Pascal for many years, mixing with British families and benefiting from an education both on and off the ship. Equiano was therefore bitterly disappointed when Pascal unexpectedly sold him back into American slavery. Stirred by this move, and now working on the merchant ships of his new owner, Equiano began trading for himself, gradually earning enough money to buy back his freedom.

As a free man, his voyages continued: to the Arctic as an assistant to a surgeon, to the Mediterranean as a manservant to an English traveller and to Central America, where he spent six months among the Miskito Indians. Eventually he settled in England, where he became a leading spokesman for the black population in London, contributing greatly to the fight for abolition. In 1787, he was appointed commissary for stores to the expedition that was to return many freed slaves to a new settlement at Freetown in Sierra Leone, but he was dismissed after disagreements with the organizers before the expedition left England. He was now free to complete his autobiography, already several years in the making.

Published in London in 1789, *The Interesting Narrative of the Life of Olaudah Equiano, or Gustavus Vasa the African, written by himself* was a bestseller. It went into eight British editions, as well as an American edition (1791), and was translated into Dutch (1790), German (1792) and Russian (1794). It continued to be read after his death, going into many more editions in the first half of the nineteenth century. Although Ukawsaw Gronniosaw's *Narrative* had already been published, Equiano's work, being written in the author's own hand, was thus the first authentic account in English of the life of an African slave.

In 1792, after the publication of his book, Equiano married Susannah Cullen of Soham, Cambridge. He then travelled widely throughout Britain, selling copies of the book and speaking publicly against slavery. He also became a regular contributor of letters and reviews to the *Public Advertiser*.

By the time of his death in 1797, Equiano had become a relatively prosperous moneylender. The fruits of his estate went to his sole surviving daughter, Johanna. His wife had died two years earlier and his four-year-old second daughter, Anna Maria, died just months after Equiano himself.

Equiano came of age at a time when the lobby for the abolition of slavery in British possessions was becoming increasingly powerful. He not only had a platform from which to speak but also displayed outstanding skills as a writer. He was able to help his contemporaries understand what it meant to be culturally an outsider from British society, and in the extract from his autobiography that follows he offers some insight into the difficulties faced by a newcomer who does not fully understand the English language.

Voyage to England

I stayed in this island for a few days; I believe it could not be above a fortnight; when I and some few more slaves, that were not saleable amongst the rest, from very much fretting, were shipped off in a sloop for North America. On the passage we were better treated than when we were coming from Africa, and we had plenty of rice and fat pork. We were landed up a river a good way from the sea, about Virginia county, where we saw few or none of our native Africans, and not one soul who could talk to me. I was a few weeks weeding grass, and gathering stones in a plantation; and at last all my companions were distributed different ways, and only myself was left. I was now exceedingly miserable, and thought myself worse off than any of the rest of my companions; for they could talk to each other, but I had no person to speak to that I could understand. In this

state I was constantly grieving and pining, and wishing for death
rather than any thing else. While I was in this plantation the
gentleman, to whom I suppose the estate belonged, being unwell, I
was one day sent for to his dwelling house to fan him; when I came
into the room where he was I was very much affrighted at some
things I saw, and the more so as I had seen a black woman slave as I
came through the house, who was cooking the dinner, and the poor
creature was cruelly loaded with various kinds of iron machines; she
had one particularly on her head, which locked her mouth so fast
that she could scarcely speak; and could not eat nor drink. I was
much astonished and shocked at this contrivance, which I afterwards
learned was called the iron muzzle. Soon after I had a fan put into my
hand, to fan the gentleman while he slept; and so I did indeed with
great fear. While he was fast asleep I indulged myself a great deal in
looking about the room, which to me appeared very fine and curious.
The first object that engaged my attention was a watch which hung
on the chimney, and was going. I was quite surprised at the noise it
made, and was afraid it would tell the gentleman any thing I might
do amiss; and when I immediately after observed a picture hanging
in the room, which appeared constantly to look at me, I was still
more affrighted, having never seen such things as these before. At
one time I thought it was something relative to magic; and not seeing
it move I thought it might be some way the whites had to keep their
great men when they died, and offer them libation as we used to do
to our friendly spirits. In this state of anxiety I remained till my
master awoke, when I was dismissed out of the room, to my no small
satisfaction and relief; for I thought that these people were all made
up of wonders. In this place I was called Jacob; but on board the
African ship I was called Michael. I had been some time in this
miserable, forlorn, and much dejected state, without having any one
to talk to, which made my life a burden, when the kind and
unknown hand of the Creator (who in very deed leads the blind in a
way they know not) now began to appear, to my comfort; for one
day the captain of a merchant ship, called the Industrious Bee, came
on some business to my master's house. This gentleman, whose name

was Michael Henry Pascal, was a lieutenant in the royal navy, but now commanded this trading ship, which was somewhere in the confines of the county many miles off. While he was at my master's house it happened that he saw me, and liked me so well that he made a purchase of me. I think I have often heard him say he gave thirty or forty pounds sterling for me; but I do not now remember which. However, he meant me for a present to some of his friends in England: and I was sent accordingly from the house of my then master, one Mr Campbell, to the place where the ship lay; I was conducted on horseback by an elderly black man, (a mode of travelling which appeared very odd to me). When I arrived I was carried on board a fine large ship, loaded with tobacco, &c. and just ready to sail for England. I now thought my condition much mended; I had sails to lie on, and plenty of good victuals to eat; and every body on board used me very kindly, quite contrary to what I had seen of any white people before; I therefore began to think that they were not all of the same disposition. A few days after I was on board we sailed for England. I was still at a loss to conjecture my destiny. By this time, however, I could smatter a little imperfect English; and I wanted to know as well as I could where we were going. Some of the people of the ship used to tell me they were going to carry me back to my own country, and this made me very happy. I was quite rejoiced at the sound of going back; and thought if I should get home what wonders I should have to tell. But I was reserved for another fate, and was soon undeceived when we came within sight of the English coast. While I was on board this ship, my captain and master named me *Gustavus Vasa*. I at that time began to understand him a little, and refused to be called so, and told him as well as I could that I would be called Jacob; but he said I should not, and still called me Gustavus; and when I refused to answer to my new name, which at first I did, it gained me many a cuff; so at length I submitted, and was obliged to bear the present name, by which I have been known ever since. The ship had a very long passage; and on that account we had very short allowance of provisions. Towards the last we had only one pound and a half of bread per week, and about the same quantity of meat, and one quart of water a day. We spoke with only one vessel the whole time we were at sea, and but once we caught a few fishes. In our extremities the captain and people told me in jest they would kill and eat me; but I thought them in earnest, and was depressed beyond measure, expecting every moment to be my last. While I was in this situation one evening they caught, with a good deal of trouble, a large shark, and got it on board. This gladdened my poor heart exceedingly, as I thought it would serve the people to eat instead of their eating me; but very soon, to my astonishment, they cut off a small part of the tail, and tossed the rest over the side. This renewed my consternation; and I did not know what to think of these white people, though I very much feared they would kill and eat me. There was on board the ship a young lad who had never been at sea before, about four or five years older than myself: his name was Richard Baker. He was a native of America, had received an excellent education, and was of a most amiable temper. Soon after I went on board he shewed me a great deal of partiality and attention, and in return I grew extremely fond of him. We at length became inseparable; and, for the space of two years, he was of very great use to me, and was my constant companion and instructor. Although this dear youth had many slaves of his own, yet he and I have gone through many sufferings together on shipboard; and we have many nights lain in each other's bosoms when we were in great distress. Thus such a friendship was cemented between us as we cherished till his death, which, to my very great sorrow, happened in the year 1759, when he was up the Archipelago, on board his majesty's ship the Preston: an event which I have never ceased to regret, as I lost at once a kind interpreter, an agreeable companion, and a faithful friend; who, at the age of fifteen, discovered a mind superior to prejudice; and who was not ashamed to notice, to associate with, and to be the friend and instructor of one who was ignorant, a stranger, of a different complexion, and a slave! My master had lodged in his mother's house in America: he respected him very much, and made him always eat with him in the cabin. He used often to tell him jocularly that he would kill me to eat.

Sometimes he would say to me – the black people were not good to eat, and would ask me if we did not eat people in my country. I said, No: then he said he would kill Dick (as he always called him) first, and afterwards me. Though this hearing relieved my mind a little as to myself, I was alarmed for Dick and whenever he was called I used to be very much afraid he was to be killed; and I would peep and watch to see if they were going to kill him: nor was I free from this consternation till we made the land. One night we lost a man over-board; and the cries and noise were so great and confused, in stopping the ship, that I, who did not know what was the matter, began, as usual, to be very much afraid, and to think they were going to make an offering with me, and perform some magic; which I still believed they dealt in. As the waves were very high I thought the Ruler of the seas was angry, and I expected to be offered up to appease him. This filled my mind with agony, and I could not any more that night close my eyes again to rest. However, when daylight appeared I was a little eased in my mind; but still every time I was called I used to think it was to be killed. Some time after this we saw some very large fish, which I afterwards found were called grampusses. They looked to me extremely terrible, and made their appearance just at dusk; and were so near as to blow the water on the ship's deck. I believed them to be the rulers of the sea; and, as the white people did not make any offerings at any time, I thought they were angry with them: and, at last, what confirmed my belief was, the wind just then died away, and a calm ensued, and in consequence of it the ship stopped going. I supposed that the fish had performed this, and I hid myself in the fore part of the ship, through fear of being offered up to appease them, every minute peeping and quaking: but my good friend Dick came shortly towards me, and I took an opportunity to ask him, as well as I could, what these fish were. Not being able to talk much English, I could but just make him understand my question; and not at all, when I asked him if any offerings were to be made to them: however, he told me these fish would swallow any body; which sufficiently alarmed me. Here he was called away by the captain, who was leaning over the quarter-deck railing and looking at the fish; and most of the people were busied in getting a barrel of pitch to light, for them to play with. The captain now called me to him, having learned some of my apprehensions from Dick; and having diverted himself and others for some time with my fears, which appeared ludicrous enough in my crying and trembling, he dismissed me. The barrel of pitch was now lighted and put over the side into the water: by this time it was just dark, and the fish went after it; and, to my great joy, I saw them no more.

However, all my alarms began to subside when we got sight of land; and at last the ship arrived at Falmouth, after a passage of thirteen weeks. Every heart on board seemed gladdened on our reaching the shore, and none more than mine. The captain immediately went on shore, and sent on board some fresh provisions, which we wanted very much: we made good use of them, and our famine was soon turned into feasting, almost without ending. It was about the beginning of the spring 1757 when I arrived in England, and I was near twelve years of age at that time. I was very much struck with the buildings and the pavement of the streets in Falmouth; and, indeed, any object I saw filled me with new surprise. One morning, when I got upon deck, I saw it covered all over with the snow that fell over-night: as I had never seen any thing of the kind before, I thought it was salt; so I immediately ran down to the mate and desired him, as well as I could, to come and see how somebody in the night had thrown salt all over the deck. He, knowing what it was, desired me to bring some of it down to him: accordingly I took up a handful of it, which I found very cold indeed; and when I brought it to him he desired me to taste it. I did so, and I was surprised beyond measure. I then asked him what it was, he told me it was snow: but I could not in anywise understand him. He asked me if we had no such thing in my country; and I told him, No. I then asked him the use of it, and who made it; he told me a great man in the heavens, called God: but here again I was to all intents and purposes at a loss to understand him; and the more so, when a little after I saw the air filled with it, in a heavy shower, which fell down on the same day. After this I went to church; and having never been at such a place before, I was again amazed at seeing and hearing the service. I asked all I could about it; and they gave me to understand it was worshipping God, who made us and all things. I was still at a great loss, and soon got into an endless field of inquiries, as well as I was able to speak and ask about things. However, my little friend Dick used to be my best interpreter; for I could make free with him, and he always instructed me with pleasure: and from what I could understand by him of this God, and in seeing these white people did not sell one another, as we did, I was much pleased; and in this I thought they were much happier than we Africans. I was astonished at the wisdom of the white people in all things I saw; but was amazed at their not sacrificing; or making any offerings, and eating with unwashed hands, and touching the dead. I likewise could not help remarking the particular slenderness of their women, which I did not at first like; and I thought they were not so modest and shamefaced as the African women.

I had often seen my master and Dick employed in reading; and I had a great curiosity to talk to the books, as I thought they did; and so to learn how all things had a beginning: for that purpose I have often taken up a book, and have talked to it, and then put my ears to it, when alone, in hope it would answer me; and I have been very much concerned when I found it remained silent.

William Thackeray

[1811–63]

William Makepeace Thackeray was born in Calcutta, the only son of Anglo-Indian parents. In 1816 his father died and Thackeray was sent back to England, to live with his aunt, Mrs Ritchie, in Chiswick. He began his private education at Chiswick Mall, where he stayed until 1822, at which point his mother and stepfather returned to England. The family then moved to Addiscombe College, where his stepfather had been appointed governor, and Thackeray was sent to school at Charterhouse in Smithfield, London, where he stayed until 1828. He then entered Trinity College, Cambridge, but left after two years without taking a degree.

In 1829 a vacation to Paris secured a lifelong love of the city. After leaving Cambridge in 1830, he travelled to Germany and spent six months at Weimar, where he met Goethe. He returned to London in 1831 and spent a short time at law school. Then, having joined the *National Standard*, a newspaper with which his stepfather was connected, he travelled to Paris as a correspondent. The newspaper failed and, with most of his patrimony lost in the Indian bank failures of 1833, Thackeray turned to his skills as a caricaturist, studying art in Paris from 1834 to 1837. By 1835 he was contributing to *Fraser's Magazine*, and the following year he unsuccessfully applied to Dickens to illustrate *The Pickwick Papers*.

Struggling in his career as a painter, in 1836 Thackeray acquired a second appointment as a Paris correspondent, this time on the radical newspaper *The Constitutional*, which was set up by his stepfather. On the strength of this new position, that same year he was married to Isabella Shawe, the daughter of an expatriate Anglo-Irish family. The newspaper folded after only one year and in 1837 Thackeray returned to London. Forced to write for a living, he contributed various reviews and articles to *The Times* and serial works to *Fraser's Magazine*, including his first real novel, *Barry Lyndon* (1844). Between 1837 and 1840, his wife gave birth to three daughters. After the birth of the third, Mrs

Thackeray, who had been showing signs of insanity, had a complete breakdown and was confined. The children went to live with Thackeray's grandmother in Paris.

During the 1840s Thackeray's reputation grew. He published a series of travel books, but his popularity was largely due to his writings for *Punch*, which began in 1842 and lasted for ten years. These included the highly successful 'Book of Snobs' (1846–7), a series of sketches which characterized the class-consciousness of the early Victorian age. His satirization of the English upper middle classes continued in the parodies of 'Punch's Prize Novelists' (1847) and the anti-heroic vision of his first major serialized novel, *Vanity Fair* (1847–8). Following the success of *Vanity Fair*, Thackeray wrote the semi-autobiographical *The History of Pendennis* (1848–50). It was during this time that he was to have his first bout of serious ill-health.

By now Thackeray had installed himself, his daughters and his grandmother at a house in Kensington. In 1848 he began a platonic relationship with Jane Brookfield, the wife of a college friend, which she was to end in 1851. The signs of unfulfilled love show in *The History of Henry Esmond* (1852), a historical novel set during the reign of Queen Anne that reflected Thackeray's growing interest in the history of the eighteenth century. In 1851 Thackeray began his series of lectures on 'The English Humorists of the Eighteenth Century' (published under that title in 1853), which was to form the basis of a lucrative lecture tour of the United States in 1852–3. During his time in the United States Thackeray tried, without success, to acquire some sort of civil or diplomatic post. This was presumably an attempt to secure for himself a more steady income, as Thackeray always felt that his writing was based on financial rather than artistic necessity.

Back in England, he returned to his theme of English social life in *The Newcomes* (1853–5). Following the publication of *The Rose and the Ring* (1855), he went back to the United States for a second lecture tour, which was to become the basis for *The Four Georges* (1860).

Attempting to enter into politics in 1857, Thackeray stood for Oxford and was narrowly beaten. In 1859 he became the founding editor of *The Cornhill Magazine*, a monthly literary journal that achieved huge success. However, suffering from increasing ill-health, he had to give up the post in 1862. He published his last works in the journal, the short novel *Lovel the Widower* (1860) and *The Adventures of Philip* (1861–2), which were said by critics to be an unoriginal rehash of his earlier works on English society. He died on Christmas Eve in 1863, leaving his final novel, *Denis Duval* (1864), unfinished.

Thackeray's biting satire of English middle-class pretence and posturing permeates the greater part of both his fiction and his non-fiction. Over a century later, the great Trinidadian writer C. L. R. James could boast of having read Vanity Fair *at least half a dozen times before he was out of his teens. Thackeray's satire was applicable to colonial Trinidad, and in fact to most middle-class societies anywhere in the British Empire. However, Thackeray's concern with the hypocrisies of English society was born out of his own ambivalence towards his 'home'. The following essay, 'A Word about Dinners' from 'Book of Snobs' (1846), was one of several which sought to 'expose' English society.*

A Word about Dinners

English Society, my beloved Bob, has this eminent advantage over all other – that is, if there be any society left in the wretched distracted old European continent – that it is above all others a dinner-giving society. A people like the Germans, that dines habitually, and with what vast appetite I need not say, at one o'clock in the afternoon – like the Italians, that spends its evenings in opera-boxes – like the French, that amuses itself of nights with *eau sucrée* and intrigue – cannot, believe me, understand Society rightly. I love and admire my nation for its good sense, its manliness, its friendliness, its morality in the main – and these, I take it, are all expressed in that noble institution, the dinner.

The dinner is the happy end of the Briton's day. We work harder than the other nations of the earth. We do more, we live more in our time, than Frenchmen or Germans. Every great man amongst us likes his dinner, and takes to it kindly. I could mention the most august names of poets, statesmen, philosophers, historians, judges, and divines, who are great at the dinner-table as in the field, the closet, the senate, or the bench. Gibbon mentions that he wrote the first two volumes of his history whilst a placeman in London, lodging in St James's, going to the House of Commons, to the Club, and to dinner every day. The man flourishes under that generous and robust regimen; the healthy energies of society are kept up by it; our friendly intercourse is maintained; our intellect ripens with the good cheer, and throws off surprising crops, like the fields about Edinburgh, under the influence of that admirable liquid, Claret. The best wines are sent to this country therefore; for no other deserves them as ours does.

I am a diner-out, and live in London. I protest, as I look back at the men and dinners I have seen in the last week, my mind is filled with manly respect and pleasure. How good they have been! how admirable the entertainments! how worthy the men!

Let me, without divulging names, and with a cordial gratitude, mention a few of those whom I have met and who have all done their duty.

Sir, I have sat at table with a great, a world-renowned statesman. I watched him during the progress of the banquet – I am at liberty to say that he enjoyed it like a man.

On another day, it was a celebrated literary character. It was beautiful to see him at his dinner: cordial and generous, jovial and kindly, the great author enjoyed himself as the great statesman – may he long give us good books and good dinners!

Yet another day, and I sat opposite to a Right Reverend Bishop. My Lord, I was pleased to see good thing after good thing disappear before you; and think no man ever better became that rounded episcopal apron. How amiable he was! how kind! He put water into his wine. Let us respect the moderation of the Church.

And then the men learned in the law: how they dine! what hospitality, what splendour, what comfort, what wine! As we walked away very gently in the moonlight, only three days since, from the —'s, a friend of my youth and myself, we could hardly speak for gratitude: 'Dear sir,' we breathed fervently, 'ask us soon again.' One never has too much at those perfect banquets – no hideous headaches ensue, or horrid resolutions about adopting Revalenta Arabica for the future – but contentment with all the world, light slumbering, joyful waking to grapple with the morrow's work. Ah, dear Bob, those lawyers have great merits. There is a dear old judge at whose family table if I could see you seated, my desire in life would be pretty nearly fulfilled. If you make yourself agreeable there, you will be in a fair way to get on in the world. But you are a youth still. Youths go to balls: men go to dinners.

Doctors, again, notoriously eat well; when my excellent friend Sangrado takes a bumper, and saying, with a shrug and a twinkle of his eye, '*Video meliora proboque, deteriora sequor,*' tosses off the wine, I always ask the butler for a glass of that bottle.

The inferior clergy, likewise, dine very much and well. I don't know when I have been better entertained, as far as creature comforts go, than by men of very Low Church principles; and one of the very best repasts that ever I saw in my life was at Darlington, given by a Quaker.

Some of the best wine in London is given to his friends by a poet of my acquaintance. All artists are notoriously fond of dinners, and invite you, but not so profusely. Newspaper-editors delight in dinners on Saturdays, and give them, thanks to the present position of Literature, very often and good. Dear Bob, I have seen the mahoganies of many men.

Every evening between seven and eight o'clock, I like to look at the men dressed for dinner, perambulating the western districts of our city. I like to see the smile on their countenances lighted up with an indescribable self-importance and good-humour; the askance glances which they cast at the little street-boys and foot-passengers who eye their shiny boots; the dainty manner in which they trip over the pavement on those boots, eschewing the mud-pools and dirty crossings; the refreshing whiteness of their linen; the coaxing twiddle which they give to the ties of their white chokers – the caress of a fond parent to an innocent child.

I like walking myself. Those who go in cabs or broughams, I have remarked, have not the same radiant expression which the pedestrian exhibits. A man in his own brougham has anxieties about the stepping of his horse, or the squaring of the groom's elbows, or a doubt whether Jones's turn-out is not better; or whether something is not wrong in the springs; or whether he shall have the brougham out if the night is rainy. They always look tragical behind the glasses. A cab diner-out has commonly some cares, lest his sense of justice should be injured by the overcharge of the driver (these fellows are not uncommonly exorbitant in their demands upon gentlemen whom they set down at good houses); lest the smell of tobacco left by the last occupants of the vehicle (five medical students, let us say, who have chartered the vehicle, and smoked cheroots from the London University to the playhouse in the Haymarket) should infest the clothes of Tom Lavender who is going to Lady Rosemary's; lest straws should stick unobserved to the glutinous lustre of his boots – his shiny ones, and he should appear in Dives's drawing-room like a poet with a *tenui avenâ*, or like Mad Tom in the play. I hope, my dear Bob, if a straw should ever enter a drawing-room in the wake of your boot, you will not be much disturbed in mind. Hark ye, in confidence; I have seen — * in a hack-cab. There is no harm in employing one. There is no harm in anything natural, any more.

I cannot help here parenthetically relating a story which occurred in my own youth, in the year 1815, at the time when I first made my own *entrée* into society (for everything must have a beginning, Bob; and though we have been gentlemen long before the Conqueror, and have always consorted with gentlemen, yet we had not always attained that *haute volée* of fashion which has distinguished some of us subsequently); I recollect, I say, in 1815, when the Marquis of Sweetbread was good enough to ask me and the late Mr Ruffles to dinner, to meet Prince Schwartzenberg and the Hetman Platoff. Ruffles was a man a good deal about town in those days, and certainly in very good society.

I was myself a young one, and thought Ruffles was rather inclined

---

* Mr Brown's MS here contains a name of such prodigious dignity out of the 'P–r–age,' that we really do not dare to print it.

to patronize me: which I did not like. 'I would have you to know, Mr Ruffles,' thought I, 'that, after all, a gentleman can but be a gentleman; that though we Browns have no handles to our names, we are quite as well-bred as some folks who possess those ornaments' – and in fine I determined to give him a lesson. So when he called for me in the hackney-coach at my lodgings in Swallow Street, and we had driven under the porte-cochère of Sweetbread House, where two tall and powdered domestics in the uniform of the Sweetbreads, viz. a spinach-coloured coat, with waistcoat and the rest of delicate yellow or melted-butter colour, opened the doors of the hall – what do you think, sir, I did? In the presence of these gentlemen, who were holding on at the door, I offered to toss up with Ruffles, heads or tails, who should pay for the coach; and then purposely had a dispute with the poor Jarvey about the fare. Ruffles's face of agony during this transaction, I shall never forget. Sir, it was like the Laocoön. Drops of perspiration trembled on his pallid brow, and he flung towards me looks of imploring terror that would have melted an ogre. A better fellow than Ruffles never lived – he is dead long since, and I don't mind owning to this harmless little deceit.

A person of some note – a favourite Snob of mine – I am told, when he goes to dinner, adopts what he considers a happy artifice, and sends his cab away at the corner of the street; so that the gentleman in livery may not behold its number, or that the lord with whom he dines, and about whom he is always talking, may not be supposed to know that Mr Smith came in a hack-cab.

A man who is troubled with a shame like this, Bob, is unworthy of any dinner at all. Such a man must needs be a sneak and a humbug, anxious about the effect which he is to produce: uneasy in his mind: a donkey in a lion's skin: a small pretender – distracted by doubts and frantic terrors of what is to come next. Such a man can be no more at ease in his chair at dinner than a man is in the fauteuil at the dentist's (unless indeed he go to the admirable Mr Gilbert in Suffolk Street, who is dragged into this essay for the benefit of mankind alone, and who, I vow, removes a grinder with so little pain, that all the world should be made aware of him) – a fellow, I say, ashamed of the original from which he sprung, of the cab in which he drives, awkward, therefore affected and unnatural, can never hope or deserve to succeed in society.

The great comfort of the society of great folks is, that they do not trouble themselves about your twopenny little person, as smaller persons do, but take you for what you are – a man kindly and good-natured, or witty and sarcastic, or learned and eloquent, or a good *raconteur*, or a very handsome man (and in '15 some of the Browns were – but I am speaking of five-and-thirty years ago), or an excellent gourmand and judge of wines – or what not. Nobody sets you so quickly at your ease as a fine gentleman. I have seen more noise made about a knight's lady than about the Duchess of Fitzbattleaxe herself: and Lady Mountararat, whose family dates from the Deluge, enters and leaves a room, with her daughters, the lovely Ladies Eve and Lilith d'Arc, with much less pretension and in much simpler capotes and what-do-you-call-'ems, than Lady de Mogyns or Mrs Shindy, who quit an assembly in a whirlwind as it were, with trumpets and alarums like a stage king and queen.

But my pen can run no further, for my paper is out, and it is time to dress for dinner.

Joseph Conrad

[1857–1924]

Joseph Conrad was born Jozef Teodor Konrad Korzeniowski in Berdyczów, Poland, into a family of landowning aristocrats. His father, a political activist and man of letters, had translated Shakespeare and Victor Hugo from English and French into Polish. As a supporter of Polish independence from Russia and a member of the National Committee of the underground movement, Conrad's father was arrested by Russian police in 1862 and the family was exiled to Vologda in Russia.

When he was seven years old, just shortly after their arrival in Russia, Conrad's mother died. On account of his father's grief and failing health, father and son were allowed to return to Poland. Soon after, his father died and Conrad, aged eleven, passed into the care of his uncle. This early experience of the pressures politics bring to bear on personal life helped to make Conrad's writing different from that of many of his Western contemporaries, whose own experience of political pressure was not felt until the outbreak of the First World War in 1914.

During these difficult and often solitary years Conrad sought refuge in books. He developed a fascination for tales of sea life and in 1874 he joined the crew of a French ship on a voyage that took him to the West Indies and Central America. The enclosed community of the ship was, to Conrad, a microcosm of the moral world, and his observation of it during his years at sea was to give him a profound understanding of human psychology.

In 1878, with virtually no knowledge of the English language, Conrad travelled to England. He joined a British ship and sailed extensively in the Far East. Then in 1886, having sailed exclusively on British ships for eight years, Conrad was made a British subject and qualified as a Master Mariner. That same year, he wrote his first story, *The Black Mate*, which he entered for a competition in the magazine *Tit-Bits*. In 1888 Conrad received his first command as Captain on a river steamer in the Belgian Congo. His experience of the brutality of imperialism had a profound effect on him and was later to be the inspiration for one of his most admired works, *Heart of Darkness*. The trip, however, took its toll and in 1894 Conrad retired from the sea.

Settling in London, Conrad began to write and by 1896 had published two novels set in the Far East, *Almayer's Folly* and *An Outcast of the Islands*. Both novels brought him critical acclaim from, among others, Henry James, Ford Madox Ford, H. G. Wells and Stephen Crane. In 1896 he married Jessie George and they had two sons, Borys and John. The family lived in a series of rented homes in the secluded countryside of Essex and Kent while Conrad wrote.

In the work that followed, most notably *The Nigger of the 'Narcissus'* (1898), *Lord Jim* (1900), *Heart of Darkness* (1902), *Nostromo* (1904), *The Secret Agent* (1907) and *Under Western Eyes* (1911), Conrad was to transform the English novel in both style and content. He abandoned the stability given by the single narrator in favour of the shifting perspective brought by several, and while his exploration of moral issues put him in the English tradition, he held the very untraditional concept of the novel as a fusion of history, psychology, sociology and poetry.

Despite his continuing critical success, Conrad was never a 'popular' writer and only one of his later novels, *Chance* (1914), brought him public acclaim. Although many praised his gift for the English language, others found his prose stiff and ornate, and as a result Conrad made little money from his writing. However, his work undoubtedly remains central to the development of the English novel.

Conrad found a 'home' in England which went some way to mirroring his first 'home' of the sea. International in flavour, full of high and low argot, forever restless, this was the England that Conrad loved. It was as if the whole world lived in London, as is made clear in the following passage from The Nigger of the 'Narcissus'. *The ship (the* Narcissus) *arrives in the capital and the whole heterogeneous mix that is contemporary London is laid before us.*

From *The Nigger of the 'Narcissus'*

A week afterwards the *Narcissus* entered the chops of the Channel.

Under white wings she skimmed low over the blue sea like a great

tired bird speeding to its nest. The clouds raced with her mastheads;
they rose astern enormous and white, soared to the zenith, flew past,
and, falling down the wide curve of the sky, seemed to dash headlong
into the sea – the clouds swifter than the ship, more free, but without
a home. The coast to welcome her stepped out of space into the
sunshine. The lofty headlands trod masterfully into the sea; the wide
bays smiled in the light; the shadows of homeless clouds ran along the
sunny plains, leaped over valleys, without a check darted up the hills,
rolled down the slopes; and the sunshine pursued them with patches
of running brightness. On the brows of dark cliffs white lighthouses
shone in pillars of light. The Channel glittered like a blue mantle shot
with gold and starred by the silver of the capping seas. The *Narcissus*
rushed past the headlands and the bays. Outward-bound vessels
crossed her track, lying over, and with their masts stripped for a
slogging fight with the hard sou'wester. And, inshore, a string of
smoking steamboats waddled, hugging the coast, like migrating and
amphibious monsters, distrustful of the restless waves.

At night the headlands retreated, the bays advanced into one
unbroken line of gloom. The lights of the earth mingled with the lights
of heaven; and above the tossing lanterns of a trawling fleet a great
lighthouse shone steadily, like an enormous riding light burning above
a vessel of fabulous dimensions. Below its steady glow, the coast,
stretching away straight and black, resembled the high side of an
indestructible craft riding motionless upon the immortal and unrest-
ing sea. The dark land lay alone in the midst of waters, like a mighty
ship bestarred with vigilant lights – a ship carrying the burden of
millions of lives – a ship freighted with dross and with jewels, with
gold and with steel. She towered up immense and strong, guarding
priceless traditions and untold suffering, sheltering glorious memories
and base forgetfulness, ignoble virtues and splendid transgressions. A
great ship! For ages had the ocean battered in vain her enduring sides;
she was there when the world was vaster and darker, when the sea was
great and mysterious, and ready to surrender the prize of fame to
audacious men. A ship mother of fleets and nations! The great flagship
of the race; stronger than the storms! and anchored in the open sea.

The *Narcissus*, heeling over to off-shore gusts, rounded the South Foreland, passed through the Downs, and, in tow, entered the river. Shorn of the glory of her white wings, she wound obediently after the tug through the maze of invisible channels. As she passed them the red-painted light-vessels, swung at their moorings, seemed for an instant to sail with great speed in the rush of tide, and the next moment were left hopelessly behind. The big buoys on the tails of banks slipped past her sides very low, and, dropping in her wake, tugged at their chains like fierce watchdogs. The reach narrowed; from both sides the land approached the ship. She went steadily up the river. On the riverside slopes the houses appeared in groups – seemed to stream down the declivities at a run to see her pass, and, checked by the mud of the foreshore, crowded on the banks. Farther on, the tall factory chimneys appeared in insolent bands and watched her go by, like a straggling crowd of slim giants, swaggering and upright under the black plummets of smoke, cavalierly aslant. She swept round the bends; an impure breeze shrieked a welcome between her stripped spars; and the land, closing in, stepped between the ship and the sea.

A low cloud hung before her – a great opalescent and tremulous cloud, that seemed to rise from the steaming brows of millions of men. Long drifts of smoky vapours soiled it with livid trails; it throbbed to the beat of millions of hearts, and from it came an immense and lamentable murmur – the murmur of millions of lips praying, cursing, sighing, jeering – the undying murmur of folly, regret, and hope exhaled by the crowds of the anxious earth. The *Narcissus* entered the cloud; the shadows deepened; on all sides there was the clang of iron, the sound of mighty blows, shrieks, yells. Black barges drifted stealthily on the murky stream. A mad jumble of begrimed walls loomed up vaguely in the smoke, bewildering and mournful, like a vision of disaster. The tugs backed and filled in the stream, to hold the ship at the dock gates; from her bows two lines went through the air whistling, and struck at the land viciously, like a pair of snakes. A bridge broke in two before her, as if by enchantment; big hydraulic capstans began to turn all by themselves, as though animated by a mysterious and unholy spell. She moved through a narrow lane of water between two low walls of granite, and men with check-ropes in their hands kept pace with her, walking on the broad flagstones. A group waited impatiently on each side of the vanished bridge: rough heavy men in caps; sallow-faced men in high hats; two bareheaded women; ragged children, fascinated, and with wide eyes. A cart coming at a jerky trot pulled up sharply. One of the women screamed at the silent ship – 'Hallo, Jack!' without looking at any one in particular, and all hands looked at her from the forecastle head. – 'Stand clear! Stand clear of that rope!' cried the dockmen, bending over stone posts. The crowd murmured, stamped where they stood. – 'Let go your quarter-checks! Let go!' sang out a ruddy-faced old man on the quay. The ropes splashed heavily falling in the water, and the *Narcissus* entered the dock.

The stony shores ran away right and left in straight lines, enclosing a sombre and rectangular pool. Brick walls rose high above the water – soulless walls, staring through hundreds of windows as troubled and dull as the eyes of over-fed brutes. At their base monstrous iron cranes crouched, with chains hanging from their long necks, balancing cruel-looking hooks over the decks of lifeless ships. A noise of wheels rolling over stones, the thump of heavy things falling, the racket of feverish winches, the grinding of strained chains, floated on the air. Between high buildings the dust of all the continents soared in short flights; and a penetrating smell of perfumes and dirt, of spices and hides, of things costly and of things filthy, pervaded the space, made for it an atmosphere precious and disgusting. The *Narcissus* came gently into her berth; the shadows of soulless walls fell upon her, the dust of all the continents leaped upon her deck, and a swarm of strange men, clambering up her sides, took possession of her in the name of the sordid earth. She had ceased to live.

A toff in a black coat and high hat scrambled with agility, came up to the second mate, shook hands, and said: – 'Hallo, Herbert.' It was his brother. A lady appeared suddenly. A real lady, in a black dress and with a parasol. She looked extremely elegant in the midst of us, and as strange as if she had fallen there from the sky. Mr Baker touched his cap to her. It was the master's wife. And very soon the Captain, dressed very smartly and in a white shirt, went with her over the side. We didn't recognize him at all till, turning on the quay, he called to Mr Baker: – 'Don't forget to wind up the chronometers to-morrow morning.' An underhand lot of seedy-looking chaps with shifty eyes wandered in and out of the forecastle looking for a job – they said. – 'More likely for something to steal,' commented Knowles cheerfully. Poor beggars! Who cared? Weren't we home! But Mr Baker went for one of them who had given him some cheek, and we were delighted. Everything was delightful. – 'I've finished aft, sir,' called out Mr Creighton. – 'No water in the well, sir,' reported for the last time the carpenter, sounding-rod in hand. Mr Baker glanced along the decks at the expectant group of sailors, glanced aloft at the yards. – 'Ough! That will do, men,' he grunted. The group broke up. The voyage was ended.

Rolled-up beds went flying over the rail; lashed chests went sliding down the gangway – mighty few of both at that. 'The rest is having a cruise off the Cape,' explained Knowles enigmatically to a dock-loafer with whom he had struck a sudden friendship. Men ran, calling to one another, hailing utter strangers to 'lend a hand with the dunnage,' then with sudden decorum approached the mate to shake hands before going ashore. – 'Good-bye, sir,' they repeated in various tones. Mr Baker grasped hard palms, grunted in a friendly manner at every one, his eyes twinkled. – 'Take care of your money, Knowles. Ough! Soon get a nice wife if you do.' The lame man was delighted. – 'Good-bye, sir,' said Belfast, with emotion, wringing the mate's hand, and looked up with swimming eyes. 'I thought I would take 'im ashore with me,' he went on plaintively. Mr Baker did not understand, but said kindly: – 'Take care of yourself, Craik,' and the bereaved Belfast went over the rail mourning and alone.

Mr Baker, in the sudden peace of the ship, moved about solitary and grunting, trying door handles, peering into dark places, never done – a model chief mate! No one waited for him ashore. Mother dead; father and two brothers, Yarmouth fishermen, drowned together on the Dogger Bank; sister married and unfriendly. Quite a lady. Married to the leading tailor of a little town, and its leading politician, who did not think his sailor brother-in-law quite respectable enough for him. Quite a lady, quite a lady, he thought, sitting down for a moment's rest on the quarter-hatch. Time enough to go ashore and get a bite and sup, and a bed somewhere. He didn't like to part with a ship. No one to think about then. The darkness of a misty evening fell, cold and damp, upon the deserted deck; and Mr Baker sat smoking, thinking of all the successive ships to whom through many long years he had given the best of a seaman's care. And never a command in sight. Not once! – 'I haven't somehow the cut of a skipper about me,' he meditated placidly, while the shipkeeper (who had taken possession of the galley), a wizened old man with bleared eyes, cursed him in whispers for 'hanging about so.' – 'Now, Creighton,' he pursued the unenvious train of thought, 'quite a gentleman . . . swell friends . . . will get on. Fine young fellow . . . a little more experience.' He got up and shook himself. 'I'll be back first thing to-morrow morning for the hatches. Don't you let them touch anything before I come, shipkeeper,' he called out. Then, at last, he also went ashore – a model chief mate!

The men scattered by the dissolving contact of the land came together once more in the shipping office. – 'The *Narcissus* pays off,' shouted outside a glazed door a brass-bound old fellow, with a crown and the capitals B.T. on his cap. A lot trooped in at once but many were late. The room was large, whitewashed, and bare; a counter surmounted by a brass-wire grating fenced off a third of the dusty space, and behind the grating a pasty-faced clerk, with his hair parted in the middle, had the quick, glittering eyes and the vivacious, jerky movements of a caged bird. Poor Captain Allistoun also in there and sitting before a little table with piles of gold and notes on it, appeared subdued by his captivity. Another Board of Trade bird was perching on a high stool near the door: an old bird that did not mind the chaff of elated sailors. The crew of the *Narcissus*, broken up into knots, pushed in the corners. They had new shore togs, smart jackets that looked as if they had been shaped with an axe, glossy trousers that seemed made of crumpled

sheet-iron, collarless flannel shirts, shiny new boots. They tapped
on shoulders, button-holed one another, asked: – 'Where did you
sleep last night?' whispered gaily, slapped their thighs with bursts of
subdued laughter. Most had clean radiant faces; only one or two
turned up dishevelled and sad; the two young Norwegians looked
tidy, meek, and altogether of a promising material for the kind
ladies who patronize the Scandinavian Home. Wamibo, still in his
working clothes, dreamed, upright and burly in the middle of the
room, and, when Archie came in, woke up for a smile. But the
wide-awake clerk called out a name, and the paying-off business
began.

One by one they came up to the pay-table to get the wages of their
glorious and obscure toil. They swept the money with care into
broad palms, rammed it trustfully into trousers' pockets, or, turning
their backs on the table, reckoned with difficulty in the hollow of
their stiff hands. – 'Money right? Sign the release. There – there,'
repeated the clerk impatiently. 'How stupid those sailors are!' he
thought. Singleton came up, venerable – and uncertain as to daylight;
brown drops of tobacco juice hung in his white beard; his hands, that
never hesitated in the great light of the open sea, could hardly find
the small pile of gold in the profound darkness of the shore. 'Can't
write?' said the clerk, shocked. 'Make a mark then.' Singleton
painfully sketched in a heavy cross, blotted the page. 'What a
disgusting old brute,' muttered the clerk. Somebody opened the door
for him, and the patriarchal seaman passed through unsteadily,
without as much as a glance at any of us.

Archie displayed a pocket-book. He was chaffed. Belfast, who
looked wild, as though he had already luffed up through a public-
house or two, gave signs of emotion and wanted to speak to the
captain privately. The master was surprised. They spoke through the
wires, and we could hear the captain saying: – 'I've given it up to the
Board of Trade.' 'I should've liked to get something of his,' mumbled
Belfast. 'But you can't, my man. It's given up, locked and sealed, to
the Marine Office,' expostulated the master; and Belfast stood back,
with drooping mouth and troubled eyes. In a pause of the business

we heard the master and the clerk talking. We caught: 'James Wait –
deceased – found no papers of any kind – no relations – no trace –
the Office must hold his wages then.' Donkin entered. He seemed out
of breath, was grave, full of business. He went straight to the desk,
talked with animation to the clerk, who thought him an intelligent
man. They discussed the account, dropping h's against one another
as if for a wager – very friendly. Captain Allistoun paid. 'I give you a
bad discharge,' he said quietly. Donkin raised his voice; – 'I don't
want your bloomin' discharge – keep it. I'm goin' ter 'ave a job
ashore.' He turned to us. 'No more bloomin' sea fur me,' he said
aloud. All looked at him. He had better clothes, had an easy air,
appeared more at home than any of us; he stared with assurance,
enjoying the effect of his declaration. 'Yuss. I 'ave friends well off.
That's more'n you got. But I am a man. Ye're shipmates for all that.
Who's comin' fur a drink?'

No one moved. There was a silence; a silence of blank faces and
stony looks. He waited a moment, smiled bitterly, and went to the
door. There he faced round once more. 'You won't? You bloomin' lot
of 'ypocrites. No? What 'ave I done to yer? Did I bully yer? Did I 'urt
yer? Did I? . . . You won't drink? . . . No! . . . Then may ye die of
thirst, every mother's son of yer! Not one of yer 'as the sperrit of a
bug. Ye're the scum of the world. Work and starve!'

He went out, and slammed the door with such violence that the
old Board of Trade bird nearly fell off his perch.

'He's mad,' declared Archie. 'No! No! He's drunk,' insisted
Belfast, lurching about, and in a maudlin tone. Captain Allistoun
sat smiling thoughtfully at the cleared pay table.

Outside, on Tower Hill, they blinked, hesitated clumsily, as if blinded
by the strange quality of the hazy light, as if discomposed by the view
of so many men; and they who could hear one another in the howl of
gales seemed deafened and distracted by the dull roar of the busy
earth. – 'To the Black Horse! To the Black Horse!' cried some. 'Let us
have a drink together before we part.' They crossed the road,
clinging to one another. Only Charley and Belfast wandered off

alone. As I came up I saw a red-faced, blowsy woman, in a grey shawl, and with dusty, fluffy hair, fall on Charley's neck. It was his mother. She sobbed over him: – 'Oh, my boy! My boy!' – 'Leggo of me,' said Charley, 'Leggo, Mother!' I was passing him at the time, and over the untidy head of the blubbering woman he gave me a humorous smile and a glance ironic, courageous, and profound, that seemed to put all my knowledge of life to shame. I nodded and passed on, but heard him say again, good-naturedly: – 'If you leggo of me this minyt – ye shall 'ave a bob for a drink out of my pay.' In the next few steps I came upon Belfast. He caught my arm with tremulous enthusiasm. – 'I couldn't go wi' 'em,' he stammered, indicating by a nod our noisy crowd, that drifted slowly along the other sidewalk. 'When I think of Jimmy . . . Poor Jim! When I think of him I have no heart for drink. You were his chum, too . . . but I pulled him out . . . didn't I? Short wool he had . . . Yes. And I stole the blooming pie. . . . He wouldn't go. . . . He wouldn't go for nobody.' He burst into tears. 'I never touched him – never – never!' he sobbed. 'He went for me like . . . like . . . a lamb.'

I disengaged myself gently. Belfast's crying fits generally ended in a fight with some one, and I wasn't anxious to stand the brunt of his inconsolable sorrow. Moreover, two bulky policemen stood near by, looking at us with a disapproving and incorruptible gaze. – 'So long!' I said, and went on my way.

But at the corner I stopped to take my last look at the crew of the *Narcissus*. They were swaying irresolute and noisy on the broad flagstones before the Mint. They were bound for the Black Horse, where men, in fur caps, with brutal faces and in shirt sleeves, dispense out of varnished barrels the illusion of strength, mirth, happiness; the illusion of splendour and poetry of life, to the paid-off crews of southern-going ships. From afar I saw them discoursing, with jovial eyes and clumsy gestures, while the sea of life thundered into their ears ceaseless and unheeded. And swaying about there on the white stones, surrounded by the hurry and clamour of men, they appeared to be creatures of another kind – lost, alone, forgetful, and doomed; they were like castaways, like reckless and joyous castaways, like mad castaways making merry in the storm and upon an insecure ledge of a treacherous rock. The roar of the town resembled the roar of topping breakers, merciless and strong, with a loud voice and cruel purpose; but overhead the clouds broke; a flood of sunshine streamed down the walls of grimy houses. The dark knot of seamen drifted in sunshine. To the left of them the trees in Tower Gardens sighed, the stones of the Tower gleaming, seemed to stir in the play of light, as if remembering suddenly all the great joys and sorrows of the past, the fighting prototypes of these men; press-gangs; mutinous cries; the wailing of women by the riverside, and the shouts of men welcoming victories. The sunshine of heaven fell like a gift of grace on the mud of the earth, on the remembering and mute stones, on greed, selfishness; on the anxious faces of forgetful men. And to the right of the dark group the stained front of the Mint, cleansed by the flood of light, stood out for a moment dazzling and white like a marble palace in a fairy tale. The crew of the *Narcissus* drifted out of sight.

I never saw them again. The sea took some, the steamers took others, the graveyards of the earth will account for the rest. Singleton has no doubt taken with him the long record of his faithful work into the peaceful depths of an hospitable sea. And Donkin, who never did a decent day's work in his life, no doubt earns his living by discoursing with filthy eloquence upon the right of labour to live. So be it! Let the earth and the sea each have its own.

A gone shipmate, like any other man, is gone for ever; and I never met one of them again. But at times the spring-flood of memory sets with force up the dark River of the Nine Bends. Then on the waters of the forlorn stream drifts a ship – a shadowy ship manned by a crew of Shades. They pass and make a sign, in a shadowy hail. Haven't we, together and upon the immortal sea, wrung out a meaning from our sinful lives? Good-bye, brothers! You were a good crowd. As good a crowd as ever fisted with wild cries the beating canvas of a heavy foresail; or tossing aloft, invisible in the night, gave back yell for yell to a westerly gale.

Rudyard Kipling

[1865–1936]

Rudyard Kipling was born in Bombay. His father, John Lockwood Kipling, was a professor at the School of Art in Lahore. Kipling's happy childhood came to an abrupt end when, at the age of six, he was sent with his sister to England. He was put into the care of a strict guardian and attended the United Services College, a public school in Devon. These unhappy schoolboy years were later to be recounted in the semi-autobiographical *Stalky & Co.* (1899).

In 1882, having left school, Kipling went back to India and worked as a journalist in Lahore on the *Civil and Military Gazette*. Aside from news items, he began to contribute his mildly satirical poetry and short stories. In 1886 his first collection of poems, *Departmental Ditties*, was published, followed by two collections of short stories, *Plain Tales from the Hills* (1888) and *Soldiers Three* (1889). These works were to bring him early recognition back in England. Having spent two years travelling around India, he returned to England, by way of the United States, in 1889.

Settling into the London literary scene, Kipling reissued his India stories and published a new collection, *Life's Handicap* (1891). That same year, during a trip undertaken to improve his health, he visited India for the last time. In 1892 he married an American, Caroline Balestier, the sister of Charles Wolcott Balestier, an author-publisher with whom Kipling had worked. Moving with his wife to her home in Vermont, Kipling wrote and published what were to become some of his most celebrated titles, among them *Barrack-Room Ballads* (1892), a collection of poems written in the ballad tradition, the short stories *Many Inventions* (1893) and his classic children's story *The Jungle Book* (1894), plus its sequel in 1895. This spell in America ended abruptly in 1896 when, following an argument with his brother-in-law, Kipling returned with his family to England.

Thereafter, Kipling remained in England, with spells in South Africa during the winter, where he voiced his support of Britain in the Boer War.

His South African experiences, together with his earlier impressions of India, are reflected in his rigidly imperialist views on 'the white man's burden'. In fact, though some of his writing showed a sensitivity to the ill-effects of colonialism, much of it displayed his enthusiasm for a ruling order, and Kipling was later to be widely criticized for his jingoistic arrogance towards people ruled by Britain. However, in the days of the British Empire, Kipling's poetry was hugely admired by many, including Queen Victoria and George V, and although he declined many offers of honours, including a knighthood and the Order of Merit, in 1907 he did accept the Nobel Prize for Literature. Among his celebrated later works were the novel *Kim* (1901), and for children the *Just So Stories* (1902) and *Puck of Pook's Hill* (1906). His autobiography, *Something of Myself*, was published in 1937, after his death.

Having lost his son in the First World War, Kipling removed himself from the public sphere and died in relative isolation. He was buried in Poet's Corner, Westminster Abbey.

Whether one chooses to view Kipling as an unreconstructed jingoist or a fundamentally more critical observer of English life, his work comes towards the end of a period in which British people instinctively viewed themselves in a global light. The poem that follows, 'The English Flag' (1891), affirms this connection to a larger world beyond the small island and suggests that such links are benign and positive, even in the face of early protests from those 'colonials' who preferred to burn the flag.

THE ENGLISH FLAG

Above the portico a flag staff, bearing the Union Jack, remained fluttering in the flames for some time, but ultimately when it fell the crowds rent the air with shouts, and seemed to see significance in the incident.

DAILY PAPERS

Winds of the Worlds, give answer! They are whimpering to and fro –
And what should they know of England who only England know? –

The poor little street-bred people that vapour and fume and brag,
They are lifting their heads in the stillness to yelp at the English
   Flag!

Must we borrow a clout from the Boer – to plaster anew with dirt?
An Irish liar's bandage, or an English coward's shirt?
We may not speak of England; her Flag's to sell or share.
What is the Flag of England? Winds of the World, declare!

The North Wind blew: – 'From Bergen my steel-shod vanguards go;
'I chase your lazy whalers home from the Disko floe.
'By the great North Lights above me I work the will of God,
'And the liner splits on the ice-field or the Dogger fills with cod.

'I barred my gates with iron, I shuttered my doors with flame,
'Because to force my ramparts your nutshell navies came.
'I took the sun from their presence, I cut them down with my blast,
'And they died, but the Flag of England blew free ere the spirit passed.

'The lean white bear hath seen it in the long, long Arctic nights,
'The musk-ox knows the standard that flouts the Northern Lights:
'What is the Flag of England? Ye have but my bergs to dare,
'Ye have but my drifts to conquer. Go forth, for it is there!'

The South Wind sighed: – 'From the Virgins my mid-sea course was
   ta'en
'Over a thousand islands lost in an idle main,
'Where the sea-egg flames on the coral and the long-backed
   breakers croon
'Their endless ocean legends to the lazy, locked lagoon.

'Strayed amid lonely islets, mazed amid outer keys,
'I waked the palms to laughter – I tossed the scud in the breeze.
'Never was isle so little, never was sea so lone,
'But over the scud and the palm-trees an English flag was flown.

'I have wrenched it free from the halliards to hang for a wisp on the
   Horn;

'I have chased it north to the Lizard – ribboned and rolled and torn;
'I have spread its folds o'er the dying, adrift in a hopeless sea;
'I have hurled it swift on the slaver, and seen the slave set free.

'My basking sunfish know it, and wheeling albatross,
'Where the lone wave fills with fire beneath the Southern Cross.
'What is the Flag of England? Ye have but my reefs to dare,
'Ye have but my seas to furrow. Go forth, for it is there!'

The East Wind roared: – 'From the Kuriles, the Bitter Seas, I come,
'And me men call the Home-Wind, for I bring the English home.
'Look – look well to your shipping! By breath of my mad typhoon
'I swept your close-packed Praya and beached your best at
    Kowloon!

'The reeling junks behind me and the racing seas before,
'I raped your richest roadstead – I plundered Singapore!
'I set my hand on the Hoogli; as a hooded snake she rose;
'And I flung your stoutest steamers to roost with the startled crows.

'Never the lotos closes, never the wild-fowl wake,
'But a soul goes out in the East Wind that died for England's sake –
'Man or woman or suckling, mother or bride or maid –
'Because on the bones of the English the English Flag is stayed.

'The desert-dust hath dimmed it, the flying wild-ass knows,
'The scared white leopard winds it across the taintless snows.
'What is the Flag of England? Ye have but my sun to dare,
'Ye have but my sands to travel. Go forth, for it is there!'

The West Wind called: – 'In squadrons the thoughtless galleons fly
'That bear the wheat and cattle lest street-bred people die.
'They make my might their porter, they make my house their path,
'Till I loose my neck from their rudder and whelm them all in my
    wrath.

'I draw the gliding fog-bank as a snake is drawn from the hole.
'They bellow one to the other, the frighted ship-bells toll;

'For day is a drifting terror till I raise the shroud with my breath,
'And they see strange bows above them and the two go locked to
    death.

'But whether in calm or wrack-wreath, whether by dark or day,
'I leave them whole to the conger or rip their plates away,
'First of the scattered legions, under a shrieking sky,
'Dipping between the rollers, the English Flag goes by.

'The dead dumb fog hath wrapped it – the frozen dews have
    kissed –
'The naked stars have seen it, a fellow-star in the mist.
'What is the Flag of England? Ye have but my breath to dare,
'Ye have but my waves to conquer. Go forth, for it is there!'

Wyndham Lewis
[1882–1957]

Percy Wyndham Lewis was born on board his American father's yacht off Nova Scotia. His mother was English and after some years spent in Maine and Maryland the family moved to England. His parents separated in 1893 and Lewis lived with his mother. He studied at Rugby, where his skills as a draughtsman were noted and won him a scholarship to the Slade School of Art in London.

In 1901 Lewis travelled to France, Holland, Germany and Spain. Having familiarized himself with the artistic movements that were developing across Europe, he returned to England and firmly established himself as an informed leader of the avant-garde in art and literature. By 1914 he was leading the Vorticist movement in painting and looking to carry the movement's principles over to literature. He sought allegiance with the poet Ezra Pound, with whom he published the Vorticist review *Blast* (1914–15). Lewis's partnerships did not last long. His polemical views and brutal independence, coupled with obsessive criticism of his contemporaries, had by the end of the First World War led to his being ostracized by the art world.

Lewis's first novel, *Tarr* (1918), met with a mixed response. His very distinctive anti-naturalistic style of expression, in keeping with the radicalism that was occurring in painting, was felt by some to be pretentious, although others, among them T. S. Eliot, praised his style for its vitality. Eliot went on to describe Lewis as 'the most fascinating personality of our time'. In his subsequent novels *The Art of Being Ruled* (1926) and *Time and Western Man* (1927), and his epic satire *The Apes of God* (1930), Lewis developed his theme of opposing all forms of domination – whether political, psychological or bureaucratic – and set out to expose what he perceived as the mindlessness of twentieth-century man in his unconscious desire to be ruled. However, just when most writers appeared to be increasingly left-wing, as Lewis himself had been so far, in his typically controversial way he began to express sympathy for the right. In 1931 he wrote about his admiration for Hitler, and he went on to express a right-wing point of view in his book *Left Wings Over Europe* (1936). The following year he published what was considered by many to be his finest novel, *The Revenge for Love* (1937).

Having returned to Canada for the duration of the Second World War, in 1945 Lewis resettled in London. In 1946 he joined *The Listener* as art critic, but left in 1951 after his eyesight failed. Despite total blindness, Lewis continued to write. Among his later works are *Rotting Hill* (1951), stories based on Notting Hill in the 1940s, and the novels *Self Condemned* (1954) and *The Human Age* (1955), both of which were written in response to his nightmarish sense of lost identity as a European during his time in Canada.

Shortly before his death in 1957 the Tate Gallery held a retrospective of his work.

In 1948, in a letter to a Canadian friend, Lewis noted that he was living in London, 'the capital of a dying empire'. To his eyes, post-Second World War Britain was falling to pieces. In letters to David Kahma, a young and aspiring Canadian writer, Geoffrey Stone, a New York-based American critic, and Edgar Preston Richardson, Director of the Detroit Institute of the Arts, Lewis was able both to maintain the transatlantic connection that was important to his thinking and his work, and to offer insight into the political and literary culture of the country that he cared for yet was growing to despise.

To David Kahma

London
25 Aug 1947

Dear Mr Kahma . . .

The situation in this country is distressing: for there is no possible end to it. As a result of two great wars for the position of cock of the walk in Europe both England and Germany are finally ruined, and naturally the rest of Europe with them. Whether the type of state socialism which will take the place of the mercantile prosperity of Europe at the beginning of the century will be a good or a bad thing for the 'Greatest Number' I cannot tell you. But the art of writing and the other arts will gradually be extinguished. Much more life is to be found in Paris than here. There always was. But it is very doubtful if it could survive another blow – such as a war or revolution. Even as it is the world of Sartre and Camus is a very sick one indeed . . .

Mr Orwell (as they call him here 'bore-well') is an excitable idiot, who spends his time affixing political labels to people. There is no foundation whatever for the rumour you mention that I become a politician. I impartially dislike all factions: and I am not susceptible as is silly Mr Orwell, to the fascination of political Stars (nor ever have been). I have always been inclined to keep a stupid old bitch known as Brittania out of dog-fights, that is all.

She is still my only political attachment (pace the London correspondent of the Partisan Rev.). – This letter has been all about myself . . . My next communication will be about yourself.

With my sincerest thanks,

To Geoffrey Stone

London, W.11
Jan. 15 1948

My dear Stone . . .

As to conditions in these islands. We now get no eggs at all, or at most one a piece every month. (But we prefer *no* eggs to *powdered* eggs). The ingredients of the bread is said by medical men to be actually injurious to health and is so dry and gritty as to be disagreeable to eat. We eat no bread. We buy baps; but they contain no yeast, which it seems is a serious deficiency. In general, absence of fats of all kinds from the diet is the worst feature . . . The water is now so heavily chlorinated it is almost undrinkable. When the taste of the chlorine wears off, you taste the sewage, which is worse. The reason for this is that it has not been possible to renew the filters at the waterworks. We have found that sometimes for a short while the water tastes quite normal again and we fill our jugs (I suppose garbage has ceased momentarily to

flow into it, or they have run out of chlorine). These are just a few
details. The most horrible thing of all is that everything gets worse
monthly and is certain never to stop getting worse. Consider. This
is the capital of a dying empire – not crashing down in flames and
smoke but expiring in a peculiar muffled way. The 47 million
people on these islands can by no means be fed because they have
to be nourished by means of imported food which a great rich
empire could buy but not the present dwindling polity in this
greatly altered world. Also, why it is certain to become worser and
worser for us is that we are in the midst of a socialist experiment
(on the Swedish pattern) and we shall be squeezed more and more.
. . . At this point (Jan 15) a series of upheavals occurred: we had
been living in the upstairs part of our apartment, the workmen
entrenched on the floor beneath. But at last they announced their
desire to come *up*. Everything had thereupon to be moved *down*.
Everything got lost: for days and nights I was living in a whirlpool
of furniture and food and blow lamps and typewriters. At last
things are relatively quiet: and it is *Jan*. 25! In the meantime your
admirable essay 'American Life and Catholic Culture' has turned
up, and I have perused it with the greatest interest. You do not say
quite enough about American Life, I think. Why not boldly
imagine a Catholic American? Where did you get your idea of a
catholic ghetto from – observation of the social ostracism of the
irish catholics in Boston? – I enjoyed the *writing* of your article
throughout. What I felt to be a mistake was the introduction in so
short a piece of a special definition of the terms 'culture' and
'civilization'. But that would be my only criticism. Are you, may I
ask, a Maritain devotee: or do you consider what he writes
dangerous doctrine, as many do? Are you on the side of the
Louvain teaching – in brief do you consider that the existence of
God can be mathematically proved, and that the missionary should
go to work on those lines? Or are you more of a mystic than that?
. . . We both hate the 'purchase tax' more than we have ever hated
anything. Next to that we loathe an expression which our
conquerors never cease to employ.

It is this: 'Too much money chasing too few goods'. – But farewell, and best wishes from Froanna and myself,

Yours

w. l.

To Edgar Preston Richardson

London, W.11
Oct. 27 1948

My dear Richardson.

It was a very pleasant surprise to see *Detroit* and the rest of the address on the envelope, and upon opening it to be with you again . . .

Let me speak of the first year of *the Peace*, upon our return. That first twelvemonth I could do nothing but struggle with the environment. England has become a very difficult place. National bankruptcy *plus* socialism is no joke. Let me say at once that I am not anti-socialist. It would be stupid to be that: at this stage in human history some form of it seems indicated – though of course it is a necessary but disagreeable phase imposed by humanity's natural backwardness and wickedness, not a splendid culmination of human genius and endeavour. But there is one piece of political information I have most painfully and unwillingly acquired. *State-socialism* (in contrast to some other types of socialism) is not a theory of the state. It is a very grave complaint to which human society is apt to fall victim. – National bankruptcy is – well, let us say very bad for the patient – for a nation suffering from state-socialism. – I read this morning that, as well as medicine, *law* is going to be nationalized. Nationalization, of course, and state-socialism are inseparable.

Conditions here are not the straightforward disaster of a country the currency of which has become worthless – as in Germany after world war i. Disaster is disguised as 'austerity'. As a result to an outsider the mere registering of actual conditions must have a sound of unwarranted complaint. – And very little complaint – alas

– is heard here: dunning rulers in the past have carefully trained this people to 'keep a stiff upper lip', to 'keep smiling', to be fine fellows who can 'take it' . . .
You cannot defeat the English. You can publicly rob them and fool them; ruin them, and eventually enslave them. But you cannot *defeat* them. They do not [as has so often been said) know when they're beaten!

. . . It all *looks* the same you see – but it isn't quite the same! It is the most hypocritical and insidious type of inflation. Most writers have crowded into safe official jobs – B.B.C., Brit. Council, or a Ministry. Literature does not benefit . . . Then, as a limit of 5 shillings per meal per person is now statutory, (plus a 'cover charge') it is impossible to nourish oneself in a restaurant. A lunch at the Café Royal for instance is just the negation of sustenance. A couple of months ago we lunched with James Sweeney and his wife at a hotel in Half Moon Street, off Piccadilly. The restaurant is well-known, smallish and expensive. (The most reckless of my dealers always takes me there for lunch). The dish that was one of the two pièces de resistance I could not eat, because it was putrid . . .
But enough of these miseries . . .

Yrs
WYNDHAM LEWIS

T. S. Eliot

[1888–1965]

Thomas Stearns Eliot was born in St Louis, Missouri. His grandfather was a prominent Unitarian minister and a zealous missionary in his efforts to advance the causes of education, religion and community, and his example was to have a profound effect on Eliot's childhood and career. In 1906 Eliot entered Harvard University, completing his BA in 1909 and his MA in 1911. While embarking on his academic career at Harvard, he became interested in the French Symbolist movement in literature and began writing his own ironic versions of Symbolist poems. In 1910 he took a year out from Harvard and attended the Sorbonne in Paris, where he took part in the demonstrations of the Camelots du Roi, a right-wing, anti-Dreyfusard organization. He returned to Harvard in 1912, and was appointed an assistant in philosophy under the guidance of Irving Babbitt and Bertrand Russell. Two years later, he was awarded a scholarship to study philosophy at Merton College, Oxford. After his arrival in 1914, Eliot made England his permanent home.

Eliot rapidly became involved with the avant-garde movement that was dominating the arts in London at the time. With the help of the poet Ezra Pound, another expatriate American whom he met in London in 1914, Eliot published his poem 'The Love Song of J. Alfred Prufrock' in *Poetry* (1915). Pound went on to act as Eliot's agent and editor, a role that led to his significant editorial contribution to Eliot's poem *The Waste Land* (1922). In 1915 Eliot married Vivien Haigh-Wood, who was from a conventional English upper middle-class family. An unhappy marriage, it was the source of Eliot's bleak vision of matrimony in his poems and plays.

During this time, to earn his living, Eliot taught in grammar schools in High Wycombe and Highgate. Then in 1917 he joined the colonial and foreign department of Lloyds Bank in London, remaining there, despite attempts to enter into the US Navy in 1918, until 1925. Meanwhile, in his spare time, Eliot's literary career was taking shape. He published a collection of his early poetry written in America, *Prufrock and Other*

Observations (1917), followed by two more collections, *Poems* (1919) and *Ara vos prec* (1920), both severe satires of English and European post-war culture. By now he was also becoming well known as a critic. He was assistant editor of *The Egoist* (1917–19) and published his polemical book *The Sacred Wood* (1920), a collection of essays on criticism, poetic drama and poets.

Due to the pressures of his professional, literary and personal life, in 1921 Eliot was on the verge of a physical and mental breakdown and was granted a period of leave from Lloyds Bank. During his months of recovery in Margate, and then in Switzerland, Eliot wrote the majority of *The Waste Land*. Unquestionably one of the landmarks of twentieth-century poetry, the poem focuses on personal (many critics say his own) and cultural ruin in post-war London, and created a new poetic form. *The Waste Land* first appeared in the inaugural issue of *The Criterion*, a highly influential literary journal which Eliot founded in 1922 and edited until 1939.

In 1925 Eliot left Lloyds and joined the publishers Faber and Gwyer (later Faber and Faber) as a director. He published a series of books on literary criticism which, along with his commentaries in *The Criterion*, firmly established him as one of the leading literary critics of the twentieth century. Meanwhile, though, Eliot had increasing problems with his cultural identity. By approaching the matter in a distinctly traditionalist way – he described himself as 'classical in literature, royalist in politics, and Anglo-Catholic in religion' – he almost inevitably, in 1927, became a member of the Anglican Church and a British citizen.

Following his conversion, Eliot published a series of poems on religious themes, including 'Ash Wednesday' (1930), which dealt with his struggle in converting to Anglicanism. It was at this point that his wife's mental and physical state, which had plagued Eliot throughout their marriage, deteriorated to such a degree that in 1932 he decided upon a legal separation. She later died in a private mental home in 1947. In the 1930s Eliot turned increasingly to verse drama in a concentrated effort to move away from the personal nature of his poetry and towards a clearer sense of social responsibility. This began with the short *Sweeney Agonistes* (1932), and was followed by the highly successful *Murder in the Cathedral* (1935), which marked the beginning of his reputation as the poet who revived verse drama. His following plays, *The Family*

Reunion (1939), *The Cocktail Party* (1950), *The Confidential Clerk* (1954) and *The Elder Statesman* (1959), were aimed more specifically at the West End and attempted to reconcile Christianity with classical drama, modern poetry and the popular play. Towards the beginning of his career in the theatre, Eliot produced what most people regard as his greatest poetic work, *Four Quartets* (1943). Comprising four philosophical and religious meditations, it was to be Eliot's last major poem.

After the war, Eliot's career as a critic subsided. The small number of reviews and essays, most of which were published between 1945 and 1947, lacked the energy of his pre-war criticism. In 1948, he received the Nobel Prize for Literature and the Order of Merit. Following this, apart from his three 'West End' plays, Eliot settled back to reap the rewards of his long writing career, and in 1957 he married his private secretary, Valerie Fletcher. By 1964 Eliot had received enormous public acclaim, including both Britain's and the United States' highest civilian honours and seventeen honorary doctorates from American, English and European institutions. He died in London in 1965.

Eliot arrived in Britain at a time of great trauma for the nation. The country was about to be plunged into the horrors of the First World War and Eliot, already well travelled in Europe, was trying to understand both the English and England. His letters to his brother Henry and his beloved cousin Eleanor Hinkley reveal his early anxieties about how he might adjust to England, but they also betray his quiet determination to take part in a society that already held a firm grip on his imagination

To Henry Eliot

28 Bedford Place, Russell Square,
London wc
Monday 8 Sept 1914

My dear Henry,
I will ask my tailor to send you some samples at once, if he has any winter goods now; he could make you a suit to my measure; as he is a cash tailor he would have to have the money before you have the suit. I will pay him if you like, when the time comes.

I fear that I have no interesting anecdotes of my adventures beyond what I have already imparted. I was interviewed by a reporter when I got here, but had nothing interesting to give him even had I been willing to communicate it. It is really much more interesting to be in London now than it was to be in Germany: the latter experience was much like the childhood's exasperation of being in an upper berth as the train passed through a large city. – In fact it was an intolerable bore. There, one was so far from any excitement and information that it was impossible to work; here in all the noise and rumour, I can work.

The quarter where I live is rather foreign anyway, being composed exclusively of boarding houses, in rows, all exactly alike except for the fancy names on them; and now we are full up with Belgian and French refugees, whole families of them, of the well-to-do sort, with babies and nurses; – we have just acquired a Swiss waiter instead of a German one who was very unpopular (one excited lady said 'what's to prevent him putting arsenic in our food?' I said 'Nothing! – he already puts blacking on my tan shoes') so I have been talking French and acquiring a war vocabulary. The noise hereabouts is like hell turned upside down. Hot weather, all windows open, many babies, pianos, street piano accordions, singers, hummers, whistlers. Every house has a gong: they all go off at seven o'clock, and other hours. Ten o'clock in the evening, quiet for a few minutes, then a couple of men with late editions burst into the street, roaring: GREAT GERMAN DISASTER! Everybody rushes to windows and doors, in every costume from evening clothes to pajamas; violent talking – English, American, French, Flemish, Russian, Spanish, Japanese; the papers are all sold in five minutes: then we settle down for another hour till the next extra appears: LIST OF ENGLISH DEAD AND WOUNDED. Meanwhile, a dreadful old woman, her skirt trailing on the street, sings 'the Rosary' in front, and secures several pennies from windows and the housemaid resumes her conversation at the area gate.

I find it quite possible to work in this atmosphere. The noises of a city so large as London don't distract one much; they become

attached to the city and depersonalize themselves. No doubt it will
take me some time to become used to the quiet of Oxford. I like
London better than before; it is foreign, but hospitable, or rather
tolerant, and perhaps does not so demand to be understood as does
Paris. Less jealous. I think I should love Paris now more than ever, if
I could see her in these times. There seems to have come a
wonderful calmness and fortitude over Paris, from what I hear; the
spirit is very different from 1870. I have a great deal of confidence
in the ultimate event: I am anxious that Germany should be beaten;
but I think it is silly to hold up one's hands at German 'atrocities'
and 'violations of neutrality'. The Germans are perfectly justified in
violating Belgium – they are fighting for their existence – but the
English are more than justified in turning to defend a treaty. But the
Germans are bad diplomats. It is not against German 'crimes', but
against German 'civilization' – all this system of officers and
professors – that I protest. But very useful to the world if kept in its
place.

Yours affy
Tom

To Eleanor Hinkley

28 Bedford Place, Russell Square
8 Sept 1914

My dear Eleanor

Here I am in Shady Bloomsbury, the noisiest place in the world, a
neighbourhood at present given over to artists, musicians,
hackwriters, Americans, Russians, French, Belgians, Italians,
Spaniards, and Japanese; formerly Germans also – these have now
retired, including our waiter, a small inefficient person, but, as one
lady observed, 'What's to prevent him putting arsenic in our tea?' A
delightfully seedy part of town, with some interesting people in it,
besides the Jones twins, who were next door for a few days, and —
who is a few blocks away. I was quite glad to find her, she is very
pleasant company, and ~~not at all uninteresting~~ quite interesting
(that's better). Only I wish she wouldn't look like German

allegorical paintings – e.g. POMONA blessing the DUKE of
MECKLENBURG-STRELITZ, or something of that sort – because she
hasn't really a German mind at all, but quite American. I was in to
tea yesterday, and we went to walk afterwards, to the Regent's Park
Zoo. The only other friend I have here now is my French friend of
the steamer, just returned from Paris, who is also very interesting, in
a different way – one of those people you sometimes meet who do
not have much discursive conversation on a variety of topics, but
occasionally surprise you by a remark of unusual penetration. But
perhaps I do her an injustice, as she does talk pretty well – but it is
more the latter that I notice. Anyway it is pleasant to be in contact
with a French mind in a foreign city like this. I like London very
well now – it has grown on me, and I grew quite homesick for it in
Germany; and I have met several very agreeable Englishmen. Still I
feel that I don't understand the English very well. I think that Keith
is really very English – and thoroughly so – and I always found him
very baffling, though I like him very much. It seemed to me that I
got to know him quite easily, and never got very much farther; and
I am interested to see (this year) whether I shall find it so with all
English; and whether the difficulty is simply that I consider him a
bit conventional. I don't know just what conventionality is; it
doesn't involve snobbishness, because I am a thorough snob myself;
but I should have thought of it as perhaps the one quality which all
my friends lacked. And I'm sure that if I did know what it was,
among men, I should have to find out all over again with regard to
women.

Perhaps when I learn how to take Englishmen, this brick wall will
cease to trouble me. But it's ever so much easier to know what a
Frenchman or an American is thinking about, than an Englishman.
Perhaps partly that a Frenchman is so analytical and selfconscious
that he dislikes to have anything going on inside him that he can't
put into words, while an Englishman is content simply to live. And
that's one of the qualities one counts as a virtue; the ease and lack
of effort with which they take so much of life – that's the way they
have been fighting in France – I should like to be able to acquire

something of that spirit. But on the other hand the French way has an intellectual honesty about it that the English very seldom attain to. So there you are.

I haven't said anything about the war yet. Of course (though no one believes me) I have no experiences of my own of much interest – nothing, that is, in the way of anecdotes, that are easy to tell – though the whole experience has been something which has left a very deep impression on me; having seen, I mean, how the people in the two countries have taken the affair, and the great moral earnestness on both sides. It has made it impossible for me to ~~take~~ adopt a wholly partizan attitude, or even to rejoice or despair wholeheartedly, though I should certainly want to fight against the Germans if at all. I cannot but wonder whether it all seems as awful at your distance as it does here. I doubt it. No war ever seemed so real to me as this: of course I have been to some of the towns about which they have been fighting; and I know that men I have known, including one of my best friends, must be fighting each other. So it's hard for me to write interestingly about the war.

I hope to hear that you have had a quiet summer, at best. Did Walter Cook ever call? If you have seen Harry [Child] let me know how he is, and that he is not starving himself.

Always affectionately

Tom

P.S. (After rereading). Please don't quote *Pomona*. It's perhaps a literary as well as a social mistake to write as one would talk. I apologize for the quality of this letter anyway.

Katherine Mansfield

[1888–1923]

Katherine Mansfield was born Kathleen Mansfield Beauchamp in Wellington, New Zealand, the fourth child of wealthy parents. In 1903 she was sent to London to complete her education at Queen's College, where she began writing for the college magazine. After graduation in 1906, she went back to New Zealand, but she harboured ambitions to return to Europe and write. By 1907 she had made several small contributions to the Australian monthly *Native Companion*, and by 1908 she had persuaded her parents to allow her to return to London to pursue her literary career. It was to be the last time she saw New Zealand.

In 1909 she married George Bowden, but left him shortly after. It was he who suggested that she contribute some of her short stories to the Fabian-socialist magazine *The New Age*. She wrote for the magazine between 1910 and 1912, submitting various feminist pieces and satires including the 'Bavarian Sketches', which were collected and published as *In a German Pension* (1911). In 1911, she met and began living with the critic John Middleton Murry. Together they founded *Rhythm*, an avant-garde literary quarterly. It was as a result of this partnership that Mansfield met D. H. Lawrence and Leonard and Virginia Woolf, all of whom were to have a great influence on her life. In 1915, after the news of her brother's death, she wrote *Prelude* (1917). The story was one of many that focused upon her childhood in New Zealand. It was also one of the earliest publications by the Hogarth Press, owned by Leonard and Virginia Woolf. By the time Mansfield published her next collection, *Je Ne Parlais Français* (1918), she was becoming well known for her skills as a short-story writer. It was at this point that tuberculosis was diagnosed and, knowing that death was imminent, she began to write at a phenomenal pace.

In 1918 she and Middleton Murry were married, and Mansfield spent the last years of her life seeking relief from her illness in France. Despite great suffering, she managed to build up a body of work that, in its experimentation with literary form, was to transform the genre of the short story. Concentrating less on plot and more on conveying the continuity of ordinary life, Mansfield developed her technique by using devices such as internal monologue, flashbacks and daydreams. Her polemical writing, concerned with themes of self-development, sexual corruption and female art, was also to make an important contribution to feminism. Among the last works to be published during her lifetime were *Bliss and Other Stories* (1920), *The Garden Party and Other Stories* (1920) and *The Dove's Nest and Other Stories* (1922). She died in France in 1923. Posthumous works include *Poems* (1923), edited by Middleton Murry, *Something Childish and Other Stories* (1924) and *The Aloe* (1930). Middleton Murry also edited Mansfield's journals and two collections of her letters.

Unlike T. S. Eliot, Katherine Mansfield did not have a place at university waiting for her. She arrived in England determined to make a career for herself as a writer. However, being both a 'colonial' and a woman, this was difficult and in her story 'The Tiredness of Rosabel' (1924) she clearly draws upon her own feelings of loneliness and isolation during her first years in Britain.

The Tiredness of Rosabel

At the corner of Oxford Circus Rosabel bought a bunch of violets, and that was practically the reason why she had so little tea – for a scone and a boiled egg and a cup of cocoa at Lyons are not ample sufficiency after a hard day's work in a millinery establishment. As she swung on to the step of the Atlas 'bus, grabbed her skirt with one hand and clung to the railing with the other, Rosabel thought she would have sacrificed her soul for a good dinner – roast duck and green peas, chestnut stuffing, pudding with brandy sauce – something hot and strong and filling. She sat down next to a girl very much her own age who was reading *Anna Lombard* in a cheap, paper-covered edition, and the rain had tear-spattered the pages. Rosabel looked out of the windows; the street was blurred and misty, but light striking on the panes turned their dullness to opal and silver, and the jewellers' shops seen through this, were fairy palaces. Her feet were horribly wet, and she knew the bottom of her skirt and petticoat would be coated with black, greasy mud. There was a sickening smell of warm humanity – it seemed to be oozing out of everybody in the 'bus – and everybody had the same expression, sitting so still, staring in front of them. How many times had she read these advertisements – 'Sapolio Saves Time, Saves Labour' – 'Heinz's Tomato Sauce' – and the inane, annoying dialogue between doctor and judge concerning the superlative merits of 'Lamplough's Pyretic Saline.' She glanced at the book which the girl read so earnestly, mouthing the words in a way that Rosabel detested, licking her first finger and thumb each time that she turned the page. She could not see very clearly; it was something about a hot, voluptuous night, a band playing, and a girl with lovely, white shoulders. Oh, Heavens! Rosabel stirred suddenly and unfastened the two top buttons of her coat . . . she felt almost stifled. Through her half-closed eyes the whole row of people on the opposite seat seemed to resolve into one fatuous, staring face . . .

And this was her corner. She stumbled a little on her way out and lurched against the girl next her. 'I beg your pardon,' said Rosabel, but the girl did not even look up. Rosabel saw that she was smiling as she read.

Westbourne Grove looked as she had always imagined Venice to look at night, mysterious, dark, even the hansoms were like gondolas dodging up and down, and the lights trailing luridly – tongues of flame licking the wet street – magic fish swimming in the Grand Canal. She was more than glad to reach Richmond Road, but from the corner of the street until she came to No. 26 she thought of those four flights of stairs. Oh, why four flights! It was really criminal to expect people to live so high up. Every house ought to have a lift, something simple and inexpensive, or else an electric staircase like the one at Earl's Court – but four flights! When she stood in the hall and saw the first flight ahead of her and the stuffed albatross head on the landing, glimmering ghost-like in the light of the little gas jet, she almost cried. Well, they had to be faced; it was very like bicycling up a steep hill, but there was not the satisfaction of flying down the other side . . .

Her own room at last! She closed the door, lit the gas, took off her hat and coat, skirt, blouse, unhooked her old flannel dressing-gown from behind the door, pulled it on, then unlaced her boots – on consideration her stockings were not wet enough to change. She went over to the wash-stand. The jug had not been filled again to-day. There was just enough water to soak the sponge, and the enamel was coming off the basin – that was the second time she had scratched her chin.

It was just seven o'clock. If she pulled the blind up and put out the gas it was much more restful – Rosabel did not want to read. So she knelt down on the floor, pillowing her arms on the window-sill . . . just one little sheet of glass between her and the great wet world outside!

She began to think of all that had happened during the day. Would she ever forget that awful woman in the grey mackintosh who had wanted a trimmed motor-cap – 'something purple with something rosy each side' – or the girl who had tried on every hat in the shop and then said she would 'call in tomorrow and decide definitely.' Rosabel could not help smiling; the excuse was worn so thin . . .

But there had been one other – a girl with beautiful red hair and a white skin and eyes the colour of that green ribbon shot with gold they had got from Paris last week. Rosabel had seen her electric brougham at the door; a man had come in with her, quite a young man; and so well dressed.

'What is it exactly that I want, Harry?' she had said, as Rosabel took the pins out of her hat, untied her veil, and gave her a hand-mirror.

'You must have a black hat,' he had answered, 'a black hat with a feather that goes right round it and then round your neck and ties in a bow under your chin, and the ends tuck into your belt – a decent-sized feather.'

The girl glanced at Rosabel laughingly. 'Have you any hats like that?'

They had been very hard to please; Harry would demand the impossible, and Rosabel was almost in despair. Then she remembered the big, untouched box upstairs.

'Oh, one moment, Madam,' she had said. 'I think perhaps I can show you something that will please you better.' She had run up, breathlessly, cut the cords, scattered the tissue paper, and yes, there was the very hat – rather large, soft, with a great, curled feather, and a black velvet rose, nothing else. They had been charmed. The girl had put it on and then handed it to Rosabel.

'Let me see how it looks on you,' she said, frowning a little, very serious indeed.

Rosabel turned to the mirror and placed it on her brown hair, then faced them.

'Oh, Harry, isn't it adorable,' the girl cried, 'I must have that!' She smiled again at Rosabel. 'It suits you, beautifully.'

A sudden, ridiculous feeling of anger had seized Rosabel. She longed to throw the lovely, perishable thing in the girl's face, and bent over the hat, flushing.

'It's exquisitely finished off inside, Madam,' she said. The girl swept out to her brougham, and left Harry to pay and bring the box with him.

'I shall go straight home and put it on before I come out to lunch with you,' Rosabel heard her say.

The man leant over her as she made out the bill, then, as he counted the money into her hand – 'Ever been painted?' he said.

'No,' said Rosabel, shortly, realizing the swift change in his voice, the slight tinge of insolence, of familiarity.

'Oh, well you ought to be,' said Harry. 'You've got such a damned pretty little figure.'

Rosabel did not pay the slightest attention. How handsome he had been! She had thought of no one else all day; his face fascinated her; she could see clearly his fine, straight eyebrows, and his hair grew back from his forehead with just the slightest suspicion of crisp curl, his laughing, disdainful mouth. She saw again his slim hands counting the money into hers . . . Rosabel suddenly pushed the hair back from her face, her forehead was hot . . . if those slim hands could rest one moment . . . the luck of that girl!

Suppose they changed places. Rosabel would drive home with him, of course they were in love with each other, but not engaged, very nearly, and she would say – 'I won't be one moment.' He would wait in the brougham while her maid took the hat-box up the stairs, following Rosabel. Then the great white and pink bedroom with roses everywhere in dull silver vases. She would sit down before the mirror and the little French maid would fasten her hat and find her a thin, fine veil and another pair of white suède gloves – a button had come off the gloves she had worn that morning. She had scented her furs and gloves and handkerchief, taken a big muff and run down stairs. The butler opened the door, Harry was waiting, they drove away together. . . *That* was life, thought Rosabel! On the way to the Carlton they stopped at Gerard's, Harry bought her great sprays of Parma violets, filled her hands with them.

'Oh, they are sweet!' she said, holding them against her face.

'It is as you always should be,' said Harry, 'with your hands full of violets.'

(Rosabel realized that her knees were getting stiff; she sat down on the floor and leant her head against the wall.) Oh, that lunch! The table covered with flowers, a band hidden behind a grove of palms playing music that fired her blood like wine – the soup, and oysters, and pigeons, and creamed potatoes, and champagne, of course, and afterwards coffee and cigarettes. She would lean over the table fingering her glass with one hand, talking with that charming gaiety which Harry so appreciated. Afterwards a matinée, something that gripped them both, and then tea at the 'Cottage.'

'Sugar? Milk? Cream?' The little homely questions seemed to suggest a joyous intimacy. And then home again in the dusk, and the scent of the Parma violets seemed to drench the air with their sweetness.

'I'll call for you at nine,' he said as he left her.

The fire had been lighted in her boudoir, the curtains drawn, there were a great pile of letters waiting her – invitations for the Opera, dinners, balls, a week-end on the river, a motor tour – she glanced through them listlessly as she went upstairs to dress. A fire in her bedroom, too, and her beautiful, shining dress spread on the bed – white tulle over silver, silver shoes, silver scarf, a little silver fan. Rosabel knew that she was the most famous woman at the ball that night; men paid her homage, a foreign Prince desired to be presented to this English wonder. Yes, it was a voluptuous night, a band playing, and *her* lovely white shoulders . . .

But she became very tired. Harry took her home, and came in with her for just one moment. The fire was out in the drawing-room, but the sleepy maid waited for her in her boudoir. She took off her cloak, dismissed the servant, and went over to the fireplace, and stood peeling off her gloves; the firelight shone on her hair, Harry came across the room and caught her in his arms – 'Rosabel, Rosabel, Rosabel' . . . Oh, the haven of those arms, and she was very tired.

(The real Rosabel, the girl crouched on the floor in the dark, laughed aloud, and put her hand up to her hot mouth.)

Of course they rode in the park next morning, the engagement had been announced in the *Court Circular*, all the world knew, all the world was shaking hands with her . . .

They were married shortly afterwards at St George's, Hanover Square, and motored down to Harry's old ancestral home for the honeymoon; the peasants in the village curtseyed to them as they passed; under the folds of the rug he pressed her hands convulsively. And that night she wore again her white and silver frock. She was tired after the journey and went upstairs to bed . . . quite early . . .

The real Rosabel got up from the floor and undressed slowly, folding her clothes over the back of a chair. She slipped over her head her coarse, calico nightdress, and took the pins out of her hair – the soft, brown flood of it fell round her, warmly. Then she blew out the candle and groped her way into bed, pulling the blankets and grimy 'honeycomb' quilt closely round her neck, cuddling down in the darkness . . .

So she slept and dreamed, and smiled in her sleep, and once threw out her arm to feel for something which was not there, dreaming still.

And the night passed. Presently the cold fingers of dawn closed over her uncovered hand; grey light flooded the dull room. Rosabel shivered, drew a little gasping breath, sat up. And because her heritage was that tragic optimism, which is all too often the only inheritance of youth, still half asleep, she smiled, with a little nervous tremor round her mouth.

Jean Rhys

[1890–1979]

Jean Rhys was born Ella Gwendolen Rees Williams, on the British island of Dominica, to a Welsh doctor and his Creole wife. She was the fourth of five children. The family lived in the capital, Roseau, but made frequent visits to her mother's family plantation, where Rhys's maternal grandmother and great-aunt lived. Rhys cherished these visits, and her novel *Wide Sargasso Sea* (1966) draws upon their reminiscences of Dominica in the mid-nineteenth century.

Rhys was educated at a convent in Roseau where, despite whites being the minority, the children were brought up to mimic the manners of English ladies. Her strong sense of identity with Dominica and her perception of England as 'unreal' meant Rhys soon grew to understand the problematic relationship between colour and class. In 1907 Rhys left Dominica for England, where she attended the Perse School in Cambridge and later the Academy of Dramatic Art in London. After two years her father's death left her without funds and, feeling that she was not wanted by her family in Dominica, Rhys chose to remain in London. For the next two years she toured England as a chorus girl with a theatre company.

Rhys's unhappy experiences with the company led her towards writing and in 1913 she began to note down everything that had happened to her. Rhys supported herself financially with the help of an ex-lover (a relationship that had ended with her having an abortion), and through various stage, modelling and waitressing jobs. Then in 1917 she met her future husband, Jean Lenglet. Lenglet told Rhys that he was a journalist (though it later transpired that he was a French spy) and within a few weeks he had proposed to her. Looking for a new beginning, Rhys accepted. In the first three years of their marriage, the couple moved between Amsterdam, Paris, Vienna and Budapest. Both worked, but they were never financially secure. In 1920 Rhys bore a son who died three weeks later. Shortly after her son's death, it became clear that in order to get money Lenglet had been selling stolen goods. Despite the fact that Rhys was pregnant again, the couple were forced to live like fugitives. They returned to Paris at the end of 1922 and, desperate to earn money, Rhys began translating Lenglet's articles to sell to English papers. It was through these efforts that she met the writer and publisher Ford Madox Ford, to whom she showed her early notebooks. That same year, in 1923, Lenglet was finally arrested and sent to prison.

Encouraged by Ford, and through him introduced to the Parisian literary set, Rhys began writing stories. By 1927, having adopted the pen-name Jean Rhys, she was developing her precise and clear style. However, she had become uncomfortably dependent upon Ford, and although he lived with his companion, Stella Bowen, she moved into their house and began an affair with him. These events were to become the basis of her first novel, *Postures* (now known as *Quartet*, 1928). By 1927, Rhys was separated from Lenglet. That same year, while on a visit to London, she met Leslie Tilden Smith, a literary agent and publisher's reader whom she later married in 1932. Smith was to play a valuable and supportive role in Rhys's career, editing her work and keeping her in contact with the publishing world.

During the 1930s, Rhys published three novels, *After Leaving Mr Mackenzie* (1930), *Voyage in the Dark* (1934) and *Good Morning, Midnight* (1939). In each, her vision becomes increasingly pessimistic and destructive as she describes the same lonely, alienated and unwanted female figure battling against the forces of class and culture. These were themes that vividly echoed her own sense of personal exile and loss. In 1936, before completing her third novel, Rhys had visited Dominica for the first time in thirty years. Although she was disappointed by the political and social changes, in a letter back to a friend she spoke of feeling a passionate sense of belonging that was so lacking in her life in Europe.

During the 1940s and 1950s Rhys disappeared completely from the literary scene. In 1945 Smith died of a heart attack and two years later Rhys married his cousin, Max Hamer. They had little money and their misfortunes culminated in Hamer being imprisoned for three years over a case of fraud. Throughout these desolate years Rhys lived in total obscurity, but despite being slowed by age and ill-health she had already begun work on the first draft of *Wide Sargasso Sea*, a novel based on an idea that had been with her since reading Charlotte Brontë's *Jane Eyre* in 1906. In the late 1950s the editor and critic Francis Wyndham sought her out in order to gain permission for a radio adaptation of her novel *Good Morning, Midnight*. Wyndham became her mentor and for the next seven years he helped her through the completion of her new novel. By now Hamer's health had broken down completely and he died in 1966, shortly before the publication of *Wide Sargasso Sea*. Rhys's new novel was well received and undoubtedly her best achievement. She wrote steadily until her death in 1979, publishing two more collections of stories, *Tigers are Better Looking* (1968) and *Sleep It Off, Lady* (1976). Her unfinished autobiography, *Smile Please*, was published posthumously in 1979.

Rhys arrived in Britain as a 'colonial' young woman from the Caribbean and, as she makes clear in 'First Steps' (from Smile Please*), she soon found herself baffled by everything, from the weather to the plumbing. Loneliness quickly enveloped her life, and this passage reflects the lifelong unhappiness that she felt trying to adapt to the country that she eventually made her home.*

First Steps

On the sea it was still warm at first and I loved it, though I could not get over the huge amount that people ate. First there was a large breakfast, all sorts of unfamiliar dishes. At eleven o'clock the steward came round with cups of Bovril. Then a huge lunch of four or five courses.

I ate my way steadily through and could scarcely walk when I got up. Then my aunt explained that we were meant to take only a little of each course. Lunch wasn't over until half-past two. At five, tea: another huge meal with cakes, bread and butter, jam. Dinner at eight o'clock was the most important meal and the longest. The orchestra playing at meals enchanted me. They gave a concert and I sang. Everyone applauded and I told my aunt that when I got to London I would go straight on to the stage. She laughed heartily.

Then, quite suddenly it seemed, it began to grow cold. The sky was grey, not blue. The sea was sometimes rough. My aunt sat on deck in a thick coat with rugs round her. There were rugs for me too, but still I shivered. It was a very grey day when we reached Southampton and when I looked out of the porthole my heart sank. Then I thought 'Now at last I shall see a train.' I had seen toy trains. They were always brightly coloured, green, red, blue, so I stood on a platform at Southampton station bewildered because I could see nothing that resembled a train.

'But I don't see the train, where is it?'

'Right in front of you,' said my aunt and stepped into what I thought was a brown, dingy little room. There were racks overhead and people sitting in the corners. This, then, was a train. I said nothing and after a while the train started.

Before long we were plunged into black darkness. A railway accident, I thought. We came into the light again. 'Was that a railway accident?' – 'No, it was a tunnel,' my aunt said, laughing.

We stayed at a boarding-house somewhere in Bloomsbury, it may have been Upper Bedford Place. The first morning I was in London I woke up very early. I lay for what seemed an age. There wasn't a sound but I wanted to see what London looked like so I got up, put on my clothes and went out. The street door must have been bolted, not locked, or perhaps the key was in the door. At any rate I got out quite easily into a long, grey, straight street. It was misty but not cold. There were not many people about, nor much traffic. I think I must have found my way into New Oxford Street and then walked to Holborn. It was all the same, long, straight, grey, a bit disappointing. I began to feel hungry, and as I had kept careful count of the turnings I was soon on my way back. It must have been about half-past seven. When I tried the door it was open and there was a maid in the passage who seemed astonished when she saw me. I said 'Good morning' but she didn't answer.

On my way to my room I passed the bathroom and thought it would be a good idea to have a bath. I felt not hot, but sticky and a little tired. So I went in and turned the hot water tap on. When the bath was half-full I undressed and got in, thinking it very pleasant. I began to feel rather happy and thought that when the water got cool

I would turn the hot tap on again. I began to sing. Then above the noise of the water came a loud voice.

'Who's that in there?'

I answered with my name.

'Turn that tap off,' said the voice. 'Turn that tap off at once.'

I turned it off. All my pleasure had gone and I got out of the bath and into my clothes as quickly as I could. When I reached my room my aunt was waiting for me. I said: 'I'm afraid the landlady is very annoyed with me.'

'Of course she's annoyed with you,' said my aunt. 'What possessed you to go into the bathroom and take all the hot water?'

'I didn't mean to take all the hot water,' I said. 'I just wanted to have a bath. After all, it's a fairly natural thing to have in the morning.'

My aunt said: 'It didn't occur to you that nobody else would have any hot water at all?'

'I never thought of that,' I said.

'I've already noticed,' said my aunt, 'that you are quite incapable of thinking about anyone else but yourself.'

I didn't answer this though there were many things I wanted to say: that English plumbing was a mystery to me, that indoor lavatories shocked me, that I thought a tap marked 'H' would automatically spout hot water, that it never occurred to me that the supply was limited and where did it come from anyway?

My aunt then explained the ritual of having a bath in an English boarding-house. You had to ask for it several days beforehand, you had to be very careful to take it at that time and no other, and so on and so on.

All through breakfast the landlady glared at me. My aunt wouldn't speak to me. I could hardly swallow my eggs and bacon. 'We are going to see the Wallace Collection this morning,' said my aunt. 'Are you ready?'

For the next few days my aunt showed me the sights: Westminster Abbey, Saint Paul's, the zoo. I don't know what reaction she expected but I know that I disappointed her. For instance I liked the outside of

Westminster Abbey but when we went in I thought it a muddle, a jumble of statues and memorial tablets. Hardly room to move, I thought. 'Don't you think it's wonderful?' she said. 'Yes, but rather crowded.' I thought Saint Paul's too cold, too Protestant. I looked for one bit of warmth and colour but couldn't find it. In the Wallace Collection I fell asleep when she left me on a bench.

As for the zoo, I simply hated it. We saw the lions first and I thought the majestic lion looked at me with such sad eyes, pacing, pacing up and down, never stopping. Then we made a special journey to see the Dominica parrot. The grey bird was hunched in on himself, the most surly, resentful parrot I had ever seen. I said 'Hello' to him but he wouldn't even look at me. 'Of course he is very old,' said my aunt. 'Nobody knows how old.'

'Poor bird,' I said.

Then the alligators and crocodiles which frightened me so much I could barely look at them. Then the snakes. Finally we went to see the hummingbirds. The hummingbirds finished me.

I believe that it is quite different now, but then they were in a little side room, the floor very dirty. Thick slices of bread smeared with marmalade or jam of some sort were suspended on wires. The birds were flying around in a bewildered way. Trying desperately to get out, it seemed to me. Even their colours were dim. I got such an impression of hopeless misery that I couldn't bear to look. My aunt finally asked me if I had enjoyed it and I said yes I had, but then and there I decided that nothing would ever persuade me to go into a zoo again.

The first time I felt a sense of wonder in England was when we, a few of the boarders at the Perse School for Girls, Cambridge, were taken to Ely Cathedral. There were no pews or chairs, only a space, empty, and the altar, and stained-glass windows. The pillars on either side were like a stone forest. I was so excited and moved that I began to tremble.

The classical mistress, Miss Patey, was in charge of the flock. Afterwards we went to have tea with one of her friends. We sat on a veranda with flagstones. I took the cup of tea that was offered to me but my hands were shaking so much that I dropped the cup, which was, of course, smashed. I mumbled some sort of apology and just for a moment the hostess looked at the pieces with a regretful face. Miss Patey apologized.

I left the Perse School after one term. I had written to my father about my great wish to be an actress, and true to his promise he wrote back 'That is what you must do.'

The Academy of Dramatic Art, then known colloquially as Tree's School after Beerbohm Tree, the manager of His Majesty's Theatre, hadn't been going very long when I went there. It had not yet become 'Royal'. I was surprised when I found I had passed the so-called entrance examination. My aunt, who disapproved of the whole affair, left me in a boarding-house in Upper Bedford Place, very excited and anxious to do my best. I was seventeen.

The Academy was divided into the As, the Bs and the Cs. The As were the new students, the Bs were half-way and I never met any of the Cs. Well-known actors and actresses would arrive to advise the Cs, but we never saw them except in passing. When matinée idols like Henry Ainley arrived, the girls would haunt the passages hoping to catch a glimpse of them, but they would pass along quickly, and also one wasn't supposed to look.

The As were taught by an actress whose Christian name was Gertrude. I have forgotten her surname. The Bs we sometimes met in a room downstairs presided over by a woman called Hetty. Here you could get coffee and sandwiches and here I met several of the Bs and came to dislike them. I thought them conceited and unkind. Once, when I left my furs behind and came back to fetch them, I heard someone say, 'Is this goat or monkey?'

I must confess that my furs, like all my clothes, were hideous, for my aunt's one idea had been to fit me out as cheaply as possible. When we bought my one dress, my everyday wear, the skirt was far too long even for those days but she said to have it altered would be too expensive. I could tuck it up at the waist and because I was so thin nobody would notice. So apparelled, I set off to be inspected by the As, the Bs and the Cs.

Miss Gertrude was quite a good teacher, I think. One of our first lessons was to learn how to laugh. This was comparatively easy. You sang the doh re ma fah soh lah ti doh, and done quickly enough it did turn out to be a laugh, though rather artificial. Our next lesson was to learn how to cry. 'And now, watch me,' said Miss Gertrude. She turned away for a few seconds, and when she turned back tears were coursing down her face, which itself remained unmoved. 'Now try,' she said. The students stood in a row trying to cry. 'Think of something sad,' whispered the girl next to me. I looked along the line and they were all making such hideous faces in their attempts to cry that I began to laugh. Miss Gertrude never approved of me.

We had lessons in fencing, dancing, gesture (*del sarte*) and elocution. In the elocution master's class there was once a scene which puzzled me and made me feel sad. It upset me because the master, whose name was Mr Heath, was the only one except for the gesture woman who gave me the slightest encouragement or took any notice of me, and Honour, the pupil who quarrelled with him, was the only one I really liked. We had even been to a matinée together, accompanied by a sour-faced maid. We were reciting a poem in which the word 'froth' occurred, and Honour refused to pronounce the word as Mr Heath did. 'Froth' said the elocution master. 'Frawth' said the pupil. For a long time they shouted at each other: 'Froth' – 'Frawth' – 'Troth' 'Frawth'. I listened to this appalled. 'Froth' – 'Frawth' – 'Froth' – 'Frawth'. At last Honour said: 'I refuse to pronounce the word "froth". "Froth" is cockney and I'm not here to learn cockney.' Her face was quite white with the freckles showing. 'I think you mean to be rude,' Mr Heath said. 'Will you leave the class, please.' Honour stalked out, white as a sheet. 'We will now go on with the lesson,' said Mr Heath, red as a beet. There was no end to the scandal. Honour was taken away from the school by her mother, who had written a book on the proper pronunciation of English. Mr Heath was either dismissed or left. This gave me my first insight into the snobbishness and unkindness that went on.

Part of our training was that every week some of us would have to act a well-known scene before Miss Gertrude, and she would criticize it and say who was right and who was wrong. We usually played a scene from *Lady Windermere's Fan* or *Paula and Francesca* by Stephen Philips. I soon got caught up with five or six other students.

A man we called Toppy was a bit of a clown and announced that he intended to go into music hall, not the straight theatre. The other man of our group, to my great surprise, asked me to marry him. Having a proposal made me feel as if I had passed an examination. He wrote me a long letter which started by saying he noticed that my landlady bullied me and that I had better get away from her by marrying him. He then talked about money. He said that as he was now twenty-one he had come into his money, and he was anxious to meet my aunt to explain matters to her. He ended the letter by saying that if I would consent we would spend our honeymoon in Africa, travelling from the Cape to Cairo. The trip did sound tempting, but I answered the letter solemnly that my only wish was to be a great actress. After some thought I crossed out *great* and put *good*. When we met afterwards at the Academy he didn't seem at all embarrassed, and never referred either to his letter or my answer.

One of the girls with whom for a time I made friends was half Turkish. She asked me to tea at her rooms and spent all the time talking about a hectic love affair. 'You don't know anything about it,' she'd say, then proceed to tell me all about it at great length. One day when I went there she was darning some stockings. She said, 'I expect you are very surprised to see someone like me darning stockings.' I said, 'No, why?' From that time on our friendship cooled. She stopped inviting me to tea.

At that time where was a dancer called Maud Allen playing at the Palace Theatre. She was a barefoot dancer as they called it then, and wore vaguely classic Greek clothes. She was, of course, imitating Isadora Duncan. A lot of people in London were shocked by her and when in one of her dances she brought in the head of John the Baptist on a dish, there was quite a row and she had to cut that bit out. One day our dancing teacher said: 'Maud Allen is *not* a dancer. She doesn't even begin to be a dancer. But if I told her to run across the stage and pretend to pick a flower she would do it, and do it well. I'm afraid I cannot say the same of all the young ladies in the class, and I advise you all to go to the Palace and watch Maud Allen. It might do you a lot of good.'

During vacation from the Academy I went to Harrogate to visit an uncle. It was there that I heard of my father's death. My mother wrote that she could not afford to keep me at the Academy and that I must return to Dominica. I was determined not to do that, and in any case I was sure that they didn't want me back. My aunt and I met in London to buy hot-climate clothes, and when she was doing her own shopping I went to a theatrical agent in the Strand, called Blackmore, and got a job in the chorus of a musical comedy called *Our Miss Gibbs*.

C. L. R. James

[1901–89]

Cyril Lionel Robert James was born in Trinidad, the son of a schoolteacher. At the age of nine he won a scholarship to the Queen's Royal College in Port of Spain. After graduating in 1918, he taught at the college and then at the Government Training College for Teachers. During this time, he began writing fiction. In 1927 he published 'La Divina Pastora', a story about rural peasant life, which was reprinted in the *British Saturday Review of Literature*. This put James into the centre of a group of liberal British expatriates and young Trinidadian intellectuals whose creative endeavours centred around the cultural development of Trinidad and the West Indies as a whole. The group set up and published a biannual literary magazine, *Trinidad*, which contained stories, poems and essays by its members. They came to be known as the Beacon Group and in 1931 a new magazine, *The Beacon*, was launched. Over the next two years, twenty-eight issues appeared. The magazine carried some of James's best stories, including 'Triumph', which initiated the still-current tradition of comic tales that recount competitive life among the urban poor. James's background, like that of many of his intellectual contemporaries, gave him very little direct social contact with lower-class blacks, but unlike other intellectuals, who offered sympathy to uneducated people while dismissing their ability to learn, James carefully studied their social alienation. The relationship between the educated and the uneducated dominates his early writing and features in his first novel, *Minty Alley* (1936).

In 1932 James left Trinidad for England. He worked first as a cricket correspondent for the *Manchester Guardian* and later as journal editor of the International African Service Bureau, the organ of George Padmore's Pan-African movement. Exposed to radical new ideas in England, James became active in British politics and joined the Independent Labour Party. In 1936 he wrote his last literary work, the play *Toussaint L'Ouverture*, based on the Haitian revolution. It was first performed the same year, with Paul Robeson in the lead role. Later James utilized the play as part of his major historical study *The Black Jacobins: Toussaint L'Ouverture and the San Domingo Revolution* (1938). Rather than celebrate the military successes of Haiti's revolution, James illuminated the strengths and weaknesses of its black leadership. He questioned the true freedom of the Haitian people under the yoke of a despotic regime, and concluded that in many ways the new system was as oppressive as the original French colonial system.

By now James had become well acquainted with Marxism and was concentrating on developing principles for an autonomous black Marxist ideology. Between 1938 and 1952 he lectured widely in the United States and published the first of his historical and polemical works, *A History of Negro Revolt* (1938). However, his Marxist theories were not acceptable in the McCarthy era and, following almost a year of internment on Ellis Island, James was expelled from the United States. During his internment he wrote a study of the work of the American writer Herman Melville, *Mariners, Renegades and Castaways* (1953).

After a period of five years in England, during which time he continued his writing and his work with the Pan-African movement, James decided in 1958 to return to the West Indies in order to contribute to the intellectual and political life of his country, Trinidad, as it prepared for political independence. He became secretary of the Federal Labour Party and for a short time edited the journal of the People's National Movement, *The Nation*. Over the next three years he gave lectures and wrote two books, *Modern Politics* (1960) and *Party Politics in the West Indies* (1962). However, following a difference of opinion with Trinidad's political leader, Dr Eric Williams, *Modern Politics* was banned and James returned to England in 1962, just days before Trinidad's independence.

Throughout the 1960s and 1970s he continued to write and lecture in Europe, America and Africa. In 1965 he returned to Trinidad as a cricket correspondent, but upon his arrival he was put under house arrest. A public outcry led to his release and he stayed for several months, during which time he founded the Workers' and Peasants' Party and started a newspaper, *We the People*. Among his later works were a popular commentary on the social role of cricket, *Beyond a Boundary* (1963), *Notes on Dialectics: Hegel, Marx, Lenin* (1971) and *Nkrumah and the Ghana Revolution* (1977). From 1981 until his death in 1989, he lived and worked in the Brixton area of London.

James is at the head of a rich twentieth-century tradition of Caribbean writers who have migrated to Britain in order to develop their literary careers. The deep desire of these writers to 'belong' is made all the more poignant by their sense of expectation. They were arriving in the 'mother country', and writers such as James were anxious to display their knowledge of the literary traditions. In 'Bloomsbury: An Encounter with Edith Sitwell' (1932) there is a swaggering ease about the manner in which James flaunts his learning, as though he wishes to remind everyone that being born in Trinidad should not be viewed as an impediment to full participation in English literary life.

Bloomsbury: An Encounter with Edith Sitwell

I have been living in London for ten weeks and will give what can only be called first impressions. I have been living in Bloomsbury, that is to say, the students' and young writers' quarter. It is as different from Clapham or Ealing suburban, as you can imagine, and is in its way distinctive, so absolutely different from life in the West Indies, that it stands out as easily the most striking of my first impressions. In later articles, I shall go more into detail about such things as have struck me – houses, food, clothes, men, women, the streets, scores of things. But for the present my chief concern will be with Bloomsbury and the Bloomsbury atmosphere. I shall best describe it by not trying to describe it at all, but by merely setting down faithfully the events of three or four days, just as they happened. If there is a lot of 'I' and 'I' and 'I', it cannot be helped. I can only give my own impressions, and what happened to me. To generalize about so large a district and such numbers of people after only ten weeks would be the limit of rashness.

I shall begin with Wednesday the eighteenth of May. I reached home from the city at about half past three having twice sat before food and both times been unable to eat. I knew from long experience that I had a sleepless night before me, and to make matters worse, my right hand which had been going for some time decided finally to go.

I tried to write and found that I could not – nervous strain I expect. I went to bed, got out of bed, went to bed again, knocked about the place a bit, tried to read, failed, in fact did not know what to do with myself. But I was in Bloomsbury, so would always find distractions.

Restlessness was the only reason which made me go to a lecture at the Student Movement House by Miss Edith Sitwell. I had promised to go with a girl whom I have met here, extremely interesting, and the only person I have ever met, who, if we are looking down a book or newspaper together, has to wait at the end of the page for me, and not by three or four lines but sometimes by ten. I had almost intended to telephone to say that I was not going, but the prospect of my own company in a room of a Bloomsbury lodging-house, aesthetically speaking, one of the worst places in the world, made me decide to summon up some energy and go to hear Miss Sitwell. I went over to my friend's room and met there, herself and another girl friend of hers who had ridden five miles to come to the lecture, and was to ride five miles afterwards to get home. We walked over to the Student House, which is a club for London students, white and coloured, but with its chief aim giving coloured students in London an opportunity to meet together and fraternize with English students and with one another. The atmosphere of the place is definitely intellectual, in intention at least.

Now I had heard a lot about Miss Edith Sitwell before. She is supposed to be eccentric, in appearance and manner at least. She and her two brothers, Osbert and Sacheverell, are a family of wealthy people who have devoted themselves to literature (chiefly poetry) and the arts. They have made quite a name for themselves as poets and critics, and although few modern writers have attracted such a storm of hostile criticism, yet that in itself is perhaps a testimony of a certain amount of virility in their work. Today, however, they have won their position and are among the first flight of the younger generation of English writers. Miss Edith Sitwell, I had been told in Trinidad, rather posed. She wore robes, not dresses, and, to judge from her photographs, was not only handsome, but distinctly evil-looking in appearance. She had an underlip that seemed the last word in spite and malice, and in nearly every photograph that I had seen a rebellious lock of hair waved formidably about her forehead.

At a quarter past eight there was the usual whisper and the lady walked into the room. If ever rumour had been lying, this certainly was a case. She did wear robes, some old brocaded stuff, dark in colour with a pattern of some kind. The waist was about six inches below where the waist of the ordinary dress is and the skirt was not joined to the bodice in a straight line but by means of many half circles looking somewhat like the rim of an opened umbrella. Women will know the kind of design I mean. But the chief thing was that she could carry the dress. She is tall and though mature, still slim and the dress fitted beautifully. But even more remarkable than the dress was the face, a thin aristocratic well-formed face, very sharp and very keen. Her eyes too, were bright and keen. The lip I saw later did look spiteful at times but it was only when she shot an arrow at some of her fellow poets and writers, and to speak the truth, she had a good many to shoot. The lock of hair I can say nothing about, because she wore a small white cap which would have kept the most rebellious locks in order. She stood on the little platform to address us, a striking figure, decidedly good-looking, and even more decidedly a personality. Perhaps the outstanding impression was one of fitness and keenness together, the same impression I had got from a bronze head of her brother, which I had seen in the Tate.

I do not intend to go into her lecture, which consisted partly of readings from her own and other works and partly of short dissertations on certain aspects of modern work, the Sitwells being essentially of the modern school. Her voice was not exceptional and she was rather hoarse but she read well. Most interesting to me, however, were the bombs she threw at writer after writer. For a sample, Mr D. H. Lawrence, who would be judged by most people as the finest English writer of the post-war period. Miss Sitwell (sparkling with malicious enjoyment) told us that in the course of a lecture at Liverpool she had defined Mr Lawrence as the chief of the Jaeger school of poetry. This was reported in the press and a few days afterwards she received a dignified letter from the famous firm of underwear makers, saying that they had noted her remark and would like to know what she meant by that reference to their goods.

Miss Sitwell replied that she had called Mr Lawrence the head of the Jaeger School because his poetry was like Jaeger underwear, hot, soft and woolly; whereupon the Jaeger Company replied that while their products were soft and woolly they begged to deny that they were in any way hot, owing to their special process which resulted in non-conductivity of heat. Miss Sitwell begged to apologize and asked the Jaeger Company if they could discover a special process for Mr D. H. Lawrence which would have the same effect of non-conductivity. Unfortunately Mr Lawrence died too soon and nothing could be done. That is a sample of the kind of compliment she distributed and it is only fair to say that she and her two brothers if they give hard knocks have received quite as many. Naturally I was very much interested in all this and soon realized that I had done very well to come. But more was to follow. Speaking of D. H. Lawrence, she said that she did not think much of his work, that even his novels were very much overrated, and that she knew a young American writer of 31 or 32 who was a far finer novelist than D. H. Lawrence. However wild horses would not draw his name from her.

Of course that was easy. I told her at once that it was William Faulkner and she rather blinked a bit, though honestly I do not think that there was much in it. Anyone who is really interested in fiction would at least have heard Faulkner's name.

As the evening progressed Miss Sitwell grew more and more animated and told us a story of that very brilliant writer who has just died, Mr Lytton Strachey. To appreciate the story properly, you must understand that Mr Strachey was a very thin, tall man, well over six feet, with a long beard and in appearance the essence of calm, assured, dignified superiority. I had heard of this and fortunately had seen, also in the Tate, first, a portrait of Mr Strachey, full size, which though a mediocre painting, gave one some idea of the man and secondly, a bust which was an admirable piece of work and gave a strong impression of his personality. To return to Miss Sitwell's story. She said that a young composer, a big bustling fellow, whose name she certainly would not tell us, had met Mr Strachey at a party. Two years afterwards he met Mr Strachey at another party, hustled up to him and said, 'Hello! I met you at a party two years ago, didn't I?' Mr Strachey drew himself up, pointed his beard in the air, and looking serenely over the head of the intruder on his peace said quietly, 'Yes, two years ago. A nice long interval, isn't it?' As soon as the meeting was over I went to her and told her that I hoped I wasn't intruding, but I would be glad to know if her young composer was not Constant Lambert. You never saw a woman look so surprised. She had to admit that it was and wanted to know how in the name of Heaven I knew that.

I do not know Constant Lambert's music at all, but since the reorganization of the *New Statesman* as the *New Statesman and Nation* he has been writing musical criticism for the new paper, and writes quite well. One day I saw in the *Tatler* or *Sketch* or some picture-book of the kind, a photograph of Mr Constant Lambert and his bride. It was his wife that interested me, however. She was a cute woman with features rather resembling someone whom I knew, and yet no two women could have looked more different. She was rather a striking little woman in her way, and I looked at the photograph for some time, paying little attention, however, to Mr Lambert himself, who was big and beefy and burly, and looked rather like a prize-fighter. But when Miss Sitwell began her story with this young composer who was so big and who came pushing his way in, then the connection was simple enough. I had one shot and it went straight home.

But before the evening was over, I am afraid I had an argument with the good lady. After the lecture proper, came questions when Miss Sitwell sat down and answered whatever anyone chose to ask. Here she was at her best, showed a wide range of reading, was terse and incisive and every now and then when she got in a particularly good shot which set the house in roars of laughter, her lower lip quivered for a fraction of a second in a fascinating way.

After a while I asked her a question on which I have definite views of my own. There is a lot of experimentation in all modern art today, in technique particularly. People are writing free verse, verse which I believe Shakespeare and Keats and Shelley would find it difficult to recognize as kindred to their own work. Some people say that poetry must find new forms. It is my belief, though only a belief, that a great poet is first and foremost a poet, that is to say a man of strong feeling and delicate nerves, and secondly a technician and interested in technique, as such only as a means of getting the best manner of expressing what he has in him; and I also incline to the belief that if a great poet were born today he could use the traditional forms of verse and write the most magnificent poetry without bothering himself about new forms of poetry and technical experiments and the other preoccupations of most modern writers. These preoccupations it seems to me are things of essentially secondary importance. But with the spread of education and multiplication of books, people with little genuine poetic fire occupy themselves with poetry and thus have to concentrate on technique. Real poetic genius they cannot cultivate, because they have not got it.

At any rate I asked her the question, quite straightforwardly.

'Do you believe that a genuine poet coming into the world today would be able to write great poetry in the old traditional form, the sonnet form for instance?' I chose the sonnet particularly. From Sir Thomas Wyatt in the sixteenth century to the present day, Englishmen have written these poems of fourteen lines. Shakespeare and Milton, Keats and Wordsworth, nearly all the great English poets have exercised themselves with the sonnet. Could a modern Shakespeare write a sonnet which would be able to take its place beside the sonnets of Shakespeare or Milton?

Miss S: 'To begin with I do not think that any modern sonnets of the first class have been written since the sonnets of Keats and Wordsworth.'

Myself: 'What about Elizabeth Barrett Browning's *Sonnet from the Portuguese*, particularly the one beginning, "If thou would'st love me, let it be for nought, Except for love's sake only."'

Miss S: (Shaking her head) 'No, as a matter of fact I think that no woman could ever write a really great sonnet. I happen to believe that technique is largely a matter of physique. Pope for instance though an invalid had very strong and beautiful hands . . . and I do not think that any woman is strong enough physically to weight the syllables as a man can in order to strengthen the lines.'

Myself: 'But you will admit that the *Ode to a Nightingale* and the *Ode to a Grecian Urn* are magnificent poetry.'

Miss S: 'Yes, certainly.'

Myself: 'But nevertheless Keats was always very frail.'

Miss S: 'Of course I do not mean that to write fine poetry a man must be big and strong like a butcher.'

It was the reply of a skilful controversialist. The audience was much amused. And as it was her lecture and not mine I let it pass. Nevertheless I think it was pretty clear to a good many in the hall that she was concerned.

But that is not all there is to it. At odd moments I have been thinking over the matter and while I cannot say that she is right I am becoming less and less able to say that she is wrong. Unfortunately for her I happened to hit almost immediately on the chief example which seemed to confound her theories at once. But on close observation even the case of Keats can be defended. Keats's poetry is very beautiful but it is not strong as the work of Shakespeare or Milton is strong; even Shelley, magnificent poet as he is, has force and fire, but not strength in the sense that Shakespeare has strength. Take for instance these two lines from one of the sonnets:

> Oh how can summer's honey breath hold out
> Against the wreckful siege of battering days.

Anyone who read that aloud can feel the almost physical weight behind the lines. One does not get it often in Keats and in Shelley. And it is particularly the kind of weight that the sonnet form, compact as it is, needs in order that every line of the fourteen should tell. It is not an easy question, and this is not the place to discuss it. Anyway, after many more questions the regular meeting ended. Then came general conversation in which those who wished went up to the platform and talked to Miss Sitwell while the audience broke up into groups. Students went up and came down, but stranger as I was, I did not go, and was talking to a girl who spoke thirteen languages, when the chairman touched me on the shoulder. Would I give my name and address to Miss S. and would I come up on the platform to speak to her? Certainly, no one was more pleased than I.

Up on the platform Miss Sitwell sat in the centre of a group of students. There was the chairman also and there was a Miss Trevelyan, some relation I believe of the Oxford historian. The talk ran chiefly on the work of the moderns. There is no need to go into what was said, except that Miss Sitwell agreed thoroughly with what I have always felt, that, for instance, to take an outstanding figure among the moderns, while one listens with the greatest interest to the music of Stravinsky, neither he nor any other modern can ever move your feelings as can Bach or Haydn, Mozart or Beethoven. It is the great weakness of most modern work. Well, it ended as all good things have to end. Miss Sitwell promised to send me a book written by her brother in traditional verse. I was bold enough to say that I hoped I would see her again. She said, yes certainly.

We may seem to have got some distance from Bloomsbury. We have not. That is Bloomsbury. Some group or society is always having lectures or talks by some distinguished person who comes and talks and is always willing to do anything for anyone who wishes assistance or guidance of some sort. On the Sunday following Miss Sitwell's lecture, Mr Sidney Dark was to speak. Still later in the term Mr Walter de la Mare is to speak on Modern Fiction. Something of that kind in music, art, literature, architecture, philosophy, history, by the most distinguished persons, day after day. You have your choice. And however distinguished the lecturers, they are always willing to do their very best for anyone who seems more than usually interested. I went to two lectures by Professor Bidet of the University of Ghent on Greece and the Near East. The lectures were in French and I found them rather difficult to follow, but the man was so interesting that I wrote him a short note asking if there were any small books on the subject, or magazine articles which he himself had written. He did not reply at once, but did so when he reached back home. He wrote that he was delighted to have heard from me, that the interest I took in his subject gave him great pleasure, that my writing him about it meant far more to him than anything which he could do for me. He sent me one of his own articles, signed, as a souvenir and told me that although he had not written as yet his book on the subject would soon be published and he would be extremely glad to send me a copy. He does not know me and in all probability never will. There is the case of John Clarke, who along with law has been doing literature, and economics, and sociology, and goodness knows what not. He attended a series of lectures on sociology given by Mrs Beatrice Webb, Lord Passfield's wife. He was not too certain of himself and wrote to her asking for some guidance. He told me that he was surprised at the result. She did not send him information of what books to read, but sent him actual manuscripts, sheets and sheets of her own work. She invited him to tea, filled him with food and knowledge and told him to come again. That is not exactly Bloomsbury, but it is the atmosphere of Bloomsbury. Anyone who lives in this place for any length of time and remains dull need not worry himself. Nothing he will ever do will help him. He was born that way.

George Orwell

[1903–50]

George Orwell was born Eric Arthur Blair in Bengal, India. In 1904 he and his older sister accompanied their mother to England. His father, a member of the Indian Civil Service, joined them after his retirement in 1912. Orwell was formally educated at St Cyprian's, a preparatory school in Eastbourne, Sussex, and at Eton. In 1922 he left Britain and joined the Imperial Police in Burma, serving for five years before a growing distaste for imperialism caused him to resign.

The next few years were spent in Paris and London, where a series of low-paying jobs left him struggling against severe poverty. Finally in 1930 Orwell became a regular contributor to *The Adelphi*, but his earlier experiences induced him to write the autobiographical *Down and Out in Paris and London* (1933). In 1934 he coined the pen-name George Orwell and published his first novel, *Burmese Days*, a work that reflected his anger over the political injustice that he had experienced and observed. This was followed by two more novels, *A Clergyman's Daughter* (1935) and *Keep the Aspidistra Flying* (1936). In 1936 he married Eileen O'Shaughnessy.

It was Orwell's flair for non-fiction that led the publisher Victor Gollancz to commission him for the Left Book Club. Gollancz was interested in a documentary account of unemployment in the north of England. The result was the journalistic landmark *The Road to Wigan Pier* (1937). In part an exploration of human misery and in part a study of socialism as a remedy, it established Orwell's growing reputation as a brilliant and polemical social commentator. His position as an unaligned democratic socialist was further clarified in *Homage to Catalonia* (1938), which told of his experiences as a volunteer for the Republican Army during the Spanish Civil War. In his fictional work, Orwell was also able to express many of his own aspirations, frustrations and political concerns.

From 1943 to 1945 Orwell contributed to *Tribune*, of which he was literary editor, and to newspapers such as the *Observer* and the

Manchester Evening News. He possessed the ability to illustrate the effects and dangers of totalitarianism through his depictions of everyday life, and it was particularly in this guise, as pamphleteer, that the clarity and colloquial nature of his writing shone through. His first wife died in 1945 and he remarried in 1949, a year before his own death. His second wife, Sonia Brownwell, coedited with Ian Angus a four-volume, posthumous compilation, *Collected Essays, Journalism and Letters* (1968), which contains over 200 of Orwell's ruminations on literature, politics and English life, and includes the famous essay 'Inside the Whale' (1940).

Orwell's most popular and universally enduring works are the two satirical novels *Animal Farm* (1945) and *Nineteen Eighty-four* (1949). The political and social resonance of the latter in particular has been especially marked, and since its publication Orwellian terms such as 'newspeak' and 'doublethink' have entered the English language. It is a bleak and bitter work on the threat of political tyranny, written as Orwell was dying of the tuberculosis he had contracted in childhood. Having spent much of his short writing career in relative obscurity, Orwell died in 1950 with a widespread reputation as a novelist, essayist and journalist.

'Confessions of a Down and Out' points to the remarkable obsession the English have with outward appearances and decorum. In matters of dress and accent, one has to 'act' as though one belongs in order to belong. To fail to do so merely invites the inevitable spiral down the staircase of social acceptability. Both a colonial and an old Etonian, Orwell certainly understood life at the higher levels of society. In this piece he reveals something of the trauma for those, including himself, who appear to have temporarily lost their footing.

Confessions of a Down and Out

I travelled to England third class via Dunkirk and Tilbury, which is the cheapest and not the worst way of crossing the Channel. You had to pay extra for a cabin, so I slept in the saloon, together with most of the third-class passengers. I find this entry in my diary for that day:

'Sleeping in the saloon, twenty-seven men, sixteen women. Of the women, not a single one has washed her face this morning. The men mostly went to the bathroom; the women merely produced vanity cases and covered the dirt with powder. Q. A secondary sexual difference?'

On the journey I fell in with a couple of Roumanians, mere children, who were going to England on their honeymoon trip. They asked innumerable questions about England, and I told them some startling lies. I was so pleased to be getting home, after being hard up for months in a foreign city, that England seemed to me a sort of Paradise. There are, indeed, many things in England that make you glad to get home; bathrooms, armchairs, mint sauce, new potatoes properly cooked, brown bread, marmalade, beer made with veritable hops – they are all splendid, if you can pay for them. England is a very good country when you are not poor; and, of course, with a tame imbecile to look after, I was not going to be poor. The thought of not being poor made me very patriotic. The more questions the Roumanians asked, the more I praised England: the climate, the scenery, the art, the literature, the laws – everything in England was perfect.

Was the architecture in England good? the Roumanians asked. 'Splendid!' I said. 'And you should just see the London statues! Paris is vulgar – half grandiosity and half slums. But London – '

Then the boat drew alongside Tilbury pier. The first building we saw on the waterside was one of those huge hotels, all stucco and pinnacles, which stare from the English coast like idiots staring over an asylum wall. I saw the Roumanians, too polite to say anything, cocking their eyes at the hotel. 'Built by French architects,' I assured them; and even later, when the train was crawling into London through the eastern slums, I still kept it up about the beauties of English architecture. Nothing seemed too good to say about England, now that I was coming home and was not hard up any more.

I went to B.'s office, and his first words knocked everything to ruins. 'I'm sorry,' he said; 'your employers have gone abroad, patient and all. However, they'll be back in a month. I suppose you can hang on till then?'

I was outside in the street before it even occurred to me to borrow some more money. There was a month to wait, and I had exactly nineteen and sixpence in hand. The news had taken my breath away. For a long time I could not make up my mind what to do. I loafed the day in the streets, and at night, not having the slightest notion of how to get a cheap bed in London, I went to a 'family' hotel, where the charge was seven and sixpence. After paying the bill I had ten and twopence in hand.

By the morning I had made my plans. Sooner or later I should have to go to B. for more money, but it seemed hardly decent to do so yet, and in the meantime I must exist in some hole-and-corner way. Past experience set me against pawning my best suit. I would leave all my things at the station cloakroom, except my second-best suit, which I could exchange for some cheap clothes and perhaps a pound. If I was going to live a month on thirty shillings I must have bad clothes – indeed, the worse the better. Whether thirty shillings could be made to last a month I had no idea, not knowing London as I knew Paris. Perhaps I could beg, or sell bootlaces, and I remembered articles I had read in the Sunday papers about beggars who have two thousand pounds sewn into their trousers. It was, at any rate, notoriously impossible to starve in London, so there was nothing to be anxious about.

To sell my clothes I went down into Lambeth, where the people are poor and there are a lot of rag shops. At the first shop I tried the proprietor was polite but unhelpful; at the second he was rude; at the third he was stone deaf, or pretended to be so. The fourth shopman was a large blond young man, very pink all over, like a slice of ham. He looked at the clothes I was wearing and felt them disparagingly between thumb and finger.

'Poor stuff,' he said, 'very poor stuff, that is.' (It was quite a good suit.) 'What yer want for 'em?'

I explained that I wanted some older clothes and as much money as he could spare. He thought for a moment, then collected some dirty-looking rags and threw them on to the counter. 'What about the money?' I said, hoping for a pound. He pursed his lips, then produced *a shilling* and laid it beside the clothes. I did not argue – I was going to argue, but as I opened my mouth he reached out as though to take up the shilling again; I saw that I was helpless. He let me change in a small room behind the shop.

The clothes were a coat, once dark brown, a pair of black dungaree trousers, a scarf and a cloth cap; I had kept my own shirt, socks and boots, and I had a comb and razor in my pocket. It gives one a very strange feeling to be wearing such clothes. I had worn bad enough things before, but nothing at all like these; they were not merely dirty and shapeless, they had – how is one to express it? – a gracelessness, a patina of antique filth, quite different from mere shabbiness. They were the sort of clothes you see on a bootlace seller, or a tramp. An hour later, in Lambeth, I saw a hang-dog man, obviously a tramp, coming towards me, and when I looked again it was myself, reflected in a shop window. The dirt was plastering my face already. Dirt is a great respecter of persons; it lets you alone when you are well dressed, but as soon as your collar is gone it flies towards you from all directions.

I stayed in the streets till late at night, keeping on the move all the time. Dressed as I was, I was half afraid that the police might arrest me as a vagabond, and I dared not speak to anyone, imagining that they must notice a disparity between my accent and my clothes. (Later I discovered that this never happened.) My new clothes had put me instantly into a new world. Everyone's demeanour seemed to have changed abruptly. I helped a hawker pick up a barrow that he had upset. 'Thanks, mate,' he said with a grin. No one had called me mate before in my life – it was the clothes that had done it. For the first time I noticed, too, how the attitude of women varies with a man's clothes. When a badly dressed man passes them they shudder away from him with a quite frank movement of disgust, as though he were a dead cat. Clothes are powerful things. Dressed in a tramp's clothes it is very difficult, at any rate for the first day, not to feel that you are genuinely degraded. You might feel the same shame, irrational but very real, your first night in prison.

At about eleven I began looking for a bed. I had read about doss-houses (they are never called doss-houses, by the way), and I supposed that one could get a bed for fourpence or thereabouts. Seeing a man, a navvy or something of the kind, standing on the kerb in the Waterloo Road, I stopped and questioned him. I said that I was stony broke and wanted the cheapest bed I could get.

'Oh,' said he, 'you go to that 'ouse across the street there, with the sign "Good Beds for Single Men." That's a good kip [sleeping place], that is. I bin there myself on and off. You'll find it cheap *and* clean.'

It was a tall, battered-looking house, with dim lights in all the windows, some of which were patched with brown paper. I entered a stone passage-way, and a little etiolated boy with sleepy eyes appeared from a door leading to a cellar. Murmurous sounds came from the cellar, and a wave of hot air and cheese. The boy yawned and held out his hand.

'Want a kip? That'll be a 'og, guv'nor.'

I paid the shilling, and the boy led me up a rickety unlighted staircase to a bedroom. It had a sweetish reek of paregoric and foul linen; the windows seemed to be tight shut, and the air was almost suffocating at first. There was a candle burning, and I saw that the room measured fifteen feet square by eight high, and had eight beds in it. Already six lodgers were in bed, queer lumpy shapes with all their own clothes, even their boots, piled on top of them. Someone was coughing in a loathsome manner in one corner.

When I got into bed I found that it was as hard as a board, and as for the pillow, it was a mere hard cylinder like a block of wood. It was rather worse than sleeping on a table, because the bed was not six feet long, and very narrow, and the mattress was convex, so that one had to hold on to avoid falling out. The sheets stank so horribly of sweat that I could not bear them near my nose. Also, the bedclothes only consisted of the sheets and a cotton counterpane, so that though stuffy it was none too warm. Several noises recurred throughout the night. About once in an hour the man on my left – a sailor, I think – woke up, swore vilely, and lighted a cigarette. Another man, victim of bladder disease, got up and noisily used his chamber-pot half a dozen times during the night. The man in the corner had a coughing fit once in every twenty minutes, so regularly that one came to listen for it as one listens for the next yap when a dog is baying the moon. It was an unspeakably repellent sound; a foul bubbling and retching, as though the man's bowels were being churned up within him. Once when he struck a match I saw that he was a very old man, with a grey, sunken face like that of a corpse, and he was wearing his trousers wrapped round his head as a nightcap, a thing which for some reason disgusted me very much. Every time he coughed or the other man swore, a sleepy voice from one of the other beds cried out:

'Shut up! Oh, for Christ's—*sake* shut up!'

I had about an hour's sleep in all. In the morning I was woken by a dim impression of some large brown thing coming towards me. I opened my eyes and saw that it was one of the sailor's feet, sticking out of bed close to my face. It was dark brown, quite dark brown like an Indian's, with dirt. The walls were leprous, and the sheets, three weeks from the wash, were almost raw umber colour. I got up, dressed and went downstairs. In the cellar were a row of basins and two slippery roller towels. I had a piece of soap in my pocket, and I was going to wash, when I noticed that every basin was streaked with grime – solid, sticky filth as black as boot-blacking. I went out unwashed. Altogether, the lodging-house had not come up to its description as cheap *and* clean. It was, however, as I found later, a fairly representative lodging-house.

I crossed the river and walked a long way eastward, finally going into a coffee-shop on Tower Hill. An ordinary London coffee-shop, like a thousand others, it seemed queer and foreign after Paris. It was a little stuffy room with the high-backed pews that were fashionable in the 'forties, the day's menu written on a mirror with a piece of soap, and a girl of fourteen handling the dishes. Navvies were eating out of newspaper parcels, and drinking tea in vast saucerless mugs like china tumblers. In a corner by himself a Jew, muzzle down in the plate, was guiltily wolfing bacon.

'Could I have some tea and bread and butter?' I said to the girl.

She stared. 'No butter, only marg,' she said, surprised. And she repeated the order in the phrase that is to London what the eternal *coup de rouge* is to Paris: 'Large tea and two slices!'

On the wall beside my pew there was a notice saying 'Pocketing the sugar not allowed,' and beneath it some poetic customer had written:

> He that takes away the sugar
> Shall be called a dirty —

but someone else had been at pains to scratch out the last word. This was England. The tea-and-two-slices cost threepence halfpenny, leaving me with eight and twopence.

E. R. Braithwaite

[1912–]

Edward Ricardo Braithwaite was born in Georgetown, Guyana (then British Guiana), and received his schooling there and in New York. His formal education continued in England at Cambridge (where in 1949 he was awarded an M.Sc. in physics) and the London University Institute of Education. His studies were disrupted by the Second World War, during which he served in the RAF from 1941 to 1945.

From 1950 to 1957 Braithwaite lived and worked as a schoolteacher in London. He described his experiences in simple and unflinching prose in *To Sir, With Love* (1959), winner of the Anisfield-Wolf award in 1960 and later a successful film starring Sidney Poitier. His book *Paid Servant* (1962) was a sequel of sorts; it depicted the social welfare work with which Braithwaite – a London County Council welfare officer (1958–60) and a human rights officer in the Parisian Veterans' Foundation (1960–63) – was intimately involved. In 1962 he also published *A Kind of Homecoming*, a nostalgically written travel book that explored his African roots.

From 1963 to 1966 Braithwaite was a lecturer and education officer for Unesco. His next novel, *Choice of Straws* (1965), was a portrayal of white working-class racial psychology that ventured into controversial ground. In 1972 he published his autobiography, *Reluctant Neighbours*, and in 1975 *Honorary White: A Visit to South Africa* appeared. He has been anthologized in a variety of journals and publications.

E. R. Braithwaite is currently living in New York.

In A Choice of Straws *(1965) Braithwaite displays a great facility for penetrating the psyche of the white English working class. In a dramatic and forthright manner, he addresses the physical and mental torment of a young man who hates the 'other' without really knowing why. The novel is a sustained* tour de force *and is much underrated.*

From *Choice of Straws*

We'd been like that for nearly an hour. Just waiting. The cold, damp, bitter-sweet stink of the place was beginning to get on my nerves, but I said nothing, waiting for Dave to make the first move about leaving. Outside, the shadows of evening had thickened with the persistent drizzle which occasionally slanted in through the paneless window of our hiding-place, to add to my discomfort. My legs were beginning to feel numb. I wanted to smoke, badly. This waiting had taken the edge off the thing as far as I was concerned, and if Dave had said let's call it off, he'd have had no argument from me. But I didn't think he would. Not Dave. Once he got on to something he'd never back out.

I thought of the people who might have lived in the very room where we were waiting. It looked out on to the street through two huge windows from which the glass had long ago been shattered by bomb blast or the marksmanship of small boys, and may have been the best room where friends were received for Sunday tea. Dead and gone, perhaps. Mother and children with father off to the wars to make Britain safe for heroes. Heroes hell! So many black buggers about the place, the ruddy heroes couldn't get a fair crack at the jobs or their own ruddy women. Bloody Spades.

Near me I could hear Dave with that faint, tuneless, whistling sound he always made when excited, more like a long breath indrawn through his teeth. I couldn't see anything of his face the way he was leaning against the wall to have a clear view of the street as far as the pub at the corner.

'Seen anything?' I asked him.

'Not yet.'

'Think he'll come?'

'He'll come.'

'Then he'd better ruddy well hurry.'

'Why, what's up?'

'Cramp in my legs.'

'Quit nagging. You'll survive.'

I was squatted on my heels beside him, to be out of the way of anyone glancing in from the street. It was Dave's idea, though I couldn't imagine who'd want to waste time looking into any of those dead houses. We'd come in here to wait because the place was open, the main door not boarded up or anything, just a huge, gaping hole in the front of the house. Even the woodwork had been ripped off. The floor was thick with dust and garbage.

'I still don't get it, how you're so sure about him.' I said it, not to start an argument, but just to show him my attitude to the whole thing, this waiting for something that might not happen.

'Look, Jack.' There was in his voice that schoolmasterish tone which always got under my skin, that way he had of making the thing seem simple and me as stupid as hell. 'Look, when we were coming to that pub at the corner, didn't you see the fellow come out, heading this way? Right. Then someone stuck his head out of the door and called him back, Doc or Jock or something like that? Okay, so it stands to reason that when he's ready he'll come out again and head this way.'

I looked up at him while he talked. Never once did he take his eyes off the road outside.

'It had better be soon.' I couldn't give him a broader hint than that.

'Oh, wrap up.'

'But how do you know he's a Spade? I didn't even get a look at his face.'

'I know. He's a Spade all right.'

'Dave.'

'What?'

'I feel funny about this one.'

'Scared?'

I didn't answer. The truth is I wasn't really scared. At least that's not the word for what I felt. After all, it wasn't the first time we'd done something like this, but always it had been done on the spur of the moment. No waiting around. We'd go up where we knew some of them lived, Brixton, Goldhawk Road, places like that, and wander around, keeping an eye out till we saw one by himself. Then we'd

have a little fun with him if we thought we could risk it. Knock him
about a bit, then push off. Always at night, when there wouldn't be
any nosy people trying to interfere. But this was different, hiding here
for more than half an hour, the place stinking as if the whole
neighbourhood had been relieving themselves in it. Dave nudged me
and I stood up alongside him. Over his shoulder the houses opposite
were glued together in a faceless dark mass all the way down to the
corner.

The door of the pub was open and someone was framed in the
broad patch of light, moving, as if talking with another inside. Then
the light was cut off.

'That's him. He's heading this way,' Dave whispered, the
excitement tight in his voice. It was too dark to see his face clearly,
but I could well imagine the grey-green eyes shining with anticipation, the thin mouth half open for breathing, pulling away from the
teeth. I often wondered if, all the time, I looked exactly like him.
Often wished there was some way of seeing myself when watching
him, to find out if the resemblance between him and me extended to
every look, every smile, everything. True, nobody but our Mum
could tell us apart, but that was on the outside, and I know I didn't
always feel the same way as he did about things. At least, I didn't
always want to; especially with everybody expecting us to even think
alike, just because we were identical twins. Sometimes I only went
along with doing something with him just because, well, just because
we were always together. Since we were little it was always the Twins
or Dave and Jack. Always Dave and Jack, even at school. Never Jack
and Dave. Kids would call to us, hey Dave and Jack, never knowing
which was which.

The man from the pub came along the far pavement. From where
we hid we could hear the tap, tap of his shoes, as if he had metal tips
on his heels.

'We'll wait till he's a little ahead, then we'll cross over and come up
behind him,' Dave whispered, pushing me towards the doorway,
where we stood, one on each side. As the man came nearer there was
clinking from something he was carrying, loud in the silent night as

he came abreast and went past. We left the house and crossed the street, our jeans, black sweaters and suède jackets mixing into the dingy wetness, silent as ghosts in our rubber-soled chukka boots. He was laughing and singing to himself, the words trailing behind him . . . She's a whole lot of woman and she sure needs a whole lot of man . . . fading away into laughter. Probably half stewed. He stopped to shift the parcel and was moving on when we reached him, one on each side.

'Hey, Spade,' Dave whispered.

The man stopped and turned.

'What the . . .' The words were cut off as Dave hit him. Dave was right. A bloody Spade. In the gloom all you could see was the dark head shape. I hit at it and heard him grunt, then we were hitting him and suddenly the crash as his parcel fell and broke and the strong smell of rum or whisky or something. I kicked him and he doubled forward, grabbing Dave and falling on top of him. I kicked him, the excitement so strong in me I wanted to shout, this was so different from the other times. The Spade was fighting, silently, like a madman. Suddenly he sprang away from Dave and came at me, hitting me in the stomach. I could hardly breathe, but Dave pulled him and they were on the ground again, the Spade hitting Dave and muttering, 'I'll kill you, you lousy fuckers, I'll kill you.'

Then Dave screamed. 'Get him off me, Jack. Get him off.' I grabbed the Spade's coat, pulling him backwards, but he flung me off and I fell. He was strong as a horse, and I was suddenly frightened. We couldn't cope with him. I got up, and the Spade was banging Dave's hand on the ground. I saw the glint of the knife just as Dave let it go, snatched it and stuck it into the Spade's back. He twisted around and came at me, and I dropped the knife, frightened, turning to run. Then I heard him cry 'Aaaah,' and when I looked around there was Dave with the knife in his hand, the Spade bent over, walking out into the middle of the street. Slowly, carefully, he knelt down, his arms folded low in front of him.

'Come on, let's get out of here,' Dave said, pulling my arm. I was watching the Spade. He made an attempt to get up, gave it up, and reached forward, braced on his hands and knees like a sprinter. Then slowly he fell over sideways, coughing.

'Come on.' Dave was pulling my arm.

We ran up the street leaving the Spade.

'Come on,' Dave urged. We ran headlong away.

Keeping as much as possible to the shadows we cut through Cable Street and a maze of alleyways towards Commercial Road, and beyond it, till we came to a narrow lane behind the big mass that is London Hospital. We took a breather against some iron railings, Dave hanging on and gasping as if he'd run out of his last breath. My face was running with the drizzle and perspiration, and inside my clothes the heat was like a steam bath. Not another soul in sight, and home seemed a thousand miles away. Dave was groaning beside me.

'Take a look at my back,' he said. 'It's hurting like hell.'

'Turn around.' I couldn't see much, with the poor light from the street lamps across the road, except the shiny wetness on his jacket. I slipped my hand underneath, felt the stickiness on his sweater and withdrew my hand, covered with blood, smelling raw and awful.

'You're bleeding, Dave.'

'Fucker had me down on those ruddy bottles. Is it bad?'

'Can't tell, but your sweater's soaked. Look at my hand.'

'Suffering Christ.' We looked at each other, the fear coming over me like a thick black fog. My brother's face was like a mirror of the things inside me. I felt weak and lost. Dave rallied quickly.

'Oh, bugger it. Come on, let's get off home.'

The lane led into Whitechapel Road, diagonally across from the Underground station. We made it through a break in the traffic just as two policemen came out of the Underground, and in our rush we nearly banged into them. We waited in the dark entrance of a tobacconist's and watched them wait at the zebra crossing while the traffic rushed by. One of them looked back towards us and said something to his mate. My heart nearly stopped beating. But then the traffic halted and they crossed over and went into the hospital gate with the neon sign 'Ambulance'. Dave was leaning weakly against the shop window. Two women came along, slowed to look in our direction, then walked on.

'Want a fag?' I asked him.

'Yes. Christ, I feel sick as a dog.'

Over the flame of my lighter I watched his face, chalk-white and running with perspiration, the fine rain like tiny diamonds in his short, curly blond hair. His blue eyes looked black in the bloodless background. The feeling of sickness came up in me.

'We'd better get you home quick, Dave. Come on, let's go down the Tube.'

He straightened up suddenly. 'You raving bonkers or something? What do you think would happen if I went down there like this? Some nosy parker'd be sure to . . . Tell you what, we'd better split up. The way those coppers looked at us, let's not take any chances.'

'What are you on about, splitting up? I can't leave you to make it home by yourself. Not like this.'

'Oh, wrap up. What do you think I'll do, pass ruddy out or something?'

'But your back.'

'Bugger my back. I'm not going to bleed to ruddy death. Look, I'll catch a bus to Leytonstone and take the Central line from there, okay? One of us by himself is fine, but together we're sure to have them staring as always.'

'Okay, Dave, okay.' From the set of his mouth I knew he'd made up his mind. No shifting him.

'But I'll wait and see you on the bus.'

'What for? Go on, scarpa before those coppers come back.'

'Mum will want to know what's up if I go in alone.'

'Tell her I'm seeing a bird home and I'll be in shortly.' He grimaced with the pain, but made an attempt to smile. 'Better keep an eye out for me, though. Go on, hop it.'

He walked across to the bus shelter, stiffly, like those toy soldiers in the comics, and stood holding on to one of the shiny metal posts. I went and stood just inside the station entrance to watch until his bus arrived and he climbed on, going upstairs. Even after it rolled away I

stayed there, stiff with fear and confused, the whole rotten evening a
heavy lump in my stomach. Please God, just let him get home safe.
Please. He looked so white and scary, like that time long ago when as
kids we'd been messing about on the diving-board at the swimming
baths and he'd slipped off and belly-landed on the water. The
attendant had fished him out white and limp like a broken doll.

'If you're going some place you'd better hurry, mate,' someone said
behind. 'There's one just in.' It was the ticket collector. I showed my
ticket and rushed down the stairs to the train. Jumping on the train, I
nearly lost the ticket. It fell out of my hand and landed on the edge of
the platform. I picked it up and put it away in my pocket. The return
half Upminster to Piccadilly Circus. That's where we'd planned to go
tonight and listen to some jazz, where we should have gone if we
hadn't changed our minds.

I sat down between a bearded student and a fat, elderly woman
with a fat little boy on her lap, and closed my eyes, wishing
desperately that I could open them again to find that the night hadn't
really happened and I'd only dreamed all those terrible things. But
the fear and worry followed me deep inside my mind wherever I tried
to hide, real as the cold sweat I could feel running down my face and
neck and alongside my ribs.

'Look, mummy, the man's crying.'

I opened my eyes to see the little boy twisted around in his
mother's tight grip, pointing a pudgy finger close to my face, his eyes
wide with surprise. With a quick, accurate movement his mother
smacked his hand down, but he continued staring, his eyes swivelled
around until I thought they'd pop out. He had a tiny mole near the
right side of his mouth, just like Dave's. Oh God, let him be okay.
Just this once. He was always the tough one. I might even reach
home to find him there ahead of me.

'Young man, are you all right?' The woman was speaking, pulling
me back to the time and place beside her.

'Yes, thanks, I'm fine,' I told her, trying to avoid looking at the four
eyes from the two fat heads which seemed perched recklessly one on
top of the other. All along the opposite seat eyes seemed to be

watching me, so I closed mine. Perspiration was running down my face and into my mouth. I wiped it with my handkerchief, smelt the rank smell and right away remembered I'd wiped my hands on it after feeling Dave's back. I opened my eyes to see if anyone had noticed. Seeing the wide streaks nearly made me sick. I pushed it into my pocket, thinking about Dave, wanting him to be okay, to reach home safe, even ahead of me. Oh God, oh Jesus God, please, please. Oh Dave.

'Something the matter, young man?'

I kept my eyes shut tight, not answering her. Why the hell didn't she mind her own ruddy fat-arsed business and leave me alone? God, it was only supposed to be a bit of a giggle, just knock him about a bit and push off. If the bloody fool hadn't got hold of Dave we'd have just given him a few and been out of it, but the bastard just wouldn't let go. Bloody Spades. They had it coming to them. After all, our Dad hadn't done anything to them, yet they'd jumped him and beat him up. And him always on about how they were human beings like anyone else and why shouldn't they come here, the only reason was they wanted work and why not. And if things had been different and there was plenty of work in their countries with good pay lots of English would be rushing over there. Well, what the hell good had all that talk done him? He'd had nothing to do with the riots in Notting Hill. He was coming home from the building site in Ladbroke Grove when they jumped out of a car and beat him up. Put him in hospital for nearly three weeks, and not a ruddy policeman in sight to lend a hand.

When he came home he wouldn't talk about it. Not to us, not to Mum. Funny thing, though, we were watching television one night and there was this Spade come on and right away our Dad got up and switched the set off. Didn't say anything, just switched off as if he couldn't bear the sight of that black face.

The first time we got one of them was at Brixton. We'd heard so much about them living up there, and this Saturday night we'd gone up West, having a wander around, and we saw this bus with Brixton on the front and Dave said how about it and we jumped on. There

were only a few of them in the High Street but too many other people
about. Perhaps as soon as it was night they disappeared into wherever
they lived. We walked about for a while but it didn't look as if
anything would turn up, then out of a side street this fellow came, in a
hell of a hurry, his overcoat collar turned up around his ears and hands
stuck in the pockets. As he passed us we noticed the black face and
glasses. We waited until he'd gone a few steps then turned and
followed. He turned by that big shop with the Bon Marché sign. There
wasn't anyone else in sight so we caught up with him. As Dave
punched him I tripped him up, flat on his face. He rolled over and then
we saw he was old, with not a single tooth in the wide open hole of a
mouth. Lying there squinting up at us, probably couldn't see much
since his glasses had fallen off. Not saying a word.

Funny thing about them. They'd either fight back, or just be there
and take it, but they'd never run or shout for help, as if they didn't
expect anyone to help them anyway.

Then there was that time we'd come out of Lancaster Gate Underground and were going up Bayswater Road on the Park side when
we passed this one, standing by himself as if he was waiting for
somebody. Dave said let's take him and we turned back, but the
Spade must have guessed what was up because just as we reached
him he pulled a knife. Must have had it in his pocket. Just flicked
open the blade and stood there looking at us, nobody saying a word.
So we left the stupid bugger standing there and went about our
business. We couldn't figure how he'd guessed.

This night after work Dave had said let's go and have a little fun.
We often went up West, sometimes two or three times a week, mostly
Friday or Saturday nights. Better than going to the local hop or even
Romford. We'd go up to Soho to the Kaleidoscope or somewhere
like that, drinking coffee or Cokes and listening to jazz. Sometimes
we'd meet up with some birds, mostly students, chat around with
them, then catch the last train home. We caught the District Line,
intending to change at Charing Cross for Piccadilly, but at Aldgate
East we just got off the train, not talking about it. When the train
reached the station Dave got up and I just followed him out.

Mum was always talking about the way we did things together. She said we were born with caul, or something like that. We even had the toothache and colds at the same time and our Dad used to laugh and say, one sneeze and the other wipe. But even they couldn't really understand about us. Like the time at Infants' school when Dave had gone out to the toilet and cut his penis with the old razor-blade he'd found, and I'd suddenly started screaming for no reason at all and they'd gone out and found Dave, standing there in the toilet not saying a word, blood over everything . . .

At Bow Road the fat woman and her son got off and two Spades got on, both in the stiff blue Underground uniform. One of them took the seat where the fat woman had been, the other standing near him, holding the overhead strap. I didn't want to watch them, but they were whispering and laughing. I couldn't help looking. The one standing was young, strong-looking, light glinting from his eyes and teeth. I wondered if the other one looked like him, the one we left lying in the road. Funny thing, I didn't give a damn about him, or these two, but thinking of them I remembered Dave, and the cold sweat started again.

'Man, the woman bawled.' The Spade sitting near me was speaking, his voice clear, but sounding a bit strange, like the way Welsh people speak, as if they really want to sing.

'So, what happened? You stopped?'

'You kidding?'

'Well, what?'

'Put my hand over her mouth so the neighbours wouldn't hear, and the bitch bit me.'

Laughter bubbled out of them.

'Man, you're lucky.'

'Lucky? How come?'

'Might have been something else.'

Again the laughter from deep inside them. Just between them. Secret. I hated those two, remembering Dave and the way that other bastard had knocked me about, I'd like to push a knife into their backs and really give them something to laugh about. The one standing looked across at me and the smile disappeared from his face as if he could read my thoughts. I could feel the other turn to look at me. Hatred for them was like a slow trembling deep inside. At the next station some passengers left and the Spades sat together opposite me. I closed my eyes so as not to have to look at them.

Lawrence Durrell

[1912–90]

Lawrence George Durrell was born in Julundur, India. His parents were colonials of Irish and English descent. Accounts of his somewhat eccentric childhood (as well as his bohemian early adulthood) can be found in affectionate detail in his zoologist brother Gerald's autobiographical books. Educated in England at St Edmund's College, Canterbury, Durrell's subsequent working life was characteristically eclectic. In his own words, he 'hymned and whored' in London, with jobs ranging from jazz pianist and composer to automobile racer and real-estate agent. In the 1930s he began what was to be a long and close correspondence with Henry Miller. Miller's own erotic novels greatly influenced Durrell's work, and when a manuscript of Durrell's failed to pass the British obscenity regulations Miller suggested that Durrell publish his now-infamous *Black Book* (1938) in Paris. Ironically, this work examines what Durrell calls 'the English Death', or the sterility of British society.

Durrell supplemented his writing with schoolteaching and employment in various diplomatic posts, both during and after the Second World War. He spent much of his life on islands in the eastern Mediterranean; by the time *The Black Book* was published, he had moved to the Greek island of Corfu. He served as a Foreign Service press officer during the 1940s and early 1950s in Athens, Cairo, Rhodes and Belgrade, and was a lecturer and the director of the Institute for the British Council in Cordoba, Argentina, from 1947 to 1948. In the 1950s he acted as the director of public relations for the British government in Cyprus. In 1957 he moved to Provence, France, and became a full-time writer.

Durrell was a novelist, dramatist, short-story and travel writer, translator, editor and critic; yet he considered himself to be principally a poet. His first book to be accepted by a major publisher was the collection of verse *A Private Country* (1943). His early poetic work blends traditional Western lyric forms with Mediterranean sensuality.

These poems are included in the compilation *Collected Poems, 1931–1974* (1980). Durrell the poet is often overlooked, and the work commonly regarded as his *chef-d'œuvre* is the fictional opus *The Alexandria Quartet*.

Comprising the volumes *Justine* (1957), *Balthazar* (1958), *Mountolive* (1958) and *Clea* (1960), the *Quartet* is an experiment with structure. It uses Einstein's space-time continuum to question our perception of reality, examining the same events from a multitude of different perspectives. Durrell frequently employed his Baroque sensibilities and a Joycean absence of plot to explore the theories of Einstein and Freud. But his flamboyant language was seen by some critics as excessive, and Durrell was often cited for his overblown metaphors and lack of subtlety.

Sappho (1959) is one of Durrell's several verse plays. It uses classical myth, dramatic principles and blank verse to explore the contemporary notion that traditional beliefs can hinder the pursuit of knowledge. Such irony seemed to be central in Durrell's life, for while he lived for the most part in the eastern Mediterranean, enjoying a tangential relationship with Britain, he was perfectly aware that British people made up a large part of his readership. His expatriate status greatly influenced his work and he himself openly acknowledged a 'love-hate' relationship with Britain.

Durrell married his first wife, Nancy Myers, in 1935; the two divorced in 1947 and Durrell was remarried in the same year to Tyvette Cohen, whom he later divorced. He had a daughter from each union, Penelope Berengaria and Sappho-Jane respectively. In 1961 he married Claude Marie Vineenden, a writer, who died in 1967. He married his fourth wife, Ghislaine de Boysson, in 1973. Durrell lived with her in Provence – wearied by his travels and perhaps by his turbulent personal life as well – in reclusive fashion. He died in 1990.

Durrell found it difficult to take Britain's grand conception of herself seriously. For him Britain would always be a stuffy, comically self-important country. His contempt is evident in 'London at Night' (1969), in which he bemoans this grubby, unsensual city that clearly holds no attraction for him: it is neither an exciting place of multicultural possibilities, as it was for Conrad, nor a crucible for investigation, as it proved to be for Orwell.

London at Night
(Walsh in Bloomsbury)

Some nights, when sleep was impossible, and he had lain awake for hours watching the yellow pools of light on the ceiling as they flickered, and listening to the growing quiet of the streets, he would get up out of his bed and stand at the window. The café opposite stayed open until three o'clock and through the steamy glass of the swing-doors he could see the groups of men and women sitting round the marble-topped tables drinking coffee; mostly tall, sallow Jews, he noticed, with long dark overcoats and rakish hats; their clothes were padded out about the shoulders to give them the appearance of physique which they did not possess. And the women, mostly Euston Road bawds, with their loud market-place voices and disease fast hollowing out their eyes and melting down their features. Across the clear sound of voices in the silent street he caught clear scraps of words, unfinished sentences which hung for a moment in the air of the darkened room, and disappeared, leaving only the ghost of meaning in his watching mind. And from this polyglot crew of ruffians and bawds, lustrous Jews who waited in the shadows of every street-corner, and loud-mouthed taxi-drivers who drank tasteless coffee as they awaited late fares, some few he selected as worthy of remembrance. He knew from habit the times of their appearance, and waited to see them come down the street and shoulder their ways into the steamy den. At eleven, for instance, a tall negress walked through the street, limping with fatigue but with a face cocked up to the sky. She hummed a song as she passed in a low, nasal voice, very melancholy but not displeasing, and, surprisingly, held a beautiful silvery-coated whippet on a lead, which followed her softly, its arched body taut and docile. Every night, as she passed, she stopped at the entrance of the café and pushed the swing-doors aside, peering around at the seated people as though seeking someone; but she never went inside, only turned back each night with a little shrug of annoyance and continued her walk. Later, shortly after two, there appeared the figures of two men, one tall and powerful, the other smaller, but sturdily made. The larger was always without a hat, and his face was small and twisted with knobs of curly hair trained back across his poll. His shoulders were large enough for him to do without a padded overcoat. His companion was dark but in a more pallid, Israelite way and carried a huge, ebony-handled stick which seemed thick enough to house the blade of a sword. They walked slowly, with a kind of nervous nonchalance, and always stayed in the café until a quarter-past-three when they both swaggered out and called a taxi to them from the cab-rank at the corner of the road. They seemed never to speak to each other.

Some nights when he found it impossible to sleep he would dress and go out for a walk in the streets, slowly treading out the deliberate sound of his feet upon the pavements, smelling the stale night smells and hearing the noises, and imagining himself in a new world – a world of which half-silence and fear were the keynotes. The stale earth in the window-boxes, sterile and exhausted, unwilling to put forth more small flowers for the dust to choke, had a sharp, rancid smell that mingled with the stale odours of basement kitchens. When he walked thus, in a land where noise was so sharp and disturbing, he found himself able to notice things and comment on them, compare and associate groups of ideas. Even if the nearer silence was unbroken there was the great purring sound of distance, the mighty pouring of blood through the arteries of the city that was never silent. He wondered how many diverse sounds, how many different causes, went to make up this giant uniform growl of silence; the gurgle of water in the underground sewers, the wailing of sirens on the river, the swishing of the late trains as they moved out on their journeys, the groan of an early cart as it crawled down through the city, the chatter of the prostitutes at the street corners, the drone of taxis, the scratching of paper as it drifted upon the pavements – all these were absorbed and became components of that blare of silence; even the small flat sound of his feet upon the pavement was absorbed into it, and made a millionth part of the activity. Sometimes he would stand quite still and strain to distinguish the separate sounds of the vast orchestra – strain until his head ached for those indistinct siren-calls, the roar of trains, but he could never distinguish anything; always a nearer sound would break down his effort, laughter from the next street, or a cry from some shuttered window.

Yet from out of all the bewildering diversities of the night-life some sounds and smells remained constant and unchanging, and for these he treasured recognition as he did for those two or three inhabitants of the café opposite his house. The wheels of a taxi on the smooth black road never made anything but the sound of a choir of gnats, even in wet or frosty weather; and those gaunt men who wheeled their barrows of fruit through the dark squares never looked anything but furtive and hunted; their filthy cloth caps were pulled down low over their faces, and they lowered their voices when they spoke as though there were something shameful in the act of peddling their rich merchandise through the midnight city.

In a little street off Fitzroy Square there was always a light in the basement, and if you stood on the gleaming glass slab fretted with metal, your body was shaken by the pulsing of the machines that baked bread all night; and at each fresh throb of sound the wholesome smell of bread came out upon you from the grating in great heartening whiffs. He would stand upon the pitted glass and let the hot draught pour out around him, permeating his clothes, while he sniffed the sweet odours of the bakery. Once, as he stood there, taking great breaths of the pure warm air, a man, clad in a white smock, came to the grating and handed him two huge hunks of newly baked bread on a long fork, inviting him to eat it, smiling very kindly upon him:

'I get lots of you poor artists round 'ere. Always 'ungry, aren't yer?'

And as Walsh let his teeth sink into the warm crumbly richness of the bread he said, after thanking the man:

'That's settled it. I'm going to be a baker.'

But there were other things that he hated. Down by Leicester Square, in the little burrows behind the theatres, he found many a bundle of rags that had once been a human being curled up asleep in the doorway where tomorrow it would be turned away to make room for a pit queue; and once, a ragged little old man with a tabby beard who was burrowing in a dustbin. Beside him on the pavement lay a very old and very worn violin with only three sound strings, and a minute parcel of his belongings, girded up in a stained handkerchief. Walsh gave him a florin, but the poor creature seemed hardly to comprehend the meaning of the act, and he stared at the coin as it lay in his creased brown palm. Then, with a sudden quick gesture, he nodded his head and turned back to the dustbin, rummaging among the scattered paper and filth. His little frog-head was ducked flat as he tried to reach some object deep in the bin, while unconsciously with his boots he trampled the little round parcel which held his belongings, trampled and tore the red handkerchief.

On these late walks Walsh would often be filled with the feeling that he alone among the living trod the gloomy streets; his moving body and the feel of his clothes hanging on him, they were the only knowledge of substance in an illusory world. Even the sleek and silent men who stood night-long at the street-corners, and the women with their chalk-pale vermilion-rouged masks hiding what little self was left them, were but puzzling symbols of actualities that existed only in the squalid turbulence of the daytime. With the knowledge that so many activities, so many interests, so many personalities lay submerged in the second-sleep of dawn, his own perceptions quickened and briskly demanded food, as if given a freedom which the day denied them.

Doris Lessing
[1919–]

The oldest of two children, Doris Lessing was born in Kermanshah, Persia. In 1925, her family moved to Southern Rhodesia and settled on the 1,000-acre farm where Lessing would spend most of her childhood. The joy of living in the adventurous African landscape contrasted sharply with her unhappy home life. Her relationship with her mother was characterized by emotional abuse and, as is evident in Lessing's autobiography, left deep psychological scars.

Lessing attended a convent boarding school and was enrolled for a brief time at an all-girls high school. However, she dropped out of the formal educational system at age thirteen. Although she had already written two full-length manuscripts and had published several short stories by the time she was eighteen, she made her living working in various secretarial positions. In 1939 she married Frank Wisdom, a civil servant who was much older than she was, and they had two children, John and Jean. After the couple's divorce in 1943, the children remained with their father.

Inspired by the charged political atmosphere that followed the battle of Stalingrad, Lessing embraced Communism. She met her second husband, a Jewish-German immigrant named Gottfried Lessing, through a Marxist organization in Salisbury. The two were married in 1945, but the union was a troubled one that existed more for convenience than any emotional involvement. It ended in divorce in 1949, after Gottfried's application for British citizenship had been approved. That same year Lessing emigrated to London, taking the couple's two-year-old son, Peter, with her. Thus began her relationship with England, a country she found to be full of 'quiet, mad maniacs – behind closed doors'. In 1950 she published her first novel, *The Grass is Singing*, which was unanimously acknowledged to be a highly accomplished debut. The protagonist is a woman whose spiritual isolation, both a product and a reflection of the racist society in which she was raised, results in a mental breakdown.

In 1956 Lessing paid a visit to Rhodesia. It was not a pleasant homecoming, for the government labelled her a 'prohibited immigrant' and restricted her travel. She subsequently returned to England and, later that year, officially left the Communist Party. Nonetheless, she remained politically active, participating in mass nuclear disarmament demonstrations in the late 1950s and serving, until 1961, on the editorial board of an independent Marxist publication, *The New Reasoner* (later the *New Left Review*). Her experiences with the Communist Party are recorded in the first three of the five *Children of Violence* novels (1952–69). In 1962 Lessing's most celebrated work, *The Golden Notebook*, was published. In it she chronicles the life of novelist Anna Wulf from the Second World War to 1957, and explores the idea that modern women are bound by the 'rules' of the society in which they live.

In the late 1960s Lessing became involved in theatre work and wrote several plays that were produced. During this time she also began to take an avid interest in Sufism, and its influence has been evident in her work. Over the course of her career Lessing has received several awards, including the Somerset Maugham Award (1954) and the Prix Medici (1976). Most recently, Lessing published the first volume of her autobiography, *Under My Skin* (1994), and a novel *Love, Again* (1996). She is acutely aware that while she is a member of the British literary establishment, she is also a white African whose sensibilities were formed in and by Africa. Her relationship with British culture and her constant struggle to reconcile her status as a woman writer and a white African figure largely in her work.

In her essay 'In Defence of the Underground' (1987), Lessing finds reason to celebrate multicultural, heterogeneous London. Given the nature of her upbringing as a white African, this is an author who fully understands the interrelationship between race, class and colonialism, and she remains optimistic about the manner in which these societal components come together in modern-day Britain.

In Defence of the Underground

In a small cigarette and sweet shop outside the Underground station, the Indian behind the counter is in energetic conversation with a young man. They are both so angry that customers thinking of coming in change their minds.

'They did my car in, they drove past so near they scraped all the paint off that side. I saw them do it. I was at my window – just luck, that was. They were laughing like dogs. Then they turned around and drove back and scraped the paint off the other side. They went off like bats out of hell. They saw me at the window and laughed.'

'You're going to have to take it into your own hands,' says the Indian. 'They did up my brother's shop last month. They put burning paper through the letter box. It was luck the whole shop didn't burn. The police didn't do anything. He rang them, and then he went round to the station. Nothing doing. So we found out where they lived and we went and smashed their car in.'

'Yes,' says the other, who is a white man, not an Indian. 'The police don't want to know. I told them. I saw them do it. They were drunk, I said. What do you expect us to do? the police said.'

'I'll tell you what you can do,' says the Indian.

All this time I stand there, disregarded. They are too angry to care who hears them and, it follows, might report them. Then the young white man says – he could be something in building, or a driver, 'You think I should do the same, then?'

'You take a good-sized hammer or a crowbar to their car, if you know where they live.'

'I've a fair old idea, yes.'

'Then that's it.'

'Right, that's it.' And he goes out though he has to return for the cigarettes he came to buy, for in his rage he has forgotten them.

The Indian serves me. He is on automatic, his hands at work, his mind elsewhere.

As I go out, 'Cheers,' he says, and then, continuing the other conversation, 'That's it, then.'

In our area the Indian shopkeepers defend their shops at night with close-meshed grilles, like chain mail – and it is not only the Indian shops.

Now I am standing on the pavement in a garden. It is a pavement garden, for the florist puts her plants out here, disciplined ranks of them, but hopeful plants, aspiring, because it is bedding-plant time, in other words, late spring. A lily flowering a good month early scents the air stronger than the stinks of the traffic that pounds up this main route north all day and half the night. It is an ugly road, one you avoid if in a car, for one may need half an hour to go a few hundred yards.

Not long ago just where I stand marked the end of London. I know this because an old woman told me she used to take a penny bus here from Marble Arch, every Sunday. That is, she did, 'If I had a penny to spare, I used to save up from my dinners, I used to look forward all week. It was all fields and little streams, and we took off our shoes and stockings and sat with our feet in the water and looked at the cows. They used to come and look at us. And the birds – there were plenty of those.' That was before the First World War, in that period described in books of memoirs as a Golden Age. Yet you can find on stationers' counters postcards made from photographs of this street a hundred years or so ago. It has never not been a poor street, and it is a poor one now, even in this particular age of Peace and Plenty. Not much has changed, though shop fronts are flashier, and full of bright cheap clothes, and there is a petrol station. The postcards show modest self-regarding buildings and the ground floor of every one is a shop of a kind long since extinct, where each customer was served individually. Outside them, invited from behind a counter to centre the picture, stand men in bowler hats or serving aprons; if it is a woman she has a hat on of the kind that insisted on obdurate respectability, for that is a necessary attribute of the poor. But only a couple of hundred yards north-west my friend sat on Sundays with her feet in the little streams, while the cows crowded close. 'Oh, it was so cold, the water'd take your breath away, but you'd soon forget that, and it was the best day of the week.' A few hundred yards north there used to be a mill. Another woman, younger than the first, told me she remembered the mill. 'Mill Lane – the name's because there used to be a mill, you see. But they pulled the mill down.' And where it was is a building no one would notice, if you didn't know what it replaced. If they had let the mill stand we would be proud of it, and they would charge us to go in and see how things used to be.

I enter the station, buy a ticket from a machine that works most of the time, and go up long stairs. There used to be decent lavatories, but now they are locked up because they are vandalized as soon as repaired. There is a good waiting room with heating, but often a window is smashed, and there is always graffiti. What are the young people saying when they smash everything they can? – for it is young people who do it, usually men. It is not that they are depraved because they are deprived, for I have just visited a famous university up north, where they have twenty applications for every place, where ninety-nine per cent of the graduates get jobs within a year of leaving. These are the privileged young, and they make for themselves a lively and ingenious social life their teachers clearly admire, if not envy. Yet they too smash everything up, not just the usual undergraduate loutishness, boys will be boys, but what seems to be a need for systematic destruction. What need? Do we know?

At the station you stand to wait for trains on a platform high above roofs and the tree tops are level with you. You feel thrust up into the sky. The sun, the wind, the rain, arrive unmediated by buildings. Exhilarating.

I like travelling by Underground. This is a defiant admission. I am always hearing, reading, I hate the Underground. In a book I have just picked up the author says he seldom uses it, but when he did have to go a few stops, he found it disgusting. A strong word. If people have to travel in the rush hour, then all is understood, but you may hear people who know nothing about rush hours say how terrible the Underground is. This is the Jubilee Line and I use it all the time. Fifteen minutes at the most to get into the centre. The carriages are bright and new – well, almost. There are efficient indicators, Charing Cross: five minutes, three minutes, one minute. The platforms are no more littered than the streets, often less, or not at all. 'Ah but you should have seen what they were like in the old days. The Tube was different then.'

I know an old woman, I am sure I should say lady, who says, 'People like you . . .' She means aliens, foreigners, though I have lived here forty years . . . 'have no idea what London was like. You could travel from one side of London to the other by taxi for half a crown.' (In Elizabeth I's time you could buy a sheep for a few pence and under the Romans doubtless you could buy a villa for a silver coin, but currencies never devaluate when Nostalgia is in this gear.) 'And everything was so nice and clean and people were polite. Buses were always on time and the tube was cheap.'

This woman was one of London's Bright Young Things, her young time was the twenties. As she speaks her face is tenderly reminiscent, but lonely, and she does not expect to persuade me or anyone else. What is the point of having lived in that Paradise Isle if no one believes you? As she sings her praise-songs for the past one sees hosts of pretty girls with pastel mouths and rouged cheeks wearing waistless petal-hemmed dresses, their hair marcelled in finger-waves, and as they flit from party to party they step in and out of obedient taxis driven by men only too happy to accept a penny tip. It was unlikely those women ever came as far north as West Hampstead or Kilburn, and I think Hampstead wasn't fashionable then, though in D. H. Lawrence's stories artists and writers live there. What is astonishing about reminiscences of those times is not only that there were different Londons for the poor and the middle class, let alone the rich, but the pedlars of memories never seem to be aware of this: 'In those days, when I was a little girl, I used to scrub steps. I did even when it was snowing, and I had bare feet, they were blue with cold sometimes, and I went to the baker's for yesterday's bread, cheap, and my poor little mother slaved sixteen hours a day, six days a week, oh those were wicked times, cruel times they were.' 'In those days we were proud to live in London. Now it's just horrid, full of horrid people.'

In my half of the carriage are three white people and the rest are black and brown and yellowish. Or, by another division, five females and six males. Or, four young people and seven middle-aged or elderly. Two Japanese girls, as glossy and self-sufficient as young cats, sit smiling. Surely the mourners for old London must applaud the Japanese, who are never, ever, scruffy or careless? Probably not: in that other London there were no foreigners, only English, pinko-grey as Shaw said, always *chez nous*, for the Empire had not imploded, the world had not invaded, and while every family had at least one relative abroad administering colonies or dominions, or being soldiers, that was abroad, it was there, not here, the colonies had not come home to roost.

These Japanese girls are inside an invisible bubble, they look out from a safe world. When I was in Japan I met many Japanese young ladies, who all seemed concerned to be Yum Yum. They giggled and went oooh – oooh – oooh as they jumped up and down, goody goody, and gently squealed with pleasure or with shock. But if you got them by themselves they were tough young women with a sharp view of life. Not that it was easy, for there always hovered some professor or mentor concerned to return them to their group, keep them safe and corporate.

A young black man sits dreaming, his ears wired to his Walkman, and his feet jig gently to some private rhythm. He wears clothes more expensive, more stylish, than anyone else in this travelling room. Next to him is an Indian woman with a girl of ten or so. They wear saris that show brown midriffs as glossy as toffee, but they have cardigans over them. Butterfly saris, workaday cardigans that make the statement, if you choose to live in a cold northern country, then this is the penalty. Never has there been a sadder sartorial marriage than saris with cardigans. They sit quietly conversing, in a way that makes the little girl seem a woman. These three got out at Finchley Road. In get four Americans, two boys, two girls, in their uniform of jeans and T-shirts and sports shoes. They talk loudly and do not see anyone else. Two sprawl opposite and two loll on either side of a tall old woman, possibly Scottish, who sits with her burnished shoes side by side, her fine bony hands on the handle of a wheeled shopping basket. She gazes ahead of her, as if the loud youngsters do not exist, and she is possibly remembering – but what London? The war? (Second World War, this time.) Not a poor London, that is certain.

She is elegant, in tweeds and a silk shirt and her rings are fine. She and the four Americans get out at St John's Wood, the youngsters off to the American School, but she probably lives here. St John's Wood, so we are told by Galsworthy, for one, was where kept women were put in discreetly pretty villas by rich or at least respectable lovers. Now these villas can be afforded only by the rich, often Arabs.

As people get into the waiting train, I sit remembering how not long ago I visited a French friend in a St John's Wood hotel. While I stood at the reception desk three Arabs in white robes went through from a back part of the hotel to the lift, carrying at shoulder level a tray heaped with rice, and on that a whole roasted sheep. The lobby swooned with the smell of spices and roast meat. The receptionist said, to my enquiring look, 'Oh, it's for Sheikh So-and-So, he has a feast every night.' And she continued to chat on the telephone to a boyfriend. 'Oh, you only say that, oh I know all about men, you can't tell me anything' – using these words, as far as she was concerned, for the first time in history. And she caressed the hair above her left ear with a complacent white hand that had on it a lump of synthetic amber the size of a hen's egg. Her shining hair was amber, cut in a 1920s shingle. Four more Arabs flowed past, their long brown fingers playing with their prayer beads, like nuns who repel the world with their rosaries. 'Hail Mary Full of Grace . . .' their lips moving as they smile and nod, taking part in worldly conversation; but their fingers holding tight to righteousness. The Arabs disappeared into the lift, presumably on their way to the feast, while the revolving doors admitted four more, a congregation of sheikhs.

Not far from here, in Abbey Road, are the studios where the Beatles recorded. At the pedestrian crossing made famous by the Four are always platoons of tourists, of all ages and races, standing to stare with their souls in their eyes, while their fingers go click-click on their cameras. All over the world, in thousands of albums, are cherished photographs of this dingy place.

This part of London is not old. When the villas were full of mistresses and ladies of pleasure it was a newish suburb. Travelling from NW6 or NW2 into the centre is to leave recently settled suburbs for the London that has risen and fallen in successive incarnations since before the Romans. Not long ago I was at lunch in the house that was Gladstone's, now a Press Club. For most of us it is hard to imagine a family actually living in a house that seems built only to present people for public occasions, but above all no one could stand on Carlton House Terrace and think: not long ago there was a wood here, running water, grazing beasts. No, Nature is away down a flight of grandiose steps, across the Mall, and kept well in its place in St James's Park. The weight of those buildings, pavements, roads, forbids thoughts of the kind still so natural in St John's Wood, where you think: there must have been a wood here, and who was St John? – almost certainly a church. Easy to see the many trees as survivors of that wood; unlikely, but not impossible.

Today I am glad I am not getting off here. The escalator often doesn't work. Only a month ago, on one of the blackboards the staff use to communicate their thoughts to passengers was written in jaunty white chalk: 'You are probably wondering why the escalators so often aren't working? We shall tell you! It is because they are old and often go out of order. Sorry! Have a good day!' Which message, absolutely in the style of London humour, sardonic and with its edge of brutality, was enough to cheer one up, and ready to make the long descent on foot.

In jump three youngsters. Yobbos. Louts. Hooligans. They are sixteen or so, in other words adolescents, male, with their loud raucous unhappy braying laughter, their raging sex, their savagery. Two white and a black. Their cries, their jeers, command everyone's attention – which is after all the point. One white youth and the black are jostling and the third, who puts up with it in a manner of stylized resignation, smiling like a sophisticated Christian martyr: probably some film or television hero. Impossible to understand what they are saying, for their speech is as unformed as if they had speech defects – probably intentionally, for who wants to be understood too well by adults at sixteen? All this aggro is only horseplay, on the edge of harm, no more. At Baker Street the two tormentors push out the third, try to prevent him from re-entering. Not so easy, this, for trains take their time at Baker Street, the all-purpose junction for many-suburbed London. The three tire of the scuffle and step inside to stand near the door, preventing others from entering, but only by their passivity. Excuse me, excuse me, travellers say, confronted by these three large youths who neither resist nor attack, but only take up a lot of room, knowing that they do, knowing they are a damned nuisance, but preserving innocent faces that ignore mutters and angry stares. As the doors begin to close, the two aggressors push out the victim, and stand making all kinds of abusive gestures at him, and mouthing silent insults as the train starts to move. The lad on the platform shouts insults back but points in the direction the train is going, presumably to some agreed destination. As we gather speed he is half-strolling, half-dancing, along the platform, and he sends a forked-fingered gesture after us. The two seem to miss him, and they sit loosely, gathering energy for the next explosion, which occurs at Bond Street, where they are off the train in dangerous kangaroo leaps, shouting abuse. At whom? Does it matter? Where they sat roll two soft-drink cans, as bright and seductive as advertisements. Now in the coach are people who have not seen the whole sequence, and they are probably thinking, Thank God I shall never have to be that age again! Or are they? Is it possible that when people sigh, Oh if only I was young again, they are regretting what we have just seen, but remembered as an interior landscape of limitless possibilities?

At Bond Street a lot of people get out, and the train stays still long enough to read comfortably the poem provided by the Keepers of the Underground, inserted into a row of advertisements.

THE EAGLE

> He clasps the crag with crooked hands:
> Close to the sun in lonely lands.
> Ring'd with the azure world he stands.
>
> The wrinkled sea beneath him crawls:

> He watches from his mountain walls.
> And like a thunderbolt he falls.

Alfred Lord Tennyson

In get a crowd of Danish schoolchildren, perhaps on a day trip. They are well behaved, and watched over by a smiling girl, who does not seem much older than they are. Tidily they descend at Green Park, and the carriage fills up again. All tourists. Is that what people mean when they complain the Underground is so untidy? Is it the xenophobia of the British again? Rather, the older generations of the British? Is what I enjoy about London, its variety, its populations from everywhere in the world, its transitoriness – for sometimes London can give you the same feeling as when you stand to watch cloud shadows chase across a plain – exactly what they so hate?

Yet for people so threatened they are doing, I think, rather well. Not long ago I saw this incident. It was a large London hospital, in a geriatric ward. 'I'm just on my way to Geriatrics' you may hear one sprightly young nurse tell another, as she darts her finger to the lift button. An old white woman, brought in because she had fallen, was being offered a bedpan. She was not only old, in fact ancient, and therefore by rights an inhabitant of that lost Eden of decently uniform pinko-grey people, but working class and a spinster. (One may still see women described on old documents, Status: Spinster.) For such a woman to be invited to use a bedpan in a public place before the curtains had even been drawn about her was bad enough. To be nursed by a man, a male nurse, something she had never imagined possible. Worst of all, he was black, a young calm black man, in a nurse's uniform. ('No, I'm not a doctor, I'm a nurse – yes, that's right, a nurse.') He turned back the bed covers, assisted the old woman on to the bedpan, nicely pulling down her nightgown over her old thighs, and drew the curtains. 'I'll be back in just a minute, love.' And off he went. Behind that curtain went on an internal drama hard to imagine by people used to polyglot and casually mannered London, whether they enjoy it or not. When he returned to pull back the curtains, ask if she was all right – did she want him to clean her up a little? – and then remove the pan, her eyes were bright with dignified defiance. She had come to terms with the impossible. 'No, dear, it's all right, I can still do that for myself.'

In a school in South London where a friend is governor, twenty-five languages are spoken.

Now we are tunnelling under old London, though not the oldest, for that is a mile, or two or three, further east. On the other side of thick shelves of earth as full of pipes and cables, wires, sewers, the detritus of former buildings and towns as garden soil is of worms and roots, is St James's Park – Downing Street – Whitehall. If someone travelled these under-earth galleries and never came up into the air it would be easy to believe this was all there could be to life, to living. There is a sci-fi story about a planet where suns and moons appear only every so many years, and the citizens wait for the miracle, the revelation of their situation in the universe, which of course the priests have taken possession of, claiming the splendour of stars as proof of their right to rule. There are already cities where an under-earth town repeats the one above it, built in air – for instance, Houston, Texas. You enter an unremarkable door, just as in a dream, and you are in an underground city, miles of it, with shops, restaurants, offices. You need never come up. There are people who actually like basement flats, choose them, draw curtains, turn on lights, create for themselves an underground, and to them above-ground living seems as dangerous as ordinary life does to an ex-prisoner or someone too long in hospital. They institutionalize themselves, create a place where everything is controlled by them, a calm concealed place, away from critical eyes, and the hazards of weather and the changes of light are shut out. Unless the machinery fails: a gas leak, the telephone goes wrong.

In the fifties I knew a man who spent all day going around the Circle Line. It was like a job, a discipline, from nine till six. *They* couldn't get at him, he claimed. He was having a breakdown. Did people go in for more imaginative breakdowns then? It sometimes seems a certain flair has gone out of the business. And yet, a few days ago, on the Heath, there approached a Saxon – well, a young man wearing clothes it would be possible to agree Saxons might have worn. A brown woollen shirt. Over it a belted jerkin contrived from thick brown paper. Breeches were made with elastic bands up the calves. A draped brown scarf made a monkish hood. He held a spear from a toy shop. 'Prithee, kind sir,' said my companion, somewhat out of period, 'whither goest thou?' The young Saxon stopped, delighted and smiling, while his companion, a young woman full of concern, looked on. 'Out,' said the young man. 'Away.'

'What is your name? Beowulf? Olaf the Red? Eric the Brave?'

'Eric the Black.'

'It isn't your name *really*,' said his minder, claiming him for fact.

'Yes it is,' we heard as they wandered off into the russets, the yellows, the scorched greens of the unforgettable autumn of 1990. 'My name is Eric, isn't it? Well then, it *is* Eric.'

Charing Cross and everyone gets out. At the exit machine a girl appears running up from the deeper levels, and she is chirping like an alarm. Now she has drawn our attention to it, in fact a steady bleeping is going on, and for all we know it is a fire alarm. These days there are so many electronic bleeps, cheeps, buzzes, blurps, that we don't hear them. The girl is a fey creature, blonde locks flying around a flushed face. She is laughing dizzily, and racing a flight or flock of young things coming into the West End for an evening's adventure, all of them already crazed with pleasure, and in another dimension of speed and lightness, like sparks speeding up and out. She and two girls push in their tickets and flee along a tunnel to the upper world, but three youths vault over, with cries of triumph, and their state of being young is such a claim on us all that the attendant decides not to notice, for it would be as mad as swatting butterflies.

Now I am going out to Trafalgar Square, along a tunnel, and there, against a wall, is a site where groups of youngsters are always bedding, crouching, squatting, to examine goods laid on boxes, and bits of cloth. Rings and earrings, bracelets, brooches, all kinds of glitter and glitz, brass and glass, white metal and cheap silver, cheap things but full of promise and possibility.

I follow this tunnel and that, go up some steps, and I am in

Trafalgar Square. Ahead of me across the great grey space with its low pale fountains is the National Gallery, and near it the National Portrait Gallery. The sky is a light blue, sparkling, and fragile clouds are being blown about by winds at work far above our level of living, for down here it is quiet. Now I may enjoyably let time slide away in one Gallery or both, and not decide till the last possible moment, shall I turn left to the National, or walk another fifty paces and look at the faces of our history? When I come out, the sky, though it will not have lost light, will have acquired an intense late-afternoon look, time to find a café, to meet friends and then . . . in an hour or so the curtain will go up in a theatre, or the English National Opera. Still, after all these years, these decades, there is no moment like that when the curtain goes up, the house lights dim . . . Or, having dawdled about, one can after all simply go home, taking care to miss the rush hour.

Not long ago, at the height of the rush hour, I was strap-hanging, and in that half of the carriage, that is, among fourteen people, three people read books among all the newspapers. In the morning, off to work, people betray their allegiances: *The Times*, the *Independent*, the *Guardian*, the *Telegraph*, the *Mail*. The bad papers some of us are ashamed of don't seem much in evidence, but then this is a classy line, at least at some hours and in some stretches of it. At night the *Evening Standard* adds itself to the display. Three people. At my right elbow a man was reading the *Iliad*. Across the aisle a woman read *Moby Dick*. As I pushed out, a girl held up *Wuthering Heights* over the head of a new baby asleep on her chest. When people talk glumly about our state of illiteracy I tell them I saw this, and they are pleased, but sceptical.

The poem holding its own among the advertisements was:

INFANT JOY

'I have no name:
I am but two days old.'
What shall I call thee?
'I happy am.

Joy is my name.'
Sweet joy befall thee!

Pretty joy!
Sweet joy but two days old.
Sweet joy I call thee:
Thou dost smile.
I sing the while
Sweet joy befall thee.

William Blake

Walking back from the Underground I pass three churches. Two of them are no longer conduits for celestial currents: one is a theatre, one derelict. In such a small bit of London, three churches . . . that other-worldly visitor so useful for enlivening our organs of comparison might, seventy years ago, have wondered, 'What are they for, these buildings, so like each other, so unlike all the others, several to a district? Administrative buildings? A network of government offices? Newly built, too!' But these days this person, she, he or it, would note the buildings are often unused. 'A change of government perhaps?' Yet certain types of buildings repeat themselves from one end of the city to the other. 'Just as I saw on my last visit, there are "pubs" for dispensing intoxicants, and centres for fast movement by means of rail. Others are for the maintenance of machines like metal bugs or beetles – a new thing this, nothing like that last time I was here. And there is another new thing. Every few yards is a centre for the sale of drugs, chemical substances.' A funny business – he, she or it might muse, mentally arranging the items of the report that will be faxed back to Canopus. 'If I put them in order of frequency of occurrence, then chemists' shops must come first. This is a species dependent on chemical additions to what they eat and drink.' Within a mile of where I live there are at least fifteen chemists' shops, and every grocery has shelves of medicines.

As I turn the corner past where the old man stood I leave behind the stink and roar of vehicles pushing their way northwards and I realize that for some minutes it has been unpleasant to breathe. Now Mill Lane, where shops are always starting up, going bankrupt, changing hands, particularly now with the trebling and quadrupling of rents and rates. Soon, I am in the little roads full of houses, and the traffic has become a steady but minor din. The streets here are classically inclined. Agamemnon, Achilles, Ulysses, and there is an Orestes Mews. Add to these names Gondar, and one may postulate an army man, classically educated, who was given the job of naming these streets. In fact, this was not so far wrong. The story was this. (True or false? Who cares? Every story of the past, recent or old, is bound to be tidied up, rounded off, made consequential.) An ex-army man, minor gentry, had a wife in the country with many children, and a mistress in town, with many more. To educate all these he went in for property, bought farmland that spread attractively over a hill with views of London, and built what must have been one of the first northern commuter suburbs . . . for remember, in the valley just down from this hill, towards London, were the streams, the cows and the green fields my old friend took a penny bus ride to visit every Sunday. The commuters went in by horse-bus or by train to the City.

Some of the buildings are Mansions, built from the start as flats, but most were houses, since converted into three flats. Hard to work out how these houses functioned. The cellars are all wet. In mine labels come off bottles in three months. Yet there was a lavatory down here. Used by whom? Surely nobody could have lived in this earthy cave? Perhaps it wasn't wet then. Now a circular hole or mini-shaft has been dug into the soil, for the damp has long ago heaved off the cement floor, and in it one may watch the water level rise and fall. Not according to the rainfall: all of us in this area know the tides have something to do with the leaking pipes of the reservoir, which from my top window looks like an enormous green field, or village green, for there are great trees all around it: the Victorians put their reservoirs underground. (They say that if you know the man who has the task of guarding the precious waters, one may be taken through a small door and find oneself on the edge of a reach of still black water, under a low ceiling where lights gleam down. One may add to this attractively theatrical picture the faint plop of a rat swimming away from sudden light, and a single slow-spreading ripple.) The top of my house is a converted attic. But the attics were not converted then. There are three bedrooms on the second floor, one too small to share. Two rooms on the first floor, now one room, but then probably dining room and sitting room. A kitchen is pleasantly but inconveniently off a veranda or 'patio' – a recent addition. It was not a kitchen then. On the ground floor is one room, once two, and 'conveniences' also added recently. A garden room, most likely a nursery. In those days they had so many children, they often had relatives living with them, and every middle-class household had at least one servant, usually more. How were they all fitted in? Where did they cook, where was the larder, how did they get the washing done? And how did they keep warm? There are minuscule fire baskets in small fireplaces in every room.

A hundred years ago this suburb, these houses, were built, and they are solid and thick-walled and all the builders who come to mend roofs or fix plumbing tell you how well they were put up, how good the materials were. 'We don't build like that now.' Nor are these experts dismayed by the wet cellar. 'You keep that clay good and wet around your foundations, and it won't shrink in these summers we are having now, and you won't be sorry.'

As I turn the corner into the street I live in the light is arranging the clouds into tinted masses. The sunsets up here are, to say the least, satisfactory.

Ivy loads the corner house, and starlings are crowding themselves in there, swooping out, swirling back, to become invisible and silent until the morning.

Wilson Harris

[1921–]

Wilson Harris was born in New Amsterdam, British Guiana (now Guyana), into a middle-class family of Amerindian, African and European heritage. He was educated at Queen's College in Georgetown, a highly regarded boys' school, where he was able to study the standard works of English and classical literature. Such reading greatly influenced his own work, which, while far from classical in structure, is rife with allegory and mythical references.

In 1939 Harris studied land surveying and from 1942 to 1958 he worked as a government surveyor. The evocative landscape of Guyana, the isolation of the jungle and the people of varying race and class all have descriptive and symbolic roles in his fiction. Harris began his apprenticeship as a writer during this surveying period, contributing poems, stories, critical essays and reviews to the literary journal *Kyk-over-al*. In 1951 he published his first volume of verse, *Fetish*, under the pseudonym Kona Waruk. His next work, *Eternity to Season*, also a collection of poetry, was published in 1954. In the same year Harris married his first wife, Cecily Carew.

The year 1959 was a turning point for Harris. He and Carew divorced, and Harris moved to Britain, where he met and married the Scottish writer Margaret Burns. Not only did he establish a new residence in London but he also decided to abandon surveying and concentrate on writing. He supplemented his income with a lecturing and academic career, and his first compilation of speeches and essays, *Tradition, the Writer & Society*, was published in 1967. Later collections are *Explorations* (1981) and *The Womb of Space* (1983).

Harris's fiction, like his poetry, does not provide 'easy' reading. His first novel, *Palace of the Peacock* (1960), was greeted with both excitement and some bewilderment. Since its publication, he has been a prolific author. While his works do contain common themes – cultural heterogeneity, the unity of humans and nature and individual redemption – his thirst for originality keeps his writing from becoming stale and repetitive. With each novel, he takes the English language even further beyond the boundaries of its conventional usage in order to explore his complex vision of the world. Other important works include *The Secret Ladder* (1963) and *Carnival* (1985).

As a lecturer, Harris has taken his ideas and experiences to universities around the world. In 1970 he was writer-in-residence at the University of the West Indies and the University of Toronto in Canada, and in 1972, 1980 and 1981–2 he was a visiting professor at the University of Texas at Austin. He was also writer-in-residence at Newcastle University in Australia, and he has guest-lectured in Denmark, India and at Yale in the United States. In 1972 Harris received a Guggenheim Fellowship. He has been the recipient of many other awards, including honorary doctorates from the University of the West Indies (1984) and the University of Kent at Canterbury (1988), and the Guyana National Prize for Fiction (1987). He most recently received an honorary doctorate from the University of Essex (1996). Despite the abundance of travel, Harris remains based in Britain, and it is here that he has produced the majority of his work. Perhaps he, like his fictional counterpart in *Da Silva da Silva's Cultivated Wilderness* (1977) hears voices 'at the heart of this great city, the regional accent of birds and bells, the voices of the past, the voices of the present'.

Although he has been a resident in Britain for almost forty years, everything Harris writes is underscored with evocations, both physical and mythical, of his native Guyana. Only Harris could describe a 'straightforward' colonial encounter between three West Indians in London, as he does in the following extract from his novel The Angel at the Gate *(1982). Harris overlays it with a disturbing edge, yet still manages to render the whole as poetic. Perhaps more so than any West Indian-born author who has resided and worked in Britain, Harris has been innovative and original in language, theme and form.*

From *The Angel at the Gate*

Lucy Brown, archetypal Jamaican tea-lady, of the electrical factory from which Sebastian had been fired in the summer of 1979, came to see Jackson during the week of the Brixton disturbances in 1981. She brought her daughter (whose name was also Lucy) – a young woman of nineteen – with her, and Jackson could see from the younger woman's manner that she did not altogether relish coming. It was her first visit to North Pole Road but her mother – who was attached to Jackson – spoke of it often. Young Lucy sniffed and cast an unappreciative glance at the spartan room with its mist of faces on the ceiling. The cat lay coiled and still in a corner.

Lucy's boyfriend had been arrested three days before in Brixton, and the older woman was unhappy over her daughter's political acquaintance. She hid her anxieties and bustled all the more strenuously with trays of tea. Few of her friends saw her as she was, sagging body, psychical exhaustion. For nothing was self-evident on the surface. She dressed to preserve a robust appearance. Her composure in public was wooden save for a sudden, occasional flicker of alarm when she became enlivened – almost ecstatic – in confessing that blessings and misfortunes came three or four in a row.

Lucy Brown (the mother) had arrived in England from Jamaica on the day Jackson fell from a ladder. Lucy (the daughter) was born in Notting Hill Gate. Her birth coincided with the death of Indian Lucy in India after which Khublall had come to Europe with his shaven head. It was all recorded in Mary's automatic writing and Angel Inn mirror's wealth of a-causal coincidence enfolding series of 'absences' and 'presences' through which to read a conception of the family of Mack the Knife.

Lucy Brown had had a difficult time as an unmarried mother bringing up the child. She had met Jackson comparatively recently, scarcely more than four years ago, by chance, when he was returning home from his portering duties in a large hotel. They were sheltering from the rain in the wide doorway of the Odeon Cinema close to his workplace and he had casually asked her, on hearing her accent, whether she was interested in having some old furniture he had decided to get rid of.

It was what she wanted and she jumped at the opportunity, and that was how she first came to visit him in North Pole Road. Spartan as his flat was, it needed cleaning at times and she cleaned kitchen, bath, sitting room, etc., everything except the garden at the back in which the cat roamed and killed the occasional bird or mouse.

It was a curious friendship since Jackson was of middle-class Jamaican origins (he no longer possessed a bean of his father's money) and she was of peasant stock from the hills and had retained traces of her accent and a modified pattern of West Indian speech.

She grew to trust him implicitly and he found himself by degrees linked to her by wry comedy, exasperated spirit, yet ominous and serious understanding.

'Oh Mr Jackson,' she said, 'I been promising myself to bring Lucy to see you these past four year. She need counsel. The girl headstrong. She won't listen to me . . .'

On the surface it seemed a familiar enough story to Jackson, the gulf between the generations. 'You look well, Lucy,' Jackson said, trying to make light of her woebegone countenance. 'I mean your dress,' he added soberly. 'It's new, isn't it?'

Lucy was wearing a full dress that disguised and suited her large figure. 'I not feeling as bright as I look, sir. And if I collapse on the road and got to be taken to hospital . . .' She lifted her dress almost unconsciously to reveal a snow-white, spotless petticoat. 'They say I would win a prize for the best-dressed tea-lady in London.' Her voice rumbled into a laugh.

Jackson smiled. Lucy, the daughter, stared into space. It was astonishing how swiftly the older woman's mood could change from sad to bright like flickering shadows in Angel Inn mirror.

'You know, Mr Jackson,' she confessed, 'there's nobody else in the world I talk to like you. You know my private feeling.' She turned to her daughter. 'I don't mean by that what you thinking Lucy. All you young people is a hard generation . . .'

'Platonic,' said young Lucy, 'how good.' Her accent was Notting Hill Gate, flat-earth English, sharp, sceptical, it stung a little, but Jackson felt oddly stimulated. Her mother ignored her except that her demeanour changed again within chameleon bite of blood. 'I frighten one day of dropping down on the road, sir. All them prying eye, prying hand, undressing, dressing me.'

'What does it matter?' Jackson said. 'You won't know a thing.' He turned to hard-edged, slightly enigmatic daughter for support but she looked away swiftly to stare into space. Why had she bothered to come, he wondered. What could he say to please her?

'*It matter*,' said the older woman. 'I would know, my hair would breathe, when strange hand touch me. Nowadays nobody care. People shooting each other in Jamaica. Call an election and bullet fly. Killing, wanting to kill, wanting to be killed, wanting to fight in the street, is *immodest . . .*' She stopped.

Immodest! The word struck him. He had never thought of it like that. What did she mean? He stared into the woman's eyes and caught the drift of half-sealed, half-unsealed consciousness as her fictional death, fictional disrobing, overshadowed the room. She was obsessed, he saw, by the thought that a dead person could come immodestly alive in the 'boudoir of the coffin, the boudoir of politics'.

What an outrageous notion! Yet it glanced through his mind as a true conception of dressed urban *angst* and peasant black humour. It drew him down into the grave of the streets, the self-advertised killed around the globe upon Marsden's towering stick converted now into Lucy Brown's height of fear, her heightened fear of violence, the theatrical deaths that one saw on television, the tall dead celebrated by fanatics, the extensions of immodest naked action, immodest prosecution of feud, unconscious strip-tease, immodest wish-fulfil-ment, hunger-fasts, hate-fasts.

Young Lucy now got up from her chair and made her way over to the vase of flowers. Her mother's eyes and Jackson's eyes followed her across the room. 'I wish she would marry a good man, not a freedom fighter, God knows what unfreedom he fighting for like in a nightmare; a good man with a bit of money in the bank, Mr Jackson. *Can't you talk to she?*'

It was the kind of half-rude, half-rhetorical question for which the West Indian peasant was famous. By 'talk' Lucy Brown meant the magical power to bind to one's will, to make someone do one's bidding. That 'talk' was equated with 'good or bad persuasion' arose

from an unconscious conviction that words were a sacred or
daemonic medium since their roots were mysteriously cast in the
rhythm of things, the implicit voice in every object one uses, implicit
trance, utterance of binding contour in every feared object, respected
object. Yet fear, Jackson wanted to say but could not, could also
breed silence – the fear that's close to ambiguous love – the fear of
nemesis that helps to unravel temptation to seduce others or to be
seduced by others.

'Three year pass,' Lucy Brown said, 'since the motorcycle accident
in 1978. Three anniversary. First anniversary '79 Sebastian Holiday
lose his job.'

Jackson did not know that Sebastian Holiday was hollow relation
to his lost 'daughter of Man' and assumed the tea-lady was referring
to someone at her workplace.

'Second anniversary '80 the recession bite deep and a lot of
redundancy follow. Third anniversary '81 Lucy Brixton boyfriend in
trouble. Can't you talk to her, Mr Jackson?'

'A day's just a day for me,' said young Lucy coldly. 'No talk will
change that.' She turned around a little from the vase of flowers.
'And anyway you do enough talking for everybody and your
anniversary's early this year, isn't it, mother? This is April not June.'

'What motorcycle accident?' said Jackson, turning away for a
moment from young Lucy's hard-edged, disturbing beauty of limb
and breast.

'It was a white boyfriend Lucy had. He die on the road in '78.'

The young woman moved away slowly from the flowers, crossed
the room and fondled the cat. Jackson's eyes were unobtrusively
glued to her. It was suddenly clear to him that there was an element
of dream in the way she walked however sceptical or cold she
seemed. On the surface her body was a wall between herself and
eclipsed antecedents. Through Mary's automatic codes however that
clothed the room and propelled her pencil across the page of a
mirror, Jackson perceived depths of characterization, hypnotic
expedition.

His eyes seemed to open. Something came back to him like a blow of silence. A file of black women walking through the hills of Jamaica. He was a boy at the time in a car on his way with his father across the island. The women were dressed in white. They carried covered trays of food and other materials on their head. There was a statuesque deliberation to each movement they made, a hard-edged beauty akin to young Lucy's that seemed to bind their limbs into the soil even as it lifted them very subtly an inch or two into space.

That lift was so nebulous, so uncertain, it may not have occurred at all. Yet it was there; it gave a gentle wave or groundswell to the static root or the vertical dance of each processional body. It also imbued the women with enigmatic privacy. Were they on their way to a wedding or a wake? To ask them was to be greeted with a smile one could not interpret. Was it the smile of secret mourning or secret rejoicing? Were they oblivious of secret, ecstatic ladder of space? Did they incline without knowing it into psychology of stasis, the stasis of the hills?

Jackson heard Lucy Brown's voice again – her obsession with sudden death in the street, her obsession with her own funeral side by side with intimate (almost naked) desire for her daughter to marry 'a good man with a bit of money in the bank'. No wonder her fear of immodest exposure possessed an involuntary compulsion or subconscious strip-tease funeral expectation (the eyes that would see her, the hands that would touch her) woven into a vision of her daughter's wedding . . .

Such unconscious or subconscious strip-tease was an aspect of enigmatic privacy laid bare in half-comedy, half-tragedy, of Angel Inn mirror. It was an aspect of strangest carnival strip-tease of oblivious mankind, obliviousness of fashionable bullet-ridden nudity in the eye of the camera, obliviousness of Stella's nudity in the street, obliviousness of Sukey Tawdrey's rag dances of refined, imperial bombast, obliviousness of Mother Diver's shawl of possessions.

All this moved like a stroke of mingled lust and sorrow in young Lucy's dream-body, hard-edged, disturbing beauty, in the mirror of spectres by which Jackson was held in Mary's 'fictional book'. A series of reflections filled his mind from nowhere it seemed. She was a stubborn young woman, no one would deny. But there was more to it than that. The file of the folk by which Mary's mirror had invested her emphasized that her feet were upon the ground but also made darkly clear the precarious linkage of secret ladder of space and static hill of earth. The link was actually broken, the static had begun to engulf them, that file of women, even in those far-off days of his boyhood.

He was witnessing – without realizing it – in that procession he saw in the hills, the regression of the dying folk into mysterious tune of love and death: mysterious attunement to a gulf or divide between sky and earth, between territorial, animal imperative and human-kind or human space within all innocent/guilty, sad/happy places where Mack the Knife had moved or settled upon and around the globe . . .

Jackson recalled with sorrow how he himself had fallen from the ladder of space and into that fall was threaded his 'lost' daughter of man. Or was it that a descent of 'daughter' was needed to match an imperfectly understood notion or 'ascent' of son – daughter of man, son of man? The question loomed in Mary's automatic book.

The question brought the hills into his room as he faced the two women and listened to Lucy Brown's appeal to 'talk' to her daughter. The silent hills were running down to the sea not up to the sky. The rivers ran down the island of his boyhood to a sea that possessed so little tidal range there was no reversal of flow back upland or inland. Until the silent hills grew again to match the faint ascent of the spidery rain into the great cloud ancestors of Anancy heaven.

'Ah,' said Jackson turning away from the Jamaican hills to the young woman of Notting Hill, 'to fulfil your mother's trust . . .' he was speaking to himself '. . . I must learn to be silent in the face of your obliviousness, I must learn to paint or sculpt what lies stranded between earth and heaven . . .' He stopped. He looked at her with longing and clouded eyes. Lucy was so young. The minute hand of the clock moved in him to embrace her as Stella had embraced Mary by the hospital gates; as Khublall had embraced his child-bride a long time ago in the riddle of death and love.

Nineteen Lucy was but she seemed younger. He wanted to touch her like a painter or a sculptor and in so doing to create *through* the mystery of temptation.

What was that temptation? Enchantment with the womb of nature, an enchantment that remained the greatest danger still in bedevilled populations around the globe.

It had led to the arousal of the furies. It had damned him across a generation, no, longer than that, it seemed, a century, two centuries, three. It had given him, only to pluck from him, his 'daughter of man'.

And now as he looked at Lucy the temptation was in flower again but with a difference. In the greatest flowering danger lies the greatest prize of artistic wisdom. Lucy was smiling at him as if she knew, yet did not know what he was saying to her, a Mona Lisa smile.

Does every lost daughter of man change into unconscious child-bride within cultures that are stranded between animal divinity and human divinity?

Samuel Selvon

[1923–94]

Samuel Selvon was born in San Fernando, Trinidad. His family was too poor to finance his education and he received no formal instruction beyond high school. His mother, who was fluent in Hindi, encouraged her son to learn the language and Selvon developed a culturally cosmopolitan identity, one that reflects his colonial upbringing in a racially mixed environment. In 1940 he joined the local branch of the Royal Navy Reserve, working as a wireless operator on minesweepers and torpedo boats until 1945, and it was during this period of relative economic stability that he began to experiment with stories and poetry. Inspired by the English writer Richard Jeffreys's passionate prose about his native England, Selvon decided to express his love for the Trinidadian landscape and culture through writing.

From 1946 to 1950 Selvon worked as a journalist in Trinidad. As subeditor of the *Guardian Weekly*, the magazine for the *Trinidad Guardian*, he made important contacts that would be helpful throughout his career. He continued to write stories and poems, publishing several in the literary journal *Bim* and selling others to the BBC. In 1947 he married Draupadi Persaud and they started a family. But in 1950 she returned to her native Guyana and Selvon, by now feeling restless and restrained by life on a small island, left for London.

Upon his arrival, Selvon realized that making a fresh start would not be easy. Initially, he stayed at the Balmoral Hostel, a place occupied by Africans, Indians and many other West Indians. He was unable to get a job as a journalist because he was not a member of the National Union of Journalists. With much effort, he managed to secure a position as a civil servant at the Indian Embassy in London, and it was during his employment there that he wrote and published his first novel, *A Brighter Sun* (1952). The novel, which tells of a Trinidadian's search for identity in a colonial society, is still heralded today as one of the most influential works in West Indian literature. However, Selvon's writing ambitions, bolstered by book sales and positive reviews, were put on hold for fifteen months when he fell ill with tuberculosis and had to be hospitalized.

In 1954 Selvon left hospital and shortly after that he received a Guggenheim Fellowship for one year. He resigned from the Embassy to pursue a career as a full-time writer. It was during this period immediately following his illness that Selvon reached the height of his productivity, writing numerous novels, articles, radio plays, television and film scripts, and short stories. In 1956 he wrote *The Lonely Londoners*, a highly acclaimed novel about immigrant life in London in which he deftly illustrates the ambivalence that many immigrants feel about living in Britain and examines what is an important and recurring theme in his work: the way in which colonies both protect individuals and hinder their personal development. Based on his experiences and observations at the Balmoral Hostel, *The Lonely Londoners* was written entirely in what Selvon calls 'the Trinidadian form of the Caribbean language'. One of its characters, Moses Aloetta, appears in several of Selvon's later books.

Although Selvon's wife rejoined him in England after his hospitalizaton, they eventually divorced. He married Althea Nesta Daroux in 1963 and they had two children. In 1978 Selvon and his family moved to Calgary, Alberta. He spent his time there writing and serving as writer-in-residence at various colleges and universities. In 1994, while on a return visit to Trinidad, he died.

Selvon has a firm grasp of the Trinidadian vernacular and the manner in which he marries it to a Joycean stream of consciousness in the following extract from his novel The Lonely Londoners *is a remarkable achievement. The frustrated sexual and material ambitions of the immigrants, and their attempts to understand the new 'English' morality that is all around them, inform both the extract and the novel as a whole.*

From *The Lonely Londoners*

Oh what a time it is when summer come to the city and all them girls throw away heavy winter coat and wearing light summer frocks so you could see the legs and shapes that was hiding away from the cold blasts and you could coast a lime in the park and negotiate ten

shillings or a pound with the sports as the case may be or else they
have a particular bench near the Hyde Park Corner that they call the
Play Around Section where you could go and sit with one of them
what a time summer is because you bound to meet the boys coasting
lime in the park and you could go walking through the gardens and
see all them pretty pieces of skin taking suntan and how the old
geezers like the sun they would sit on the benches and smile
everywhere you turn the English people smiling isn't it a lovely day
as if the sun burn away all the tightness and strain that was in their
faces for the winter and on a nice day every manjack and his brother
going to the park with his girl and laying down on the green grass
and making love in the winter you would never think that the grass
would ever come green again but if you don't keep your eyes open it
look like one day the trees naked and the next day they have clothes
on sometimes walking up to the Bayswater Road from Queensway
you could look on a winter day and see how grim the trees looking
and a sort of fog in the distance though right near to you you ain't
have no fog but that is only deceiving because if somebody down the
other side look up by where you are it would look to them as if it
have fog by where you are and this time so the sun in the sky like a
forceripe orange and it giving no heat at all and the atmosphere like a
sullen twilight hanging over the big city but it different too bad when
is summer for then the sun shine for true and the sky blue and a
warm wind blowing it look like when is winter a kind of grey nasty
colour does come to the sky and it stay there and you forget what it
like to see blue skies like back home where blue sky so common
people don't even look up in the air and you feeling miserable and
cold but when summer come is fire in the town big times fete like
stupidness and you have to keep the blood cool for after all them
cold and wet months you like you roaring to go though to tell truth
winter don't make much difference to some of the boys they blazing
left and right as usual all the year round to talk of all the episodes
that Moses had with woman in London would take bags of ballad
Moses move through all the nationalities in the world and then he
start the circle again everybody know how after the war them rich

English family sending to the continent to get domestic and over
there all them girls think like the newspapers say about the
Jamaicans that the streets of London paved with gold so they coming
by the boatload and the boys making contact and having big times
with the girls working during the day and coming round by the yard
in the evening for a cuppa and to hit one or two but anyone of Moses
encounter is big episode because coasting about the Water it ain't
have no man with a sharper eye than he not even Cap could ask him
for anything and one summer evening he was walking when he spot
a number and he smile and she smile back and after a little
preliminary about the weather Moses take her for a drink in the
pub and after that he coast a walk with she in Kensington Gardens
and they sit down on the grass and talk about how lovely the city is
in the summer and Moses say how about coming to my yard she
went but afterwards Moses nearly dead with fright because the
woman start to moan and gasp and wriggle and twist up she body
like a piece of wire when Moses ask she what happen she only
moaning Moses start to get cold sweat because he know that if
anything happen to the woman and the police find her in his yard
that he wouldn't stand a chance the way how things against the boys
from in front so he begin to rub the woman down and pat she and try
to make she drink some water what happen to you Moses ask
frighten like hell that the woman might conk off on his hands the
woman only gasping and calling out for her mother and Moses
sweating just then the bell ring and Moses went to the door and see
Daniel Daniel he say boy a hell of a thing happening here man I just
pick up a woman up the road and bring she in the yard and it look
like if she dying what Daniel say as if he don't understand wait here
Moses say and he run back in the room listen he tell the woman my
friend come and you have to go put on your clothes by the time
Moses went and call Daniel inside the woman was calm and cool as
if nothing happen she look all right to me Daniel say eyeing the piece
as if he ready to charge but Moses was too frighten to keep the
woman around though she sit down on the bed and begin to talk
calmly boy he tell Daniel you wouldn't believe me but the woman did

look as if she going to dead you only lying because I happen to come round while you have she here Daniel say but Moses so relieve that she looking all right that he didn't bother with Daniel he just tell her to come and go right away so he take her out to the Bayswater Road to catch a bus the heel of my shoe is coming off she say will you come with me to get it fixed sure Moses say but as soon as they hop on the bus and it begin to drive off Moses hop off again and leave she going to Marble Arch what a gambol does go on in the park on them summer nights oh sometimes the girls wishing it would get dark quickly and you have them parading all down the Bayswater Road from the Arch to the Gate and you could see them fellars going up and talking for a minute and if they agree they go in the park or somewhere else together and if not the fellar walk on but these fellars that cruising they could size up the situation in one glance as they pass by and know if they like this one or that one you does meet all sorts of fellars from all walks of life don't ever be surprised at who you meet up cruising and reclining in the park it might be your boss or it might be some big professional fellar because it ain't have no discrimination when it come to that in the park in the summer see them girls in little groups here and there talking and how they could curse you never hear curse until one of them sports curse you if you approach one and she don't like your terms she tell you to — off right away and if you linger she tell you to double — off but business is brisk in the park in the summer one night one of them hustle from behind a tree pulling up her clothes and she bawl out Mary the police and if you see how them girls fade out and make races with the tight skirts holding the legs close together and the high heels going clopclop but that was no handicap when they take off it have some fellars who does go in the park only to cruise around and see what they could see you could always tell these tests they have on a coat with the collar turn up and they hand in they pocket and they breezing through the park hiding from tree to tree like if they playing hide and seek one night Moses was liming near the park and a car pull up that had a fellar and a old-looking woman in it the fellar start to talk friendly and invite Moses home for a cup of coffee and Moses

went just to see what would happen and what happen was the fellar
play as if he fall asleep and give Moses a free hand because it have
fellars who does get big thrills that way but Moses didn't do anything
because he know what the position like and even though the fellar
offer him three pounds he smile and was polite and tell him that he
sorry good night introducing Galahad to the night life Moses explain
to him about short time and long time and how to tackle the girls
and he take Galahad one night and let him loose in the park Galahad
say I going to try and he broach a group under the trees about a
hundred yards from the corner by the Arch but from the time he
begin to talk the girl tell him go — off Galahad stand up to argue but
Moses pull him away those girls not catholic at all Galahad say
Moses say it have some of them who don't like the boys and is all the
fault of Cap because Cap don't like to pay let us cut through the park
and go by Hyde Park Corner Galahad say when they reach there
Moses pick up a sharp thing who was talking to two English fellars
and he take her to the yard afterwards the girl tell him how she used
to take heroin at one time and she show him the marks on her arm
where she inject the kick Moses stay with the thing regularly for a
week then he get tired and tell Cap he have a girl if he interested and
Cap give the usual answer so Moses tell him to come in the yard in
the night that the girl would be there Cap went and Moses left the
two of them in the room and went for a walk when he come back
three hours later Cap was in the bathroom and the thing was
standing up before the gas fire warming up the treasury your friend
have any money she ask Moses yes Moses say he have bags of money
he is the son of a Nigerian king and when he goes back home he will
rule more than a million people the girl ask Moses if he want
anything take it easy Moses say when Cap come back Moses tell him
to drop the girl up the road and the girl went with Cap thinking that
he have plenty of money when Cap get to the corner he tell her to
wait he going to change a five-pound note as he don't go around with
small change and he left the girl standing up there and never went
back meantime Moses sit down on the bed and the bed fell down
when Cap come back he say Cap you are a hell of a man you break

my bed Cap say sorry Moses say this is the third time you break my
bed Cap say it was warm and nice in the bed Moses say what I will
tell the landlord this thing happening so often and he had was to put
a box and prop up the bed to sleep summer does really be hearts like
if you start to live again you coast a lime by the Serpentine and go for
a row on the river or you go bathing by the Lido though the water
never warm no matter how hot the sun is you would be feeling hot
out of the water but the minute you jump in you start to shiver and
have to get out quick but it does be as if around that time of the year
something strange happen to everybody they all smiling and as if
they living for the first time so you get to wondering if it ain't have a
certain part of the population what does lie low during the cold
months and only take to the open when summer come for it have
some faces in the Water that Moses never see until summer come or
maybe they have enough money to go Montego Bay in winter and
come back to the old Brit'n when they know the weather would be
nice listen to this ballad what happen to Moses one summer night
one splendid summer night with the sky brilliant with stars like in the
tropics he was liming in Green Park when a English fellar come up to
him and say you are just the man I am looking for who me Moses say
yes the man say come with me Moses went wondering what the test
want and the test take him to a blonde who was standing up under a
tree and talk a little so Moses couldn't hear but Blondie shake her
head then he take Moses to another one who was sitting on a bench
and she say yes so the test come back to Moses and want to pay
Moses to go with the woman Moses was so surprise that he say yes
quickly and he went with the thing and the test hover in the
background afterwards he ask Moses if he would come again and
Moses say yes it look like a good preposition to me I don't mind and
he carry on for a week the things that does happen in this London
people wouldn't believe when you tell them they would cork their
ears when you talk and say that isn't true but some ballad happen in
the city that people would bawl if they hear right there in Hyde Park
how them sports must bless the government for this happy hunting
ground the things that happen there in the summer hard to believe

one night two sports catch a fellar hiding behind some bushes with a flash camera in his hand they mash up the camera and beat the fellar where all these women coming from you never know but every year the ranks augmented with fresh blood from the country districts who come to see the big life in London and the bright lights also lately in view of the big set of West Indians that storming Brit'n it have a lot of dark women who in the racket too they have to make a living and you could see them here and there with the professionals walking on the Bayswater Road or liming in the park learning the tricks of the trade it have some white fellars who feel is a big thrill to hit a black number and the girls does make them pay big money but as far as spades hitting spades it ain't have nothing like that for a spade wouldn't hit a spade when it have so much other talent on parade don't think that you wouldn't meet real class in the park even in big society it have hustlers one night Moses meet a pansy by Marble Arch tube station and from the way the test look at him Moses know because you could always tell these tests unless you real green you have a lovely tie the pansy say yes Moses say you have a lovely hat yes Moses say you have a very nice coat yes Moses say everything I have is nice I like you the pansy say I like you too Moses say and all this time he want to dead with laugh I have a lovely model staying in my flat in Knightsbridge the pansy say she likes to go with men but I don't like that sort of thing myself would you like to come to my flat sure Moses say we will go tomorrow night as I have an important engagement tonight I will meet you right here by the station the test say but so many people are here Moses say I might miss you if you don't see me you can phone but what will we do when I come to your flat Moses say playing stupid and the test tell him what and what they wouldn't do one night he and Galahad was walking up Inverness Terrace when a car pass going slow and the door open and a fellar fling one of the sports out the poor girl fall down and roll to the pavement all the other sports in the area rally and run up to she and pick she up and ask she what happen she say she went with the fellar but he didn't want to pay and she give him two cuff in his face and he pitch she out the car another night a big Jamaican fellar

take two home and had them running out of the house and he throw
their clothes for them from the window people wouldn't believe you
when you tell them the things that happen in the city but the cruder
you are the more the girls like you you can't put on any English
accent for them or play ladeda or tell them you studying medicine in
Oxford or try to be polite and civilize they don't want that sort of
thing at all they want you to live up to the films and stories they hear
about black people living primitive in the jungles of the world that is
why you will see so many of them African fellars in the city with their
hair high up on the head like they ain't had a trim for years and with
scar on their face and a ferocious expression going about with some
real sharp chicks the cruder you are the more they like you the whole
blasted set of them frustrated like if they don't know what it is all
about what happen to you people Moses ask a cat one night and she
tell him how the black boys so nice and could give them plenty thrills
people wouldn't believe or else they would cork their ears and say
they don't want to know but the higher the society the higher the
kicks they want one night Moses meet a nice woman driving in a car
in Piccadilly and she pick him up and take him to a club in
Knightsbridge where it had a party bags of women and fellars all
about drinking champagne and whisky this girl who pick him up get
high and start to dance the cancan with some other girls when they
fling their legs up in the air they going around to the tables where the
fellars sitting Moses sit down there wondering how this sort of thing
happening in a place where only the high and the mighty is but with
all of that they feel they can't get big thrills unless they have a black
man in the company and when Moses leave afterwards they push
five pounds in his hand and pat him on the back and say that was a
jolly good show it have a lot of people in London who cork their ears
and wouldn't listen but if they get the chance they do the same thing
themselves everybody look like they frustrated in the big city the sex
life gone wild you would meet women who beg you to go with them
one night a Jamaican with a woman in Chelsea in a smart flat with
all sorts of surrealistic painting on the walls and contemporary
furniture in the G-plan the poor fellar bewildered and asking

questions to improve himself because the set-up look like the World
of Art but the number not interested in passing on any knowledge
she only interested in one thing and in the heat of emotion she call
the Jamaican a black bastard though she didn't mean it as an insult
but as a compliment under the circumstances but the Jamaican fellar
get vex and he stop and say why the hell you call me a black bastard
and he thump the woman and went away all these things happen in
the blazing summer under the trees in the park on the grass with the
daffodils and tulips in full bloom and a sky of blue oh it does really
be beautiful then to hear the birds whistling and see the green leaves
come back on the trees and in the night the world turn upside down
and everybody hustling that is life that is London oh Lord Galahad
say when the sweetness of summer get in him he say he would never
leave the old Brit'n as long as he live and Moses sigh a long sigh like a
man who live life and see nothing at all in it and who frighten as the
years go by wondering what it is all about.

James Berry

[1924–]

James Berry was born in Boston, Jamaica. His early years were spent chiefly out of doors, 'shut away from the world' in the coastal village of Fair Prospect. He worked in America during his late teens, then returned to Jamaica for a brief period of time before emigrating to war-ravaged London in 1948. Berry believes that Britain's sense of dislocation at that time enabled him, as a black Jamaican, to settle with relative ease. He arrived in London without prearranged lodging, but soon found a room in Brixton which he shared with another West Indian. Berry took to London immediately and was overwhelmed by the abundance of books and accessible libraries he found.

Berry worked as a telegraphist with Post Office International Telegraphs (now British Telecom) from 1951 to 1977, before making the decision to write full-time. Initially, he wrote short stories, but he is best known for his poetry. In 1977 Berry received a C. Day Lewis Fellowship. It was during this period, as a writer-in-residence at a London comprehensive school, that he developed a passion for tutoring and an interest in multicultural education.

In 1979 Berry published his collection *Fractured Circles* and in 1981 he won first prize in the National Poetry Competition for 'Fantasy of an African Boy'. In his poetry he explores Jamaican and British cultures. He also uses both Standard English and what the poet/historian Edward Kamau Brathwaite terms 'Nation Language'. The experience of being black in Britain is crucial to his writing, as is clearly visible in the character of 'Lucy', a Caribbean immigrant living in Britain whose experiences are chronicled in her letters to a friend back home in *Lucy's Letters and Loving* (1982).

Other collections of Berry's poetry include *Chain of Days* (1985) and *When I Dance* (1988), a volume of children's poems for which he won the Signal Poetry Award in 1989. His fiction – compiled in *A Thief in the Village* (1987) and *Anacy-Spiderman* (1989) – has also been successful, and in 1985 Berry won the GLC Mary Seacole Prize for his short stories.

He is a celebrated reader of his own writing and has performed on radio and television.

The two poems from Berry's 'Lucy' collection reveal the immigrant's concern with, and love for, British traditions, in this instance the Royal Family.

FROM LUCY: ENGLAN' LADY

You ask me 'bout the lady. Me dear,
old centre here still shine
with Queen. She affec' the place
like the sun : not comin' out oft'n
an' when it happ'n everybody's out
smilin', as she wave a han'
like a seagull flyin' slow slow.

An' you know she come from
dust free rooms an' velvet
an' diamond. She make you feel
this an-an'-on town, London,
where long long time deeper than mind.
An' han's after han's die away,
makin' streets, putt'n' up bricks,
a piece of brass, a piece of wood
an' plantin' trees: an' it give
a car a halfday job gett'n' through.

An' Leela, darlin', no, I never
meet the Queen in flesh. Yet
sometimes, deep deep, I sorry for her.

Everybody expec' a show
from her, like she a space touris'
on earth. An' darlin', unless
you can go home an' scratch up

you' husban', it mus' be hard
strain keepin' good graces for
all hypocrite faces.

Anyhow, me dear, you know what
ole time people say,
'Bird sing sweet for its nest'.

FROM LUCY: CARNIVAL WEDD'N', 1981
(marriage of Prince of Wales and Lady Diana Spencer)

Leela, bes' pop girl over all Brit'n
splice up the number one bachelor catch.
An', darlin', another worl', another
time, another way to ca'culate everything.

Everybody come great. All pilgrims come
showin' they rich. From worl' great houses,
from poverty places, they come grand.
Then, Leela, all stragglers follow
or watch from window or streetside.
This, me dear, wasn't wedd'n,
this was CARNIVAL ROYAL.

Darlin', on night before, in big park,
fireworks get fired off to music. An', girl,
on hilltops, all aroun' ol' Brit'n
fires leap in darkness. Then when
rum-bars closed down, folks cover
the groun', me dear, sleepin' in parks
an' at London streetside, knowin',
long time, hotels all full.

Then, girl, sun come shine on all
sort of uniform of ages an' hero
decoration. An' like human stars

come down from sky, couple stir up
wonders an' wishes. An', Leela,
want to see top class get show-off
in clothes. Want to see
top style an' the glare
of never-endin' money stacks.
Darlin', this was a differen' Jon-Kanoo.

An' everybody stan' up burstin' smiles.
No eye is big enough to see. Too many
people so much, no foot can move,
excep' carriages with the grand folks
creepin', an' shinin' more from endless
han' wavin' from tophats
to skirts in Union Jack.

An' when she climb church steps, darlin',
as all the time, bridal veil is longer
than ribbons of highest maypole.
Sweetheart, here was life
what scoop in wishes an' dreams.

Here's choir music that full up High
Church. Here's grand people sittin'
neat neat like Hope Gardens
in June. An' High Bishop now is
holy man from afar. An', darlin',
veiled before the altar,
no eyes ever shine more
a happy dream. Nobody did ever
hol' a han' for one gol' ring
with so many eyes an' thoughts on it.

An' conquering done, she leave.
She go down church steps.
She leave with her 'pretty amazing' boy
in he uniform of high-sea captain.

An' they drive back to Palace
received like home-comin' heroes.
This, me dear, was a time beforetime
with sweet parties jump-up.

An' rubbish get lef' in London streets,
Leela, was a thousan' time more than
Long Bay square, on banana market day.
But, with that new new name, me dear,
she had one-hundred-thousan' letters
of good-luck to read. She had
halfacre roomfuls of gifts to go over.
She has a lifetime among things
from every age of castles and jewels.

Darlin', you know as I know,
that whether Royalty black or Royalty white,
an' Royalty your Royalty, is your Royalty.

Remember, 'When you hear family row,
play deaf; but when you see
family food, nyam it'.

Jon-Kanoo: Jamaican masquerade celebration, with chief character-dancer by
that name.
Nyam: to eat, particularly in a hungry manner.

Ruth Prawer Jhabvala

[1927-]

Ruth Prawer Jhabvala was born in Cologne, Germany, to a Polish-Jewish father and a German-Jewish mother. In 1939 the twelve-year-old Ruth, her brother and her parents fled from the Nazis to England. She quickly learned to speak English and was educated at Hendon County School in London. In 1948 Jhabvala became a British citizen. In 1951, after receiving an MA in English literature from the University of London, she married a Parsee architect named Cyrus S. H. Jhabvala and moved to New Delhi. Thus Jhabvala was introduced to the country which has figured most prominently in her writing, and to a lifestyle which she initially found exciting but later tired of and described as being like 'living on the back of an animal'.

Jhabvala began writing and publishing fiction in India. Her first novel, *To Whom She Will* (1955; published in the US as *Amrita*), is an elegantly written comedy of manners that examines the disparity between romantic love and the Indian custom of arranged marriages. Jhabvala, the mother of three daughters, was particularly struck by Indian cross-gender and cross-cultural relationships. Her 1965 novel, *A Backward Place*, tells of three European women and their reactions to the Indian society. In other works she dissects the local customs and manners from the unique perspective of a female expatriate. Her tone ranges from one of sardonic amusement to unveiled criticism, and there is a frank ambivalence towards India in her writing. In 1972 Jhabvala acknowledged that her status left her 'stranded in the middle' of the British and Indian cultures, and that 'the central fact of all my work . . . is that I am a European living permanently in India'.

In 1975 Jhabvala published her Booker Prize-winning novel, *Heat and Dust*, which is the story of an Englishwoman who sacrifices her Western liberty for the love of an Indian prince. However, despite her acclaim as an 'Indian' writer, Jhabvala was becoming increasingly uneasy in India. In 1975, with her husband's encouragement, she moved to the United States. Since then, she has divided her time between New York and

London, collaborating on film and television scripts, while she continues to write fiction. Although the influences of her life in India are still covertly evident, in *In Search of Love and Beauty* (1983) Jhabvala focuses for the first time on the German-Jewish background of her childhood and in *Three Continents* (1987) she explores her enduring feelings of exile.

As a screenwriter she has enjoyed a long-term partnership with the American film director James Ivory, and her many screenplays for Merchant–Ivory productions include adaptations of E. M. Forster's *Room with a View* (1986) and *Howards End* (1992). In 1983 she received the British Academy of Film and Television Arts Award for her screenplay of *Heat and Dust*. Other awards include a Guggenheim Fellowship in 1976, a MacArthur Foundation Fellowship in 1984 and two Academy Awards for screenwriting.

The following extract from Jhabvala's novel Three Continents *addresses the theme of loneliness and the degree of isolation which British society, in particular London, can impose upon an individual. Jhabvala's life and work have been a testament to displacement, but out of this state of homelessness she has created a remarkable body of work.*

From *Three Continents*

It was a strange time for me in London. Although everyone else was very busy working for the movement, I had nothing to do except wait for those few hours when Crishi came to be with me; if he came, that is. I went around on my own, traveling on the tops of buses, walking through the parks in the rain. I went to museums and looked at pictures and antiquities, and went to see films in multiple cinemas, and when one was finished, I went in another one. I was so crazy with sex at the time, I went to some porno ones too, and that was strange, with all those men in raincoats, sitting very still and concentrated. Altogether London was strange to me – very different from the way I had known it on my previous stays there. The streets, the stores, and especially the museums seemed to be full of tourists, busloads of them with camera equipment and foreign languages I didn't always recognize. Sometimes it seemed to me that the only English people I saw were museum attendants and policemen directing the flow of travelers into the right channels. When I look back on that time it was very often Saturday afternoon with everything in our neighborhood of tall Edwardian houses shut tight, except for a little general store run by an Indian family who kept open late into the night though not many customers came, everyone having gone away for the weekend.

I could always visit the other house, where Bari Rani and the girls lived on a permanent note of high-pitched excitement. Usually they were getting ready to go out, and the baths were running and girls shrieking and charging into each other's bedrooms to exchange articles of clothing, perfumes, and makeup. Sometimes I went along with them, but I contributed nothing to their shopping expeditions, not buying anything for myself and unable to give sound advice on their purchases; nor to their parties, where they never noticed that I wasn't having as fabulous a time as they were. Their phones rang a lot, very often from Bombay, and the Bari Rani would talk for hours and had no difficulty hearing above the noise of the LPs the girls were playing. She often said to me, 'We must have a long talk, Harriet,' and I think she meant to, but it couldn't happen because she was continually being called away to the phone or to advise on an outfit; or she was fighting with Teresa, the Indian Christian girl they had brought with them, who had been their nanny and now was their companion and help. Teresa had an Indian boyfriend, and so did all the girls. I had difficulty keeping the girls' boyfriends apart because they were all handsome and polite and exquisitely dressed, and fantastic dancers, as were the girls. Everyone talked in a lilting English with Hindi phrases thrown in – they talked constantly but no one had to listen and in fact it all sounded the same, all on one high note, more like singing than talking.

The girls were a few years younger than I – the eldest, Priti, had her seventeenth birthday around this time – and I knew that, like everyone I had gone to school with, they were very interested in sex.

They talked and read about it and discussed it, with each other and their friends; but here too I couldn't contribute, for although by this time I thought of nothing else either, it was in a different way. They knew nothing about the kind of sex I was going through, and I didn't want them to know; it was as though I were protecting them. Probably they thought I was frigid, as everyone usually did, and I preferred a hundred times to have them think that than to know the reality. Only Crishi knew the reality, and it amused him no end. 'What would Aunt Harriet say?' was his standard crack whenever he involved me in some act he knew about. Aunt Harriet was one of his favorite jokes – he had seen her only that one time at Grandfather's funeral, but he made her into this sort of archetypal figure to which he claimed I would revert. Whenever I hesitated to perform some new thing he wanted me to do, he said 'There, see, you've reverted already.' He had many Aunt Harriet stories. He said she always had to wear a brooch on her blouse so people could tell which was front Harriet and which was back; and once he came with a very serious face, saying a dead woman had been found and they were about to carry her off to the mortuary when he saw her and cried 'No wait stop! That's no corpse, that's my Aunt Harriet.' And so on. The frigidity of Anglo-Saxon women was a favorite subject with him, and the more we did at night the more jokes he made by day.

Unable to stay another minute alone in the flat, or cope with the romantic-girl atmosphere in the other house, I would walk miles in the hope of tiring myself out and dropping off to sleep till Crishi came. It was getting into fall, damp and chilly, and though the leaves were still on the trees and still green for the most part, they kept being blown off and lay on the paths and were trodden into mulch. Sometimes I sat on a wet bench in Hyde Park and got even more wet from the leaves dripping down on me. Lonely men wandering by stopped, and some sat with me to talk but I didn't answer them much, so they soon wandered off again, sadder than ever. Once man – quite an old man with a hat on that he didn't take off – lay down on the grass near me, and it took me awhile before I realized he was masturbating, so I moved. I thought it was terrible that people, and even old people, should have these sensations, and be tortured by them. Another man must have witnessed this and he followed me and offered to call the police. He said it was disgusting and such persons must be stopped. I said no it's all right, and walked faster and he walked faster too, and then it seemed he had to protect me and wouldn't leave me. He said London was a very dangerous place, very bad people around, and a girl like me shouldn't be walking in the park. He said in his own country no girl ever walked alone, and if she did, she was picked up by the police and sent back to her family. He didn't say which his country was but referred to it constantly, so that practically every sentence started with 'In my country . . .' He was short, muscular, dark in a Middle Eastern way. His clothes were quite clean and whole but looked as though he might have bought them secondhand, maybe found them hanging in a market on a Sunday morning. After a while, walking with me, he took my hand, very nicely and respectfully, so that I felt I had to leave it there. His hand was very very warm, even hot, as if the climate of his country were stored in it. The rain kept on squeezing down the way it does in London, out of spongy colorless clouds. All around us in the park were these magnificent tall old trees, and when we came out there were these magnificent tall old buildings looming up into the wet air. He kept on talking, about his country and other general topics, still holding my hand very respectfully; sometimes he tickled my palm but stopped at once when he saw I didn't like it. We went down a tube station, and since he had only enough money for one ticket, I bought my own. It was a long underground ride, anonymous and ghostlike, as though I had just died and didn't know where I was bound for and neither did the other people who got in and out as the doors slid open at the stations; there was an unending stream of them, all smelling damp as if in their grave clothes. I felt completely passive and had stopped noticing that he was holding my hand.

When we got off and emerged up a long escalator, it was still raining from the same drained sky and over streets and streets and streets of identical houses. They were smaller houses than the ones where we lived, and grimier, and there were more gaps where some had been torn down and weeds grew in their foundations. There were also more shops – laundromats, a few supermarkets, a few very small shops going out of business and others already gone and boarded up; every block had at least one Pakistani or Bangladeshi restaurant and a donna-kebab place. We turned in to a doorway beside one of these places and walked up a very dark staircase. On the first landing he stopped and kissed me and his lips were as hot as his hand. He said his name was Salim. There was a dense smell of kebabs and the oil in which they had been fried many times. We walked up one flight more and he unlocked a door and invited me into his room. It was poorly furnished but he kept it nice with a tablecloth and photographs. He had made his bed before going out and there was a blue cotton cover on it. A pair of dark trousers was folded over the only chair. He hung them in the wardrobe so I could sit down. There was an awkward silence, for it was difficult to find anything to say. He had a clock, ticking with a tinny sound, and this seemed the most prominent object in the room except for the wardrobe, which was a very bulky piece of furniture and leaned forward slightly as though about to crash down.

He made tea on a tiny portable stove he had by the open fireplace. The tea was very good, very strong with creamy milk and much sugar and some other taste that may have been cloves. I wished I could have drunk it and said thank you and good-bye, but of course that was not what we had come for on that long underground ride. I looked at the photographs that stood on the tablecloth as on a little altar. There were some old people, some children, some young men in military uniform; when I looked at them, he explained who they were and at the same time he put his hand on my knee. I moved this knee slightly and in my embarrassment asked more questions in fast succession. He answered them and put his hand back on my knee. I picked up a studio photograph of a young man – I thought it was he but he said no, it was his brother. 'Dead,' he said, and I had hardly made sounds of regret, when he added 'Shot.' He slid his hand farther up my thigh, and feeling shocked and sorry about his brother, I didn't like to stop him. He leaned forward from the bed and pressed his lips on mine. His chin felt rough and stubbly – he may have shaved in the morning but probably needed to do so at least twice a day. He smelled like a person who tried to keep himself clean but did not have adequate bathing facilities. He was now breathing hard and tried to make me get off the chair and join him on the bed. I said 'I must go. My husband's waiting.' I'm sure I sounded like Aunt Harriet. If I had had gloves, at this point I would have put them on.

I had forgotten how much stronger men are than women. It wasn't that he was a rough or brutal man – on the contrary – but that his need was great. After all, he was away from his wife, his family, and lived alone in this little room in a rainy city of endless row houses. He even tried to argue with me – he said, quite reasonably, 'Then why did you come?' I couldn't say for the tea; I couldn't say anything. I felt I had to go through with it. But anyway there was no choice anymore. Lying under him on the lumpy bed onto which he had thrown me, watching his contorted, sweating face, I stroked his cheek because I felt sorry to have roused him so far. He didn't take long and afterward appeared to feel satisfied and grateful. I also felt grateful – that it was over, for one thing, and for another that I hadn't enjoyed it: not at all, there had been no gratification of any kind for me. I realized that my ravenous need was not that of one physical animal for another but for one particular human being – for Crishi, for my husband, whom I loved.

George Lamming

[1927–]

George Lamming, the only child of an unmarried mother, was born on the former sugar estate of Carrington Village, Barbados. He was educated on a scholarship at Combermere School and in 1946 moved to Trinidad, where he worked as a teacher until 1950. During this time, Lamming was involved with the Caribbean literary journal *Bim*, and was an active member of the independence organization, the People's National Movement. In 1950 he moved to England, coincidentally travelling on the same ship as the Trinidadian writer Samuel Selvon. In 1951 Lamming became the host of a book review programme for the BBC West Indian Service in London.

Lamming published his first novel, *In the Castle of My Skin*, in 1953. The book, which earned him the Somerset Maugham Award in 1957, reads as both a memoir of an individual's childhood and the collective biography of a West Indian village during the decline of the plantation system. Lamming's work ranges in tone from the despair of *The Emigrants* (1954) to the powerfully hopeful *Season of Adventure* (1960), and he explores the complexity of the West Indian experience as affected by the process of decolonization and national reconstruction. In *Of Age and Innocence* (1958), Lamming cites the immigrant experience in Britain as a catalyst for social and political change back in the Caribbean, and the non-fiction essays in his collection *The Pleasures of Exile* (1960) describe the experience of a writer moving from the Caribbean to a metropolitan culture.

Lamming is deeply committed to West Indian politics, and during a period of literary silence from 1960 to 1972 he remained involved in political developments. In 1965 and 1967 he was co-editor of the Barbados and Guyana independence issues of *New World Quarterly*, and in 1967 he spent a year as writer-in-residence at the University of the West Indies in Kingston, Jamaica. In 1972 he published two books within the same year, *Water with Berries* and the historical novel *Natives of My Person*. In 1974 he edited the anthology *Cannon Shot and Glass*

Beads, which is a collection of black responses to white politics and culture. Since then, he has continued to be a political organizer and has lectured and taught in the Caribbean and overseas. In 1976 he received a British Commonwealth Foundation Grant, which enabled him to travel to major universities in India and Australia. Lamming has been the recipient of several awards and fellowships, including a Guggenheim Fellowship in 1954.

Lamming's novel The Emigrants *is, alongside Samuel Selvon's* The Lonely Londoners, *probably the most important contemporary novel of migration to Britain. The following extract reveals the West Indian characters' deep love of Britain, and the powerful mythology of the country which they carry with them as part of their baggage. The importance of the moment of arrival is brilliantly captured, and one cannot help but feel that for these immigrants, life in Britain will never again be touched with such joyful innocence.*

A Voyage

THE TRAIN

Look Lilian look de ol' geyser quiet in de corner like de whole worl' come to a standstill . . . he eyes don't wink when he pull that pipe an' he lookin' only Gawd knows where he looking like he ain't got eyes in his head . . . is the way they is in dis country . . . no talk till you talk. No speak till you speak, no notice till you notice, no nothin' till you somethin' . . . 'tis what ah mean when ah says England . . . when you lan' up in Englan', ol' man, when you lan' up here.

Tornado, . . . but Tornado these people tell lies too bad. And we say back home you got to look hard to find the truth, but Tornado de truth doan' even hide round here. . . . I go back where ah went to tell de woman she ain't put sugar in de tea, an' you know,

ol' man, you know she swear she put . . . in broad
daylight Tornado she swear to my face she put as if
she think ah doan' know what sugar taste like, me,
Tornado, who been eating sugar before ah drink tea,
the woman tell me to the front o' my face she put
sugar in dis tea, taste it Tornado, taste it for yuhself
an' tell me if ah mad or she stupid.

Sugar ration, ol' man, that's why. If she say she
put she put but what she put yuh won't taste,
partner, p'raps if you been lookin' when she servin'
you might ah see somethin' in the spoon, but what it
is you won't taste, not in yuh tea 'cause sugar ration
in this country.

What ain't ration in dis country Tornado is there
anything ain't ration in dis country.

> Things haven't been the same since the war.
> Where do you chaps come from? The West Indies?
> Been there several times myself. Had a nephew was a
> Governor there some years ago.

Would you have a cup of tea? With or without?
(What she mean with or without.)
Milk and sugar?
(What she mean milk an' sugar.)
Good. Won't be a minute.
Say Tornado what wrong wid dese people at all?
You doan' mean to say people drink tea when it ain't
got milk. They ain't that poor un, un, Tornado, no
tell me de truth, dey aint so poor they can't spare a
drop o' milk in they tea, an' what kin' o talk is dis
'bout with or without. Is it ol' man that they doan'
like sugar. What wrong wid dem at all. With or
without. O Christ Tornado, will take a long time
'fore I forget dat . . . with or without.

They have funny taste, partner. You goin' get
some surprises. You wait.

'Ave 'alf pint o' bitter John?

My name aint John.

Oh no 'arm meant. Jes' gettin' to know you. 'Alf a
pint for me an' my pal . . .

'Ere's yours, John, an' yours, darkie . . .

'E isn't no darkie. 'E's 'avin' a drink with me, an'
that makes 'im my pal. Understand?

Well w'at you'd 'ave me say. Ah don't know
fercetn't the guy's name. Alllll the best.

Say Tornado. The thing they call bitter. You know
what ah mean. Well ain't it just like mauby. Same
kind o' taste an' same kind o' look in the glass. Is
that they sell instead of rum? Where you go to get
something strong.

You know larger beer in down town Port-o'-
Spain. Well that's what they call bitter. An' you goin'
to swell yuh guts up wid it here, an' it got a good
advantage, 'tis the only advantage, ol' man, it won't
ask you to trot. It goin' leave you as sober as a
gallon o' mauby, an' instead o' vomit as you vomit
back home, it'll be pissing as you never piss before.

See the chap over yonder standin' like a black
Goliath. He win a football pool las' year. Sixty
thousand pounds. 'Tis w'at every spade hope to
happen to him when he sen' in the pools.

What spade got to do with it. What you mean by
spade.

The spades? That's me, an' you. Spades. Same
colour as the card. Ever see the Ace o' spades, ol'
man. If ever ah win o' football pool I'll do just the
opposite to what he do. Instead o' settling down here
I'll go home. I'll live like a lord. I'll show Belmont
an' Woodbrook an' the whole lot of bullshitters livin'
round St Clair, I'll show them the difference between
the rich an' the rest. Ah got a feelin' some one o' we

who make this trip goin' win a football pool.

How many people go in for dis thing, the pool.

De whole country. Is a sort of legal racket, an' dese people'll do anything you only got to tell dem it legal. So long as the law give the signal to go ahead, they doan' ask where, when, or why, they go ahead. They like to know what they can do an' what they can't do, an' since they know the pools is alright they all take to it like fish to water. De whole country, an' a next reason, 'course, 'tis 'cause it give them another reason for buying the evening news. You have no idea what newspaper mean to dese people.

We got train back home but ah never see train that big. It big for so. There was train in Barbados too but not for the same sort o' purpose at all. The train we had at home was more a excursion thing. They use to use it to take the Sunday School children to Batsheba, and the Rocks. But when the war come along they scrap everything. Train days come to an' end there an' then.

This big alright but they say in the States these things bigger. They had to make a law dat no man should build a train more than a mile long. 'Cause they use to be a lot o' fightin' when the train arrive. People in the back carriage was more than a mile where they goin' long after the front carriage folks get out.

I never thought ah would have set eyes on England.

If you'd tell me that ten years ago, ol' man, I would have say you tryin' to poke fun at my head.

But the worl' get small, small, ol' man.

An' also too somethin' happen between people an' people. As soon as people get to handlin' money, they get a new sort o' insight 'bout things. If you an' me ever go back folks goin' start lookin' at we in a different way. Till every Tom, Dick an' Harry start to come, an' it get so common that it won't mean nothin' no more to go to England. Would be like goin' from Trinidad to Tobago.

Feel vaguely that have been here before just as after four years
in the other island felt had always lived there. For a moment
seemed had forgotten where I was. Stretch of land over yonder
reminds so much of home. Every inch cultivated. Earth has
colour of clay, and every row even and distinct as though they
had measured them. Only light is different. Wish it wouldn't rain
for haven't got any rain clothes and heavy coat. They say rain in
England is fatal. Put your head in brief case if it comes. Once
your head is covered, remember, you're alright.

Tornado de ground feel harder than back home.
W'at dat mean.

You on strange ground, partner. Yuh foot got to
get acclimatized.

Take off thy shoes from off thy feet for the place
thou standest is holy ground.

People doan' go barefoot here, partner, so you
better tell yuh toes to make peace wid yer boots.

Do you know if there were any stowaways on the
ship?

Why do you ask me?

Come on. If you know anything speak up. There's
nothing to be afraid of.

I don't know. But the chaps standing around here
didn't stowaway.

Why do you people come here. Can't you get
work at home?

Have a cigarette?

How many o' these did you bring?

Look I want a drink. Sorry but you'll have to find
out all this later.

Do you chaps know if there were any stowaways
on the ship?

What you take me for the Almighty Gawd.

Just a question. You know of the Metropolitan
Police.

There ain't nothing in dis country Ah don't know
'bout. Ah also know dere's one thing 'bout the
English people. They doan' interfere in nobody
business.

No stowaways I take it.

If you want to know I'll tell you. Dere's one but
they catch him an' they goin' take him back to
France for trial. Two months in a French jail an'
after back where he come from.

You don't know what a French jail is like?

Listen partner, police or no police if you ask me
the wrong question I'll tell you where to get off.
There's more in the mortar than the pestle. All you in
dis country got more for me than I got for you.

Is work scarce at home?

For some people. If you go down there they'll
make you inspector o' police. Before the sun hit you
twice you won't know who you is. 'Cause the power
you'll command after that will simply take   .
possession o' you. Ol' man you'll get in de spirit.
Know what that mean. You'll become one wid
Gawd.

In the land of the blind . . .

'Tis the other way round. In the land o' de one eye
the blind is king.

You see, partner, if you can't see, we'll all start
thinkin' that's w'at we got eyes for, not to see.

You know Bustamante?

Ask him. He come from Jamaica.

Me take to Mr Manley more.

Who's Manley?

Him know 'bout Busta, but him ain't know 'bout
Mr Manley. Me always say English people got
everything upside down. The wrong things catch
they eye.

Are there any communists in Jamaica?
Not since Stalin lef'.
When was he there?
He born there.

     Come to study?
     Where do you chaps come from? You don't mind
me asking, do you. My sister's a missionary in
Africa, says it's a nice place, and your people very
good people. She adores the Africans. Says we
haven't been very nice always but things are
changing. Your people are gradually getting to
understand us, and the future promises to be
brighter. That's what I've always said, you know.
Understanding. As soon as people get to understand
one another life is easy.

Is it true what the papers say about unemployment?

Of course it is. Don't you expect it. Wherever there's an economic
contradiction in the whole process of production and distribution
you'll find that. Wages dropping. Prices soaring. Finally slump. We
haven't got to that yet but I give us three years. This country is
heading for an economic suicide, and all because they won't face
facts. There's going to be hard times ahead, but all you've got to do is
keep on the right side of the fence. Don't listen to the lies you hear.
People are so blinded by lies in this country that they see an enemy
whenever a friend stands up to speak the truth. But history is an open
book, and those who read and understand realize that their duty is to
change. The key word is change. Before anything like peace and
prosperity can come about in this country the whole economic
structure of the society must be changed. They are people who lie
and fight and would even die to keep the old order. They want to
build a new house on old, tottering foundation. You must be careful.
Keep on the right side of the fence and play your part in the struggle.

     You speak excellent English for a foreigner. Much
     better than the French.

     How nice of you to say that. 'F course the better

classes get much the same standard of education as
you do. I'm really from the middle class. Among us,
that is my circles an' my circles' circles there isn't an
upper class. In a sense you might say we were the
upper class.

Where is this may I ask?

Grenada. One of the islands. My father is a
magistrate. Was educated here in England.

Where is Grenada? I don't seem to recall the
name.

Don't you know? You're kidding. Were you at
university?

No, but here is a map of the world. We might look
for it.

Excuse, old man, but how much you think I should give
the baggage man.

W'at you talkin' 'bout?

As a tip.

Tell him you hope de weather change.

WILL PASSENGERS TAKE THEIR SEATS PLEASE

You see dat chap over dere. Well he vex as hell to see we here
on dis train. Long ago only he could come, an' when he see dis
he start to feel he not as rich as he should be. You know that
fellow from Trinidad. Whole family solicitors. They spend six
months here and six months at home. Every year. He got a
young woman wid him.

'Tis he wife. You doan' know she . . . Chinese girl from
Woodbrook. Come into prominence when the Yanks was at Point
Cumana. When the Yanks went back home everybody say she
days did come to a end. But only Gawd know how it happen, ol'
man, my friend pick it up, an' who goin' help him wid it now is
anybody guess.

I wasn't in Trinidad when the Yanks was there.

Well you miss something, ol' man. The Yanks turn Trinidad
upside down, an' when they finish they let we see who was who.
They is a great people, those Yankee people. It take a man like
Lord Kitchener to put they fame in poetry.

WILL PASSENGERS KEEP THEIR HEADS WITHIN THE TRAIN
            What him get drunk on so?
            The limeys know how to get drunk on bitter. They
make up they min' before they take a sip. Doan' pay
him no mind.
            Him turn real stupid but me no say for certain
him ain't better man than the one me see back down
yonder who let coal pot in he mouth make dumb
man outta him.

WILL PASSENGERS KEEP THEIR HEADS WITHIN THE TRAIN
            England's a pleasant place
            For those that are rich and free
            But England ain't no place
            For guys that look like ye.
            Good night Irene, Good night,
            Pam, pan paddan pam pam.

WILL PASSENGERS KEEP THEIR HEADS WITHIN THE TRAIN
    On the hill beyond where the grass is, green,
greener than the hedges here, in the sun, look, like a
print of plaster made against plain, look a white
horse. Did you see the white horse. If you look now
you can see it, where the grass is, green, greener than
the hedges here. And the sun makes it real like an
animal in stride. It looks as if it had been set on the
side so that one flank of ribs rests on the grass, and
the sun seems brighter there, the grass green, greener,
than the hedges here. Now. The horse. The buildings
have come between us. You won't see it for some

time, that white horse like a plaster print on the
grass. Look how the buildings slip past. And these,
obviously these were destroyed. Destroyed by fire.
Two, three, four of them, all in a row. These, oh,
these were hit from above. Bombed. The War.
Everything seemed so preserved nearer the sea that it
didn't register. The War. But there was a War. These
buildings were bombed. That is, bombs fell on them,
and they went up in flames, leaving as a memorial of
their destruction what you see now. The War. It was
fought here, and you read about it. Heard about it.
Saw people who had seen it. And now the buildings.
Of course they were bombed. And this is the first
time you have been to a country that was bombed.
Now you are in the war zone. England. Am I really
in England. Remember the battles. England was
always the place that fought battles, the country with
some enemy, but England, it was Britain the books
said, For Britain. It was Britons, Britons never never
shall be slaves. This is England. Look you just missed
it. Ah, there again, there it is, the white horse. Gone.
There ah, there it is. White against the grass. Who
put it there. Look. There again. Ah, it's gone. Gone.
All the buildings are solid here. These were not
bombed. Or perhaps these were rebuilt. They have
blocked out the white horse. Forever. The white
horse is gone. Only the buildings now.

How long you been sleepin'?

WILL PASSENGERS KEEP THEIR HEADS WITHIN THE TRAIN

Look partner dat's where they make the blades,
partner, all yuh shaving you say you shave you do
cause o' that place. Look it, ol' man, they make yuh
blades there.

Ponds, ol' man, look Ponds. They make cream

there. All those women back home depend on what happen in there. Look, Ponds Cream. Look Tornado you see that. Paint. They make paint there. Look. Paint. You dint see that, partner. You see that. They make life there. Life. What life partner. Where you say they make what.

Life partner. Read it. Hermivita gives lie. You ain't see it.

In the same direction, look, they make death there, ol' man. Look. Dissecticide kills once and for all. Read partner. Look what they make.

They make everything here on this side. All England like this.

Peter Porter

[1929–]

Peter Porter was born in Brisbane, Australia, and lived his early childhood in the shadow of his mother's illness. She died when he was nine. Porter remained in Brisbane for the duration of his formal education and from 1947 to 1948 worked there as a journalist. In 1951 he moved to England, where he has lived ever since.

For ten years, Porter worked as a clerk, bookseller and advertising writer in what he would later refer to as 'temperate London, our educated city'. He married Jannice Henry in 1961 and the couple had two daughters. The year of his marriage Porter published his first collection of poetry, *Once Bitten, Twice Bitten*. In 1968 he began to earn a living from freelance writing and broadcasting. He has also, since 1970, been a university lecturer and has been writer-in-residence at various English, Scottish and Australian universities.

In 1974 his wife committed suicide, an event he has written about in several poems, including 'Exequy'. The majority of his themes, however, seem to have been inspired, as one critic put it, by a 'queasy fascination with the London scene, consumer goods, and casual sex', all seen with the eyes of a 'privileged outsider'. As an Australian, Porter is 'alienated', according to his compatriot Clive James, by his 'European sensibility', and perhaps to counteract his alienation he has, through his writing, 'set about imaginatively possessing Europe'.

Since 1961 Porter has produced a substantial body of poetry that has earned him recognition as a satirist and rhetorician, and has prompted comparisons with W. H. Auden. In addition to publishing collections of his own work, Porter has been represented in numerous anthologies. In 1976 he received the Cholmondeley Award and in 1983 he won the Duff Cooper Memorial Prize for *Collected Poems*. He also won the Whitbread Prize in 1988 and was a recipient of the Gold Medal for Australian Literature in 1990.

Porter's poem 'An Ingrate's England' (1989) reveals a great ambivalence about his relationship to Britain. After nearly forty years as a resident, the poet is still attempting to write and think his way into the essential fabric of the country.

AN INGRATE'S ENGLAND

It is too late for denunciation:
That the snow lingers on the sill
And that there are too many newspapers
Is the same as telling yourself
You've given this country forty years
Of your days, you're implicated
In the injustices of pronouns
And the smarter speech of sycamores.

This is the England in your flesh,
A code enduring Summer while
Tasteless birds flap at the edge of
Civilizing concrete. Some have found it
Necessary to reimagine Nature
And stop importing Wordsworth
To shame the bugles from the evening air –
You were born in not the colonies but God.

Yet the brain cannot be Gloucestershire
And vents of human hate are viewed
As old cathedrals across osiers.
The selling of the past to merchants
Of the future is a duty pleasing to
The snarling watercolourist. Prinny
Used to ride by here, and still the smoke
Of loyalist cottages drips acid rain on voices.

The trains in their arched pavilions leave
For restless destinations, their PA Systems
Fastidious with crackle; nobody

Will ask you to identify yourself
But this will lead to hell, the route
The pilgrims take – down the valleys
Of concealed renewal to the pier-theatre,
The crinkle-crankle wall, the graveyard up for sale.

J. G. Ballard

[1930–]

James Graham Ballard was born in Shanghai, China, where he spent the first sixteen years of his life. During the Second World War he was interned in a civilian prisoner-of-war camp. In 1946 he was repatriated to Britain, but the vision of a ravaged and desolate post-war Shanghai left a powerful impression on him and was to influence his writing in the years to come. His urban landscapes appear as places of numbing destruction (London as 'a city of hell'), or lose their identities completely in the face of chaos.

After attending King's College, Cambridge, where he studied medicine but left without taking his degree, Ballard worked at odd jobs and, in the early 1950s, served in the Royal Air Force. In 1954 he married Helen Matthews and the two settled near London. His first short stories, written in the early 1960s and later published as *Terminal Beach* (1964), appeared in the British science-fiction magazines *Science Fantasy* and *New Worlds*. Ballard gradually gained a reputation for science-fiction writing that transcended the traditions of the genre and his explorations of psychological 'inner space' earned him respect among purveyors of science fiction's 'New Wave' movement.

It is widely acknowledged that Ballard's canon can be divided into 'serious', more demanding work and lighter 'entertainments'. His first novel, *The Wind from Nowhere* (1962), would most likely fall into this second category. It was followed by *The Drowned World* (1962), *The Drought* (1965; previously issued as *The Burning World* in 1964) and *The Crystal World* (1966), a trilogy which explored the disintegration of civilization in the face of environmental catastrophe.

In 1964 Helen Matthews died. The loss of his wife, with whom he had three children, had a profound effect on Ballard's writing. His production of short stories decreased and his fiction became increasingly sombre. *Crash* (1973), which was seen as a cult triumph by some but as unnecessarily provocative by others, explored themes of violence, sexual perversion and moral and emotional sterility. Two stories of Robinson

Crusoe-type castaways, *Concrete Island* (1974) and *High Rise* (1975) followed *Crash*. In the former, the protagonist is trapped on a traffic island; in the latter, a luxury apartment building becomes the isolated setting for social savagery.

In 1984 Ballard received the Guardian Prize for *Empire of the Sun* (1984), a largely autobiographical novel set in Shanghai during the Second World War. *Empire of the Sun*, which decries the senselessness and brutality of war, also won the James Tait Black Memorial Prize in 1985. His subsequent works include *Running Wild* (1988) and *The Kindness of Women* (1991).

In 1966 many of Ballard's essays and reviews were collected in *A User's Guide to the Millennium*.

In stark contrast to Lawrence Durrell, Ballard sees London as not decadent enough. His 'First Impressions of London' (1993) is a commentary upon Britain, which to his eyes never recovered from the ravages of the Second World War.

First Impressions of London

My image of London was formed during my Shanghai childhood in the 1930s as I listened to my parents' generation talk nostalgically of West End shows, the bright lights of Piccadilly, Noël Coward and Gertie Lawrence, reinforced by a Peter Pan and Christopher Robin image of a London that consisted entirely of Knightsbridge and Kensington, where 1 per cent of the population was working class and everyone else was a barrister or stockbroker. When I actually arrived in 1946 I found a London that looked like Bucharest with a hangover – heaps of rubble, an exhausted ferret like people defeated by war and still deluded by Churchillian rhetoric, hobbling around a wasteland of poverty, ration books and grotesque social division.

To understand London now one has to grasp the fact that in this city, as nowhere else in the world, World War II is still going on. The spivs are running delis and restaurants, and an occupying arm of international bankers and platinum-card tourists has taken the place of the American servicemen. The people are stoical and underpaid, with a lower standard of living and tackier services than in any comparable Western capital. The weary camaraderie of the Blitz holds everything together. Bombs should fall tonight but probably won't, but one senses that people would welcome them.

How to improve London? Launch a crash programme to fill the city with pirate TV stations, nightclubs, brothels and porn parlours. London needs to become as decadent as Weimar Berlin. Instead, it is merely a decadent Bournemouth.

Eva Figes

[1932–]

Eva Figes was born Eva Unger in Berlin, Germany, into an affluent Jewish family. Her father was imprisoned in Dachau following Kristallnacht (9–10 November 1938). Eventually, he managed to procure visas for himself and his family, and in 1939 Eva, her parents and her brother fled to England. Figes later received a scholarship to Queen Mary College, University of London, where she received a BA in English.

In 1952 Figes began working as an editor at a London publishing house. In 1954 she married John George Figes, with whom she had two children. It was after the breakdown of their marriage that she wrote her first novel, *Equinox* (1966), which tells of one critical year in a woman's life. She then left publishing and began writing and translating full-time. In 1967 she won the Guardian Fiction Prize for her second novel, *Winter Journey*, which chronicles a day in the life of a confused, elderly man. Figes wrote several more novels before publishing a personal memoir, *Little Eden: A Child at War* (1978), in which she recounts her experiences during the 1940–41 Blitz of Britain. In this book the sense of personal alienation and 'statelessness' that she shares with many of her fictional characters is evident.

Figes has often been termed a 'modernist', for her novels digress from traditional forms. In keeping with her desire to reshape conventions, she questions accepted sexual stereotypes and in her writing she often addresses the issue of female estrangement from the mainstream of power. Her later works include *Ghosts* (1988) and *The Tree of Knowledge* (1990). Her latest novel, *The Knot*, was published in 1996.

The following extract from Figes's personal memoir Little Eden: A Child at War, *reveals the pain and anxiety of being both Jewish and German in the England of the 1930s and 1940s.*

From *Little Eden: A Child at War*

In London, for the past year, apart from a few weeks in Scotland waiting for a German invasion which never came, I had been trying very hard to get myself accepted in the childhood network of streets, school and playground whose laws were strange to me. I was foreign, used to large households with servants. All my life I had been sheltered, not only from the realities of poverty, but from the much harsher realities of life in Germany. As a small child I did not look particularly Jewish, and I could not have told you what the word meant. The adult world was wrapped in mysteries, sensed tension not understood, but always I was cushioned from the impact of harsh reality. My father had been arrested while on a business trip to Düsseldorf, so his continued absence was easily explained. He was simply 'away' on business. My nursemaid, who later died of cholera in a concentration camp, organized a singsong in a back room away from the street while the smashing and looting, the beating and killing, went on four floors below at street level. All the servants had instructions to lie, and they must have been quite good at it. My nursemaid only got caught out once: when I stopped outside a shop displaying brown uniforms and leather belts and boots, and asked what they were for. She did not answer, she had no answer ready, which is why I remember that shop so vividly. But the smashed shop windows did not make much impression, because my question was promptly answered by prearrangement: they are being repaired. My brother and I could see that the shops were being repaired, so the aftermath of the Kristallnacht faded into everyday reality.

But our sheltered and comfortable existence ended the day my father came back from concentration camp. From that moment on I felt caught up in a drama, which started with the housemaid Edith waiting for us on the pavement in her black and white uniform. We got off the tram with the nursemaid and I saw her standing outside the main house door, without even a coat slung over her shoulders. The nurse was told not to bring us indoors, but to take us straight on to our grandparents. Herr Unger had scarlet fever.

We spent some time with my grandparents, where I slept on a sofa and we had English lessons in the afternoons from a young German woman and learned a few words and phrases which later proved quite useless. After a while my grandparents, who only had a small flat and one servant, were given a rest, and we were moved to my other, widowed grandmother, who lived in gloomy and palatial splendour in a vast apartment on the Kurfürstendamm. Here I caught only a brief glimpse of my mother, who turned up to settle a row which had flared up between my grandmother and the nurse, whose nerves appeared to have reached breaking point.

The day we were finally brought back home was also memorable. My father stood in the living room, looking pale and thin. But we knew he had been ill. What I had not been led to expect was the state of the apartment: the living room was almost bare of furniture, and the carpets had disappeared. My father grinned at my puzzled astonishment on seeing familiar surroundings so changed.

'We're going to England,' he said, and our excitement changed to terror when we made too much noise at the passport office and a man in military uniform with a swastika armband frightened us into round-eyed silence when he shouted at us to keep quiet and glared down at us from his desk while he examined the passports. And when we went to the British Embassy my father only had to warn us once: we waited in the old-fashioned hallway in subdued awe, quiet as mice. By now, aged six, I had learned that officialdom was to be feared, understood that bureaucrats exercised powers of life and death over people and, judging by the Nazi at the passport office, they could exercise it arbitrarily, depending on their mood and how you behaved.

Crowded into two cars, accompanied by two grandmothers, my grandfather, and an aunt, we drove in a rather sombre mood, like a funeral cortège, to the airport at Tempelhof. It was a bleak, overcast day. During the customs formalities it began to hail and I saw my grandfather outside the plate-glass windows peering in to try and catch a final glimpse of us. He looked very forlorn outside, with the hailstones coming down on him, though he did not seem to notice them. He had not seen me: I pulled at the bottom of my father's coat to draw his attention but he was much too busy to take any notice. Afterwards, settled in the aeroplane, they were only a remote group of tiny figures standing outside the building, waiting for the plane to take off. We were told to wave, but I do not suppose they even saw us.

My brother, aged four, caused a last-minute diversion by announcing in a loud voice that, contrary to instructions, he had not spent his pocket money. He had it on him. He knew that from now on we would be poor, so if father ran short of cash he could rely on him to help out. The whole plane smiled at the pudgy small boy with ash-blond hair who thought himself a responsible man with just over one mark in his pocket, but my mother's smile was strained and anxious. I had been taken into a small shop a few days earlier and instructed to spend my money on anything, whether I wanted it or not, but my brother's childhood instinct for hoarding money had more than a touch of high drama on this occasion. He felt self-important and spoke in a very loud voice. By now I knew enough to be anxious in case we were all taken off the plane at the last minute.

But we took off, leaving everything behind. For years I was to take off, in a recurring dream, leaving them all behind, under that dark menacing sky.

My father had depicted England as the promised land with its own mythology: policemen with funny helmets, a city of buildings streaked black and white, regularly enveloped in dense fogs of legendary oddness, old railway stations where the taxis came right inside the station. Reality became, first a sordid boarding-house off the Finchley Road where I was scared to go to sleep at nights, then a small suburban flat where the furniture which we had brought from Berlin would not fit. Large Persian carpets lay rolled up against the wall as they were far too long for the small floors, sideboards and wardrobes and beds took up so much space that there was no room left to move. We rapidly acquired a new mythology of England: small rooms, draughty windows without double glazing, no central heating, outside plumbing which froze and started an indoor flood at the first sign of winter, and open coal fires which scorched your face whilst your back remained icy.

I started school, and my difficulties began. They did not really resolve themselves until I passed the eleven-plus and moved on to the local grammar school, but the period of fifteen months I spent in Cirencester was a welcome respite from the private war in which I found myself involved for so many years, no doubt one reason why it turned out to be such a special time.

When I came to Cirencester in 1940 I was raw with the effort of a year in which I had tried, oh so hard, to acclimatize not just to a foreign country in language and geography. If I had moved to Mayfair or Kensington I doubt whether I would have noticed any change. The foreign country was made up of a network of small, jerry-built semi-detached houses where children ran loose in the quiet residential streets, uncontrolled by adults. Nursemaids were unheard of, mothers did their own housework and allowed their children out of doors until dark: to fight, climb trees, invent dangerous games, sneak into back gardens for missing balls, roam from street to street and house to house until dusk or hunger drove us home. To my amazement my mother, who now did her own housework, allowed me to run wild and asked no questions. It was as though that other world of supervised walks, decorum and curtsies, separate meals in the day nursery, had been totally negated, by more than mere absence of money.

I liked being poor. I saw much more of my mother, and playing with gangs of children in the streets was exciting, an endless adventure. But I suffered from a handicap: from the day I was introduced into a classroom of forty staring children in my odd foreign clothes, only able to speak a few words, writing a peculiar script which my teacher dismissed as scribble, I was branded. I was allowed to join in girls' games on sufferance, and made to feel excluded from more secret rites. Even though I quickly learned the language and the tribal customs of alley and playground, the fact that I had arrived as a foreign child was never forgotten or forgiven, and with the rise of anti-German feeling after the outbreak of war my nationality was always good for abuse. The girls were the worst: they mostly played in groups, and my acceptance seemed to depend entirely on the mood of the acknowledged leader, whose hostility immediately infected the others. My troubles were offset but perhaps also exacerbated by the fact that as a shy, withdrawn little foreigner I quickly became the object of chivalrous attention from several small boys in the class, who invited me to tea, brought me flowers from their back garden, and came to call for me on their way to school. My popularity with boys only made the girls more standoffish and hostile, since they were openly jealous.

I learned to hate that school anyhow, for its crass teaching methods, but I was never to live down my German origin there, long after my English was perfect and I could conform to the patterns of the playground with the rest. I never knew when I would be accused next of being one of the hated enemy, except that I knew I would be. I was conscious of injustice, since my father was a soldier in the British army, which was more than most of their fathers were. But somehow these things were never open to discussion. I was too hurt and confused, my accusers too confident in their self-righteous prejudice.

Perhaps I suffered no more than any intelligent and sensitive child in such a group, but this particular group always had a stick to beat me with, and I never knew when they would take it into their heads to turn on me. At the dinner table 'shiny' spoons were much sought after as a status symbol. As a mark of friendship girls would go and get one for their friends from the cutlery tray. Nobody ever offered to find one for me. Conscious of a slight, I acquired one of the rare shiny spoons and took to keeping it in my purse, ready for the next day's meal. A few days later I found a gang of girls waiting for me as I came out of school. As usual there was a leader. They accused me of stealing cutlery and made me open my purse. I was marched off to one of the 'dinner ladies', who not only would not listen to my explanation, but dismissed me with the words: 'No English child would ever do a thing like that.' I tried to keep my head high, the tears back, as I walked home, followed by the jeers and catcalls of my classmates.

By next morning those girls were friendly once more, treated me as though nothing had happened. It was just one of those things, part of the fun and games of everyday life, and perhaps they had already forgotten the incident. But I never forgot it. Unfortunately I was proud as well as an enemy alien, and in later years I took to spending a lot of my free time in the home for parentless German-Jewish children next door to the school, where I could feel accepted as part of a strongly bonded group. Although I knew I was lucky in comparison to these children, I sometimes envied them for being all together under one large roof. It was fun there, like a permanent holiday camp, and the youth leaders always accepted me and made me welcome, when I came to join in their games. They lived openly and proudly, whilst my family was trying to hide, become English, or at least merge into the background and avoid giving any possible offence to English neighbours. Rule one: never speak German.

But in the summer of 1940 my private war was still intermittent. I had a lot of fun, climbing trees, playing cowboys and Indians, learning to chant, with appropriate actions:

> Underneath the spreading chestnut tree
> Mister Chamberlain said to me:
> If you want to get your gasmask free,
> Join the blinking ARP.

Of course gasmasks were distributed free anyhow. We had been fitted out, along with a queue of other people, in the front room of a semi-detached house stacked high with brown cardboard boxes. They caused a lot of hilarity at school when we had gasmask drill, giggling at each other in our weird rubber muzzles. We then had to march, or rather, stumble, in disorderly file down the long corridors to the school cloakrooms, which had been reinforced to double as air-raid shelters. It was hard going, since we could not see our feet and the celluloid window steamed up almost immediately. It was hot, and smelt funny, of rubber, and breathing was hard, suffocating work. We would have liked the Mickey Mouse masks, but these were only issued to very young children, who were much admired and envied in consequence.

During the short summer of 1939 there had been several excited reunions with friends or relatives who had managed to get out of Germany. My father's older sister arrived, minus her luggage. A family with two sons, with whom I used to play in the old days, came to visit us on their way to the States. All this stopped with the outbreak of war. My grandparents had sent me a postcard with their photographs, passport size, pasted to it. I used to look at it a lot once the separation had become final, the silence broken only by a rare Red Cross letter. Some things, many things, had been left too late. It was better not to talk about them too much, not then, or even half a lifetime later. To do so was to arouse feelings of guilt and recrimination, even against the dead, which could never be stilled.

V. S. Naipaul

[1932–]

Vidiadhar Surajprasad Naipaul was born in the small town of Chaguanas, Trinidad. In 1938 he and his family moved to Port of Spain. Naipaul attended Queen's Royal College from 1942 to 1949, and in 1949 he won a Trinidadian government scholarship to study abroad. In 1950 he left Port of Spain for University College, Oxford, where he decided that once he had taken his degree he would become a writer.

In 1954 Naipaul worked in the cataloguing department of the National Portrait Gallery in London – one of the few non-literary jobs he ever held. Between 1954 to 1956 he also worked for the BBC, as a writer and editor for the programme *Caribbean Voices*. In 1955 he married a former Oxford student, an Englishwoman named Patricia Ann Hale, and by 1958 was a regular contributor to the *New Statesman*. During this time, Naipaul began to write short stories which were later collected in the volume *Miguel Street* (1959), winner of the Somerset Maugham Award in 1961. His first published work, however, was the Dickensian comedy *The Mystic Masseur* (1957), which describes its main character's estrangement from Hinduism and his subsequent rise to prominence as a guru. In 1961 he published *A House for Mr Biswas*. This novel, which many critics consider his masterpiece, is a fictionalized account of his father's life.

The Middle Passage (1962), a non-fictional examination of Caribbean society, is the first of Naipaul's travel books. He recounts his journeys to India in both *An Area of Darkness* (1964), written with the help of a Phoenix Trust Award, and *India: A Wounded Civilization* (1977). During the earlier visit, Naipaul wrote his first novel with an English setting, *Mr Stone and the Knights Companion* (1963). From 1963 to 1979 he continued to publish novels at regular four-yearly intervals. In 1971, having already received all of Britain's other leading literary prizes, Naipaul was awarded the Booker Prize for *In a Free State*; he was shortlisted for the Booker Prize again with *A Bend in the River* (1979). In late 1979 and early 1980 Naipaul travelled in the Middle and Far East, gathering material for *Among the Believers: An Islamic Journey* (1981).

Although he continued to write non-fiction during the mid-1980s, Naipaul, beset by illness and devastated by the deaths of his younger sister and his brother, Shiva (also an acclaimed writer), did not write another novel until 1987. That year he published *The Enigma of Arrival*, a deeply personal work that is at once an elegy for the vanishing English landscape and a reflection upon individual loss.

A perennial nominee for the Nobel Prize for Literature, Naipaul was knighted in 1990. His 'diasporic sensibility' has given power and purpose to his substantial body of work. When writing about Trinidad in particular, Naipaul has often been harsh and uncomplimentary. This has led many critics to question his right to be considered a 'Third World writer', yet Naipaul insists that his work – in which he seems to uphold the core values of Western civilization while keeping a concerned and often ironic eye on his Caribbean and Indian background – is born not of anger but of acceptance. In 1994 his 'novel' *A Way in the World* suggested that Naipaul was becoming both increasingly frustrated with the novel form and more purposefully meditative. A pillar of the British literary establishment, Naipaul continues to live in England.

V. S. Naipaul's fictional account of his first encounter with England, from The Enigma of Arrival *(1987), suggests a tone that is entirely different from that of his West Indian-born contemporaries. The writing is elegant and detached, but there is a nervous hesitancy to the voice that one feels is a by-product more of the narrator's youth than of any fundamental lack of confidence that Naipaul may have in his own abilities. As in C. L. R. James's essay, Naipaul's West Indian narrator is quick to display his cultural knowledge, and one imagines that it will not be long before the young man penetrates the veneer of English diffidence and begins to vigorously engage with and challenge the society.*

The Journey

After the grey of the Atlantic, there was colour. Bright colour seen from the train that went to London. Late afternoon light. An extended dusk: new, enchanting to someone used to the more or less equal division of day and night in the tropics. Light, dusk, at an hour which would have been night at home.

But it was night when we arrived at Waterloo station. I liked the size, the many platforms, the big, high roof. I liked the lights. Used at home to public places – or those I knew, schools, stores, offices – working only in natural light, I liked this excitement of a railway station busy at night, and brightly lit up. I saw the station people, working in electric light, and the travellers as dramatic figures. The station lights gave a suggestion (such as the New York streets had already given me) of a canopied world, a vast home interior.

After five days on the liner, I wanted to go out. I wanted especially to go to a cinema. I had heard that in London the cinemas ran continuously; at home I was used to shows at fixed times. The idea of the continuous show – as the metropolitan way of doing things, with all that it implied of a great busy populace – was very attractive. But even for London, even for the metropolitan populace of London, it was too late. I went directly to the boardinghouse in Earls Court, where a room had been reserved for me for the two months or so before I went to Oxford.

It was a small room, long and narrow, made dark by dark bulky furniture; and bare otherwise, with nothing on the walls. As bare as my cabin on the *Columbia*; barer than the room I had had in the Hotel Wellington for that night in New York. My heart contracted. But there was one part of me that rejoiced at the view from the window, some floors up, of the bright orange street lights and the effect of the lights on the trees.

After the warm, rubbery smell of the ship, the smell of the air conditioning in enclosed cabins and corridors, there were new smells in the morning. A cloying smell of milk – fresh milk was rare to me: we used Klim powdered milk and condensed milk. That thick, sweet smell of milk was mixed with the smell of soot; and that smell was overlaid with the airless cockroachy smell of old dirt. Those were the morning smells.

The garden or yard or plot of ground at the back of the house ran to a high wall. Behind that high wall was the underground railway station. Romance! The sound of trains there all the time, and from very early in the morning! Speaking directly to me now of what the Negro in the New York hotel had spoken: the city that never slept.

The bathrooms and lavatories were at the end of the landing on each floor. Or perhaps on every other floor – because, as I was going down, there came up a young man of Asia, small and small-boned, with a pale-yellow complexion, with glasses, and an elaborate Asiatic dressing gown that was too big for him in the arms; the wide embroidered cuffs hid his hands. He gave out a tinkling 'Goo-ood morning!' and hurried past me. Was he Siamese, Burmese, Chinese? He looked forlorn, far from home – as yet, still full of my London wonder, my own success in having arrived in the city, I did not make the same judgement about myself.

I was going down to the dining room, in the basement. The boardinghouse offered bed and breakfast, and I was going down to the breakfast. The dining room, at the front of the house, sheltered from the noise of the underground trains, subject only to the vibration, had two or three people. It had many straight-backed brown chairs; the walls were as blank as the walls of my room. The milk-and-soot smell was strong here. It was morning, light outside, but a weak electric bulb was on; the wall was yellowish, shiny. Wall, light, smell – they were all parts of the wonderful London morning. As was my sight of the steep narrow steps going up to the street, the rails, the pavement. I had never been in a basement before. It was not a style of building we had at home; but I had read of basements in books; and this room with an electric light burning on a bright sunny day seemed to me romantic. I was like a man entering the world of a novel, a book; entering the real world.

I went and looked around the upper floor afterwards, or that part of it that was open to guests. The front room was full of chairs, straight-backed chairs and fat low upholstered chairs, and the walls were as bare as the walls everywhere else. This was the lounge (I had been told that downstairs); but the air was so still, such a sooty old smell came off the dark carpet and the tall old curtains, that I felt the room wasn't used. I felt the house was no longer being used as the

builder or first owner had intended. I felt that at one time, perhaps
before the war, it had been a private house; and (though knowing
nothing about London houses) I felt it had come down in the world.
Such was my tenderness towards London, or my idea of London.
And I felt, as I saw more and more of my fellow lodgers – Europeans
from the Continent and North Africa, Asiatics, some English people
from the provinces, simple people in cheap lodgings – that we were
all in a way campers in the big house.

And coming back night after night – after my tourist excursions
through London – to this bare house, I was infected by its mood. I
took this mood to what I saw. I had no eye for architecture; there had
been nothing at home to train my eye. In London I saw pavements,
shops, shop blinds (almost every other one stencilled at the bottom *J.
Dean, Maker, Putney*), shop signs, undifferentiated buildings. On my
tourist excursions I went looking for size. It was one of the things I
had travelled to find, coming from my small island. I found size,
power, in the area around Holborn Viaduct, the Embankment,
Trafalgar Square. And after this grandeur there was the boarding-
house in Earls Court. So I grew to feel that the grandeur belonged to
the past; that I had come to England at the wrong time; that I had
come too late to find the England, the heart of empire, which (like a
provincial, from a far corner of the empire) I had created in my
fantasy.

Such a big judgement about a city I had just arrived in! But that
way of feeling was something I carried within myself. The older
people in our Asian-Indian community in Trinidad – especially the
poor ones, who could never manage English or get used to the
strange races – looked back to an India that became more and more
golden in their memory. They were living in Trinidad and were going
to die there; but for them it was the wrong place. Something of that
feeling was passed down to me. I didn't look back to India, couldn't
do so; my ambition caused me to look ahead and outwards, to
England; but it led to a similar feeling of wrongness. In Trinidad,
feeling myself far away, I had held myself back, as it were, for life at
the centre of things. And there were aspects of the physical setting of

my childhood which positively encouraged that mood of waiting and withdrawal.

We lived, in Trinidad, among advertisements for things that were no longer made or, because of the war and the difficulties of transport, had ceased to be available. (The advertisements in American magazines, for Chris Craft and Statler Hotels and things like that, belonged to another, impossibly remote world.) Many of the advertisements in Trinidad were for old-fashioned remedies and 'tonics'. They were on tin, these advertisements, and enamelled. They were used as decorations in shops and, having no relation to the goods offered for sale, they grew to be regarded as emblems of the shopkeeper's trade. Later, during the war, when the shanty settlement began to grow in the swampland to the east of Port of Spain, these enamelled tin advertisements were used sometimes as building material.

So I was used to living in a world where the signs were without meaning, or without the meaning intended by their makers. It was of a piece with the abstract, arbitrary nature of my education, like my ability to 'study' French or Russian cinema without seeing a film, an ability which was, as I have said, like a man trying to get to know a city from its street map alone.

What was true of Trinidad seemed to be true of other places as well. In the book sections of some of the colonial emporia of Port of Spain there would be a shelf or two of the cheap wartime Penguin paperbacks (narrow margins, crudely stapled, with the staples rusting quickly in our damp climate, but with a wonderful colour, texture, and smell to the paper). It never struck me as odd that at the back of those wartime Penguins there should sometimes be advertisements for certain British things – chocolates, shoes, shaving cream – that had never been available in Trinidad and were now (because of the war, as the advertisements said) no longer being made; such advertisements being put in by the former manufacturers only to keep their brand names alive during the war, and in the hope that the war would turn out well. These advertisements – for things doubly and trebly removed from possibility – never struck me as odd; they came to me as an aspect of the romance of the world I was working towards, a promise within the promise, and intensely romantic.

So I was ready to imagine that the world in which I found myself in London was something less than the perfect world I had striven towards. As a child in Trinidad I had put this world at a far distance, in London perhaps. In London now I was able to put this perfect world at another time, an earlier time. The mental or emotional processes were the same.

In the underground stations there were still old-fashioned, heavy vending machines with raised metal letters. No sweets, no chocolates came from them now. But for ten years or so no one had bothered to take them away; they were like things in a house that had broken down or been superseded, but remained unthrown away. Two doors away from my boardinghouse in Earls Court there was a bomb site, a gap in the road, with neat rubble where the basement should have been, the dining room of a house like the one in which I lived. Such sites were all over the city. I saw them in the beginning; then I stopped seeing them. Paternoster Row, at the side of St Paul's Cathedral, hardly existed; but the name still appeared on the title page of books as the London address of many publishers.

My tramps about London were ignorant and joyless. I had expected the great city to leap out at me and possess me; I had longed so much to be in it. And soon, within a week or less, I was very lonely. If I had been less lonely, if I had had the equivalent of my shipboard life, I might have felt differently about London and the boardinghouse. But I was solitary, and didn't have the means of finding the kind of society I had had for the five days of the Atlantic crossing.

There was the British Council. They ran a meeting place for foreign students like me. But there one evening, the first time I went, I found myself, in conversation with a bored girl, turning to the subject of physical pain, a fearful obsession of mine, made more fearful with the war (and one further explanation of the austerities I practised at various times). I began to talk of torture, and persevered, though knowing it to be wrong to do so; and was so alarmed by this further distortion of myself (more distorted than my behaviour during the flight to New York, first with the Negro in Puerto Rico, then with the Englishwoman in the seat beside me) that I never went to that British Council place again, for shame.

I had only the boardinghouse and that curious, mixed, silent company of English people, Europeans in limbo, and a few Asiatic students to whom English was difficult. And perhaps that boarding-house life might have meant more to me if I were better read in contemporary English books, if, for example, I had read *Hangover Square*, which was set in the very area just eleven years or so before. A book like that would have peopled the area and made it romantic and given me, always needing these proofs from books, some sharper sense of myself.

But in spite of my education, I was under-read. What did I know of London? There was an essay by Charles Lamb – in a schoolbook – about going to the theatre. There were two or three lovely sentences – in another schoolbook – about the Embankment, from 'Lord Arthur Savile's Crime'. But Sherlock Holmes's Baker Street was just its name; and the London references in Somerset Maugham and Waugh and others didn't create pictures in the mind, because they assumed too much knowledge in the reader. The London I knew or imaginatively possessed was the London I had got from Dickens. It was Dickens – and his illustrators – who gave me the illusion of knowing the city. I was therefore, without knowing it, like the Russians I was to hear about (and marvel at) who still believed in the reality of Dickens's London.

Years later, looking at Dickens during a time when I was writing hard myself, I felt I understood a little more about Dickens's unique power as a describer of London, and his difference from all other writers about London. I felt that when as a child far away I read the early Dickens and was able with him to enter the dark city of London, it was partly because I was taking my own simplicity to his, fitting my own fantasies to his. The city of one hundred and thirty years before must have been almost as strange to him as it was to me; and it was his genius to describe it, when he was an adult, as a child might have described it. Not displaying architectural knowledge or taste; not using technical words; using only simple words like 'old-fashioned' to describe whole streets; using no words that might disturb or unsettle an unskilled or unknowledgeable reader. Using no word to unsettle a child far away, in the tropics, where the roofs were of corrugated iron and the gables were done in fretwork, and there were jalousied windows hinged at the top to keep out the rain while letting in light and air. Using, Dickens, only simple words, simple concepts, to create simple volumes and surfaces and lights and shadows: creating thereby a city or fantasy which everyone could reconstruct out of his own materials, using the things he knew to re-create the described things he didn't know.

To Dickens, this enriching of one's own surroundings by fantasy was one of the good things about fiction. And it was apt that Dickens's childlike vision should have given me, with my own child's ideas, my abstract education and my very simple idea of my vocation, an illusion of complete knowledge of the city where I expected this vocation to flower. (Leaving room at the same time, fantasies being what they are, for other, late-nineteenth-century ideas of size and imperial grandeur, which neither Buckingham Palace nor Westminster nor Whitehall gave me, but which I got from Paddington and Waterloo stations and from Holborn Viaduct and the Embankment, great Victorian engineering works.)

I had come to London as to a place I knew very well. I found a city that was strange and unknown – in its style of houses, and even in the names of its districts; as strange as my boardinghouse, which was quite unexpected; a city as strange and unread about as the Englishness of *South Wind*, which I had bought in New York for the sake of its culture. The disturbance in me, faced with this strangeness, was very great, many times more diminishing than the disturbance I had felt in New York when I had entered, as though entering something that was mine by right, the bookshop which had turned out to have very little for me after all.

And something else occurred in those very early days, the first days of arrival. I lost a faculty that had been part of me and precious to me for years. I lost the gift of fantasy, the dream of the future, the far-off place where I was going. At home I had lived most intensely in the cinema, where, before the fixed-hour shows, the cinema boys, to shut out daylight or electric street light, closed the double doors all around and untied the long cords that kept the high wooden windows open. In those dark halls I had dreamt of a life elsewhere. Now, in the place that for all those years had been the 'elsewhere', no further dream was possible. And while on my very first night in London I had wanted to go to the cinema for the sake of those continuous shows I had heard about, to me the very essence of metropolitan busyness, very soon now the idea of the cinema, the idea of entering a dark hall to watch a moving film, became oppressive to me.

I had thought of the cinema pleasure as a foretaste of my adult life. Now, with all kinds of shame in many recesses of my mind, I felt it to be fantasy. I hadn't read *Hangover Square*, didn't even known of it as a book; but I had seen the film. Its Hollywood London had merged in my mind (perhaps because of the associations of the titles) into the London of *The Lodger*. Now I knew that London to be fantasy, worthless to me. And the cinema pleasure, that had gone so deep into me and had in the barren years of abstract study given me such support, that cinema pleasure was now cut away as with a knife. And when, ten or twelve years later, I did return to the cinema, the Hollywood I had known was dead, the extraordinary circumstances in which it had flourished no longer existing; American films had become as self-regardingly local as the French or English; and there was as much distance between a film and me as between a book or a painting and me. Fantasy was no longer possible. I went to the cinema not as a dreamer or a fantasist but as a critic.

I had little to record. My trampings about London didn't produce adventures, didn't sharpen my eye for buildings or people. My life was restricted to the Earls Court boardinghouse. There was a special kind of life there. But I failed to see it. Because, ironically, though feeling myself already drying up, I continued to think of myself as a writer and, as a writer, was still looking for suitable metropolitan material.

Metropolitan – what did I mean by that? I had only a vague idea. I meant material which would enable me to compete with or match certain writers. And I also meant material that would enable me to display a particular kind of writing personality: J. R. Ackerley of *Hindoo Holiday*, perhaps, making notes under a dinner table in India; Somerset Maugham, aloof everywhere, unsurprised, immensely knowing; Aldous Huxley, so full of all kinds of knowledge and also so sexually knowing; Evelyn Waugh, so elegant so naturally. Wishing to be that kind of writer, I didn't see material in the campers in the big Earls Court house.

Penelope Lively

[1933–]

Penelope Lively (née Greer) was born in Cairo, Egypt. She and her family moved to England in 1945. Lively attended boarding school in Sussex and received a BA in history from St Anne's College, Oxford. In 1957 she married Jack Lively, with whom she has two children.

Lively has been a BBC presenter for a radio programme on children's literature and a reviewer for several magazines and newspapers, but it is for her fiction that she is best known. She began her writing career as a children's author. Her first book, *Astercote*, was published in 1970 and was followed by, among others, *The Ghost of Thomas Kempe*, winner of the 1973 Carnegie Medal. She won the Whitbread Award for *A Stitch in Time* (1976), the tale of a young girl who becomes obsessed with an ancient embroidery sampler.

In 1977 Lively wrote her first 'adult' novel, *The Road to Lichfield*, which was short-listed for the Booker Prize. Five more novels followed in the next ten years, and in 1987 Lively won the Booker Prize for *Moon Tiger*, her most structurally ambitious and complex novel to date. The heroine in *Moon Tiger* is a historian who, as she is dying of cancer, constructs a new history for herself and the world. In this novel, as in virtually all of her work, Lively reveals a preoccupation with the elusive nature of time, the processes of death and renewal, and the connection between past and present. As she writes in *Going Back* (1975, later reprinted as an 'adult' book in 1990), events become 'islands in a confused and layered landscape' where 'the things that should matter . . . get forgotten'.

Lively's prose is precise, intelligent and eminently readable. Her more recent novels, including *City of the Mind* (1991), have explored the materialism and oppressiveness of Margaret Thatcher's London in the 1980s. She has recently published the novels, *Cleopatra's Sister* (1993) and *Heatwave* (1996), and a memoir, *Oleander, Jacaranda: A Childhood Perceived* (1994). She currently lives in Oxfordshire and London.

The young woman in the extract from Lively's exquisite memoir
Oleander, Jacaranda *exhibits a painful desire to attach herself to an*
unknown world. The nature of her colonial upbringing in Egypt suggests
that arriving in Britain will simply form a continuum with her old life,
but the society that she confronts is alien in many surprising and difficult
ways.

From *Oleander, Jacaranda*

Lucy and I left for England in a troopship. It was early spring 1945.
The troopship – the *Ranchi* – was *en route* from the Far East and
India with a cargo of the armed forces bound for home and
demobilization. She stopped off at Suez to pick up some more, and
along with them a small consignment of women and children; seven
thousand troops, one hundred women and children. Can it really
have been seven thousand? That is the legendary figure that has lain
in my head ever since. We never saw them. We boarded the ship and
were immediately segregated in a civilian ghetto well out of the way
of the licentious soldiery, presumably in the interests of our own
well-being. I remember only crowded dormitories with bunk beds,
and queuing for the bathroom with the two saltwater showers, and
the sense of those hordes elsewhere. There was the stamp of boots
overhead, and sometimes distant sounds of revelry. It was a far cry
from the P & O and the Bibby Line. No deck chairs and solicitous
stewards.

My mother was staying in Cairo with the man she was going to
marry. My father would tie up his affairs in the Sudan and follow us
to London in a few months. The war was not yet over, but the end
was in sight. On the *Ranchi* everyone was elated – the invisible
troops, the other expatriate women. Lucy was exuberant. Everyone
was heading home, except for me, who was going into exile.

I was twelve, poised for adolescence, though a lot more childlike,
probably, than any adolescent of today. I had little idea what lay
ahead, but I knew that something had come to an end. I remember a

feeling of sobriety rather than of grief. I remember gazing theatrically at the spit of land at the mouth of the canal, as the ship headed for the open sea, and thinking that I was seeing the last of Egypt. I decided to keep a diary of this momentous journey, and began it by listing all the other ships we had seen berthed at Suez, along with further observations about military activities in the area. Lucy, a patriot to the core, became anxious about the implications of this, and mentioned the matter to the NCO supervising our ghetto, who said gravely that there might indeed be a security risk. Lucy told me to start again and stick to descriptions of our daily routine. This was not the sort of thing I had in mind at all, and I threw the diary away.

The journey is a blank now – perhaps in consequence of that affront. I remember only incessant lifeboat drills on the deck, when everyone stood about and grumbled, and nights when we lay in our bunks hearing distant muffled thuds, which were apparently depth charges. There were not supposed to be any German U-boats around in the Mediterranean, but there was always the possibility, and when we turned into the Bay of Biscay and eventually up the Irish Channel, the thuds became more frequent.

We were to dock at Glasgow. The ship entered the mouth of the Clyde, and the shoreline became visible. The seven thousand caught their first glimpse for several years of their native land and headed as one man for the port decks. There were frantic loudspeaker exhortations, and after a few minutes the ship rode level once more. It was getting dark anyway, a dank spring evening. By the time we tied up I was in my bunk, asleep.

I woke to an unnatural stillness, and monstrosity. Framed in the porthole was an immense hairy foot. A hairy hoof. I stared in disbelief, and rose to see my first Clydesdale horse, carrying out haulage duties on the quayside. It was pouring with rain, and bitterly cold. I knew that I had arrived in another world.

We took an overnight train to London, sitting up in a crammed compartment reeking of people in damp clothes, with Lucy on a high, pouring out our life histories to anyone who would listen, revelling in the camaraderie of her own language, her own country. I was acutely embarrassed, and poleaxed by the cold and what I could see out of the windows, as the train crept south in the grey dawn. The whole place was green, bright green. Grass, from end to end. How could this be?

I was dimly aware of the arrangements. I was to be consigned to the care of my grandmothers – my paternal Harley Street grandmother in London and my maternal Somerset grandmother. My father would come to England as soon as he was able to. My mother would stay on at Bulaq Dakhur with her new husband. I was going to boarding school. I knew all this, vaguely, and fended it off. For the moment, I had to come to terms with this stupefying environment: the inconceivable cold, the perpetually leaking sky, that grass.

My London grandmother met us off the train. I was almost as tall as she was now and did not remember her at all. Today I can feel a wholehearted admiration for my grandmothers. They were both over seventy and had valiantly agreed to take on a twelve-year-old whom neither had set eyes on for six years. In their heads there must have been an engaging small child. What they now received was an anguished adolescent, for whom the world had fallen apart. For the next two years they shunted me from one to the other, with anxious instructions about clothing requirements and dental appointments.

They represented a classic English polarization – the town and country cultural divide. My Harley Street grandmother was the widow of a surgeon. She was still living in what had been both the family home and his consulting rooms – a five floor house in that long sombre street. Today there is an array of brass plates at the entrance of number 76. Back then, it was far from unusual for a single successful medical practitioner to occupy the entire house. My grandfather had died during the war, and my grandmother was now living like a squatter in her own house, entrenched within the old consulting room on the ground floor, which was the only room that could be kept warm. The rest of the building towered around her, the rooms shuttered and the furniture under dust covers. Some of the windows had been blown out in the blitz and never replaced; there were makeshift arrangements with boarding, and the occasional gaping hole.

Living there with my grandmother was a relative called Cousin Dorothy. She was elderly, in delicate health, stone deaf, and distinctly unpleasant. She seemed to be the quintessential poor relation but also to have my grandmother dancing attendance on her. She spent her days in the most comfortable armchair, hogging the fire, swathed in shawls, and she used an ear trumpet. She took an instant dislike to me, correctly identifying a rival for my grandmother's attentions, and never referred to me except as 'the girl'. In the basement was Nellie the cook, governing her own, subterranean territory, which seemed to stretch away into infinity. The house was a classic example of the optimum-size early-nineteenth-century terrace mansion. It had all the accessories: an immense coal hole under the pavement, a satellite cottage in the mews behind, sculleries and larders and a wine cellar and lowering kitchen ranges and a food lift on a pulley that could be wound from top to bottom of the house. From my grandmother I learned the correct terminology for various sections, which is why I am one of the few people left to call the well between the basement of a London house and the pavement the area, and to know what the leads are (the open rooftop of a jutting extension at the back of the house – the sort of thing that would be made into a roof garden these days).

In that house my grandmother had brought up six children, and there she now held out in a sort of gallant defiance of circumstances. She was a strong personality, a forceful woman with a robust sense of humour and artistic leanings. She was not a cosy grandmother but a down-to-earth one, who set about what she no doubt saw as the rehabilitation of this waif washed up on her doorstep. No point in weeping and gnashing teeth. The child must learn to adapt. I was plunged at once into the day-by-day negotiation with shortages and bureaucratic regulations which was the hallmark of the times. Each day my grandmother sallied forth with a string bag in search of provisions. Offal was the supreme trophy. On days when she achieved this Holy Grail, she would plunge down into the basement calling for Nellie, and the two of them would pore in rapture over the bloody puddle of liver or kidneys. Lucy and I were officially nonpersons, of course. The first task of all was to establish our existence and equip us with identity cards and ration books. Long hours in Marylebone Town Hall, waiting our turn to be quizzed by a hard-faced functionary. At last we achieved recognition. I had a blue ration book, as a person under sixteen. The functionary, thawing for an instant, pointed out portentously that I'd be entitled to bananas on that. My sense of disorientation was intensified. Why should people get excited about bananas?

My Somerset grandmother lived with my aunt Rachel in a place of red earth, steep lanes, flower-filled hedge banks, the long slack skylines of Exmoor, and the slate-grey gleam of the Bristol Channel. She also was a widow, and at Golsoncott too life had been pared down, whittled away to a shadow of pre-war indulgence. But certain proprieties were observed. Dinner at eight, for which my grand-mother changed from her daytime tweeds into a floor-length housecoat and her pearls. The time-honoured routine of church attendance, chairmanship of the village hall committee and the Women's Institute, household shopping in Minehead on Tuesdays, a rigorous daily stint in the garden. To go there from Harley Street was to move from one cultural zone to another – even I could see that, with my fragile grasp of social niceties. The staccato scattershot of Cockney was replaced by the ruminative buzz of Somerset speech. In each place the other was looked upon with mistrust and contempt. In Somerset everyone said I'd soon have some roses in my cheeks once I'd shaken off that smoky London air. In London they wondered what a child could possibly find to do down there. My Somerset grandmother visited London once a year. She called it 'going up to town' and had special clothes which she wore on no other occasion. She would go to a theatre or concert, take lunch or tea with relatives, and retreat thankfully after three days to her rose garden and her embroidery. My Harley Street grandmother, for whom the wild-erness began at Croydon, made a ritual trip to Kew Gardens in the spring and a quarterly day-return outing to see her sister in Staines, from which she would return complaining of the distance.

The journey to Somerset was itself a sort of acclimatization, from the moment you reached Paddington and the Great Western Railway train with its sternly regional black-and-white photographs of Glastonbury Tor and Saint Michael's Mount and Clovelly. At Taunton you crossed the frontier for real, changing into the branch line to Minehead, Norton Fitzwarren, Bishop's Lydeard, Crowcombe, Stogumber . . . The line is still there, but mockingly reborn as a 'scenic railway'. Back then, it wasn't scenery – it was a serious progress from A to B. People got on and off at every stop: schoolchildren, women returning from a day's shopping in Taunton, visiting relatives. Myself alighting at Washford to be met by my grandmother in the old Rover with the running board, and the medallion of Saint Christopher alongside the speedometer.

My Somerset grandmother was a strong personality also, but differently so. She too took me in hand, and was eventually to do so alone when my Harley Street grandmother died within a couple of years. Her method was a kind of benign and tactful digestion of me within the calm parameters of her own concerns. She swept me up into a routine of brisk walks, local commitments, gardening chores, and fireside evenings. She was the voice of authority, but she was also affectionate and companionable. She teased me when I began to strike adolescent attitudes, and punctured my burgeoning vanity. She came to say good night to me in bed every night, humming her way along the corridor. She could be both stern and indulgent. She had a youthful sense of the ridiculous. Once, the elastic in my knickers broke when we were out shopping in Minehead and they fell to the ground: we fled to the car and laughed ourselves into incoherence. And as I grew up, and became myself more opinionated, we frequently disagreed – energetically but without rancour. I came out as an agnostic, and went through the Ten Commandments with her to demonstrate that agnosticism was not synonymous with amorality – that I still held much the same views as she did on what is right and what is wrong. I queried her Conservatism – though I was not the first to do that. My aunt Rachel had always held somewhat socialist views, which had been reinforced by her wartime experience working with an evacuee organization in East London.

In the fullness of time, Golsoncott became the approximation of a home, and my grandmother and aunt central to my life. But in those early months and years of exile I was still an alien, walking that landscape always with a faint sense of incredulity. Sooner or later, surely, I would wake up and find myself at Bulaq Dakhur. This was all a mistake, and eventually it would be proven so and normality would be restored. Sometimes I felt as though I were in suspension, dumped here in this alien other world while somewhere else real life was still going on, golden and unreachable; at other times I was swept by the grim apprehension that all this was true. It was really happening, and would continue to do so.

An enforced metamorphosis took place, during that spring and summer of 1945. I moved slowly from disbelief to resigned acceptance, and aged it seemed by about ten years. The war ended, and I hardly noticed, immersed in becoming someone else. At the most practical level, I had to be kitted out with a new wardrobe. Friends and relatives were called upon to sacrifice their clothing coupons. I must apparently have a tweed coat and flannel skirt and thick jerseys. Knee-length socks, serge knickers, Chilprufe vests, and a fearful woollen corset called a Liberty bodice. Lisle stockings and garter belt, for heaven's sake. I, who had never in all my life worn anything other than a cotton frock. I protested. You're in England now, said Lucy grimly. She didn't need to remind me.

At some point during that first summer Lucy went away. I cannot now identify a moment of departure. She was there for a while, and then she was not. And in the autumn I went to boarding school, to embark on the slow calvary that was to last until I was sixteen.

Lucy moved on to spend many years with another family, where she received more consideration than I think she had from mine. I remained in contact with her until the end of her life. On one occasion when I was visiting her, not long before her death, she remarked suddenly that she had been having a clear-out and had come across some old letters of mine. Would I like to have them? I said I would. She couldn't remember right now where she'd put them, she said. She would send them.

In due course she did so. There were dozens of them, beginning that summer of 1945 and running on for the next few years. The later ones, when I was fifteen or sixteen, were unexceptional – long chatty accounts of what I had been doing. Grumbles about school. Adolescent posturing. Family gossip. It was the early ones that brought me up short, as I sat reading in my study through a long morning more than forty years later. They too were garrulous screeds about school, about the grandmothers, about what I had seen and done, but every now and then they broke down and became something else. They became love letters, and out of them there burst a raw anguish, a howl of abandonment and despair. I read them close to tears, incredulous, realizing that I remembered neither the writing of them nor the distress. It was possible to feel an acute and entirely detached pity. And when I had finished reading the letters I destroyed them all, because I knew that I could never bear to read them again, and because I knew also that I would not wish anyone else ever to do so. That sad child was gone, at rest, subsumed within the woman that I now am. And I think now of what it must have been like to be on the receiving end of those pathetic cries. Did she reread them before she pushed them into the large manila envelope and posted them off to me? I think not. I suspect that she also, in her own way, had long since buried that traumatic separation.

The events and the impressions of those early months and years in what was allegedly my own country are compressed now into a medley of sensation, much of it physical. There was the cold, which was beyond anything I would have thought possible. In the famously hard winter of 1947 the snow came in through the blitzed windows at Harley Street and lay in unmelting drifts on the stairs. Staying with relatives somewhere in the country, I used to creep into bed with all my clothes on. At my boarding school on the south coast you had to break the ice on the dormitory water jugs in the mornings before you could wash. I thought I would die of the cold: it would have been a merciful release.

This was England, then. But it bore no resemblance whatsoever to that hazy, glowing nirvana conjured up in the nostalgic chatter to which I had half listened back in Egypt. Back in the real world. Nobody had mentioned the cold. Or the rain. Or the London dirt, which was not the aromatic organic dirt of Egypt but a sullen pervasive grime which left your hands forever grey and every surface smeared with soot. In my mind I had created a place which seems like those now outdated advertisements for environmentally destructive products like petrol or cigarettes – all soft-focus landscape, immutable good weather, gambolling animals, and happy laughing folk. I had never seen such advertisements, and I suspect the image was based on Mabel Lucie Attwell illustrations spiced with Arthur Rackham and Beatrix Potter. Certainly I would not have been surprised to find toadstool houses and the odd gnome, or people wearing poke bonnets and pinnies. I might well have felt on home ground then – I had grown up with that kind of thing, in a sense.

What I was confronted with was something that was in no way soft-focus but disconcertingly precise. The weather was precise and inescapable, the topography was precise and daunting, what was expected of me was precise but coded. The gambolling animals had been turned into offal, and the happy laughing folk were transformed into the po-faced raincoated ranks at bus stops or on railway platforms. Moreover, all the others knew their way around. They had the maps and the passwords. They did not so much exude happiness or laughter as an implacable confidence. This was their place. They had wrapped it round them and pulled up the drawbridge.

I believe I have some idea of how the refugee feels, or the immigrant. Once, I was thus, or nearly so. I had concerned relatives, of course, and I spoke the language but I know what it is like to be on the outside, to be the one who cannot quite interpret what is going on, who is forever tripping over her own ignorance or misinterpretation. And all the while I carried around inside me an elsewhere, a place of which I could not speak because no one would know what I was talking about. I was a displaced person, of a kind, in the jargon of the day. And displaced persons are displaced not just in space but in time; they have been cut off from their own pasts. My ordeal was a pale shadow of the grimmer manifestations of this experience, but I have heard and read of these ever since with a heightened sense of what is implied. If you cannot revisit your own origins – reach out and touch them from time to time – you are forever in some crucial sense untethered.

I was used to a society in which people were instantly recognizable, defined by dress and appearance. An Egyptian could easily enough be distinguished from a European; someone who was English was unlike someone who was Greek. And the same was true here in England, it seemed, except that I could not see it. They all looked much the same to me, the raincoated London throngs. I could hear differences of speech, but these were confusing rather than illuminating. And the subtle code of appearance was quite beyond me. There were sartorial requirements which applied to me also, it seemed. You must never go out without gloves and an umbrella. Well, the umbrella made sense – but the gloves were purely symbolic, so far as I could see. They indicated what sort of person you were. They indicated what sort of home you came from and quite possibly vouched for your character as well, for all I knew. Where are your gloves? my grandmother would enquire on the Harley Street doorstep, kindly but sternly. And back inside I would have to go, to equip myself with my credentials before we could set forth.

And then there was the matter of the divorce. My parents had not split up, in the brisk and neutral phraseology of today; they were divorced, a word that reeked of taboo. I soon learned that the situation should not be mentioned, or at least mentioned only by adult relatives in an awkward undertone. At my boarding school there were very few other girls with divorced parents. The headmistress summoned me to a private interview and made it clear that my position was unfortunate but distinctly reprehensible, and the most expedient behaviour was to lie low about it.

I tried to hitch myself to this place in the most basic way. I tried to find my way around it. In Somerset I pottered in the lanes and fields, contentedly enough. In London I roamed about, alone for the most part. Sometimes my grandmother took me on excursions, and succeeded in transmitting to me something of her own partisan enthusiasm for the city she had lived in all her life. But she encouraged me also to take off on my own – sensibly enough, though this now seems a surprising indulgence. Perhaps London was a safer place for a loose teenager in those days than it is now. I rode buses hither and thither, collecting those differently coloured tickets – rose, lilac, buff, sixpence, ninepence, one and six – and learning how the place fitted together.

It was a landscape still scarred and pockmarked by the blitz. Houses leered from boarded windows or simply yawned with cavernous black rectangles. They dripped plaster and sprouted greenery. Paving stones would give way to a sudden wasteland of dirt and rubble. Railings were replaced by planks and lengths of rope. There were sudden eloquent gaps. A space in a terrace of houses where you would see ghostly staircases running up exposed walls, or a spine of cast-iron fireplaces with mantelpieces, and the unexpected intimacy of floral wallpaper. Or a sudden plunging hole filled with rubble and the jungle growth of buddleia and willow herb that had swarmed into the vacuum.

It seems now a long way from the London of today – a slow, scruffy, dirty place in which the traffic crept along sedately and you woke in the mornings to the sound of hoofs, the leisurely clop of the United Dairies pony, delivering the milk. Coal was shot down under the pavements, a sackful at a time – black treasure measured out into the grate lump by lump. At Harley Street there was the one fire in the consulting room, monopolized by Cousin Dorothy, and elsewhere frigid expanses, as cold as out of doors. Little hissing gas fires in the bedrooms, those brittle grey columns in front of which you could get your legs nicely scorched if you sat close enough. I would retreat to mine and find solace in a bar of Fry's chocolate and a book from the dust-covered glass-fronted bookcases in the drawing room. My grandmother was a devotee of Charlotte M. Yonge. I read *The Daisy Chain* and *The Heir of Redclyffe* from end to end, to oblige, with my knees scarlet and the back of me shivering. And Harrison Ainsworth and G. F. Henty and John Buchan, more fodder from the shelves in this new world where even the fiction was otherwise. No Arthur Ransome at Harley Street, and if there was any Greek mythology I never found it.

Friends and relations rallied round. There were theatre visits, lunches, and teas. I was posted off for weekend visits, clutching my railway ticket, correctly gloved, with my umbrella strapped to my suitcase. I must have been a dismaying guest – incongruously tall, like a bolted lettuce, socially inept, crippled by homesickness.

I no longer know which of these family friends it was who hit on the idea of taking me to see the heart of the city, the bomb-flattened area around Saint Paul's. He was someone who had developed an intense interest in the topographical history of the area and had discovered the way in which the bombs had stripped away the layers of time. He had taken to going down there, map in hand, to trace what was revealed. He suggested I come with him on one of these weekend excursions.

The place was deserted. Saint Paul's rose from a wasteland of rubble, cropped walls, and sunken lakes of pink willow herb. The effect was one not of destruction but of tranquil decay, like some ruined site of antiquity. Street signs tacked to surviving shreds of wall plotted the layout of the place: Cheapside, Bread Street, Watling Street. We wandered around, peering down into the willow herb lakes (DANGER! KEEP OUT!), inspecting the untidy little cliffs of walling, matching what we saw against my companion's street plan of the pre-war City. He also had a plan of the medieval boundary wall. He showed me how this was reflected in the street pattern. He gave me a genial history lesson, most of which I could not follow because what I knew of English history was confined to the patriotic rantings of *Our Island Story*, but I paid attention. I became distinctly interested. I floated free of the prison of my own discontents and enjoyed the fresh air of an abstract interest. I caught a glimpse of what it is like to have adult concerns. Look, said my companion, here is a stretch of the actual medieval wall, which must have been embedded within and beneath this blitzed building – look at the flint and ragstone. And then he led me to his *pièce de résistance*. Here, he said with triumph, here is a Roman bastion. This was one of the corners of the oldest wall of all, the original Roman wall.

Roman? *Roman*, had he said? But what did this mean? We had Romans down in Egypt. Had had Romans, time was. I knew about Romans. They came from Rome and Italy and surged all over Egypt and Palestine, building forts and temples and things which had fallen down but bits of which you could still see. They dropped their money everywhere: most of it was in the Alexandria museum. They built the Alexandria catacombs. They were responsible for Pontius Pilate. So how then could there be Romans right up here, in England?

I pondered this, staring at that unexceptional bit of wall. Evidently *Our Island Story*, in its potted hagiography of Boadicea, had not made it clear who it was she had been up against. Perhaps I asked my companion to explain matters. If so, I don't remember. What I do remember, with a clarity that is still exhilarating, is the sudden sense of relevances and connections which were mysterious and intriguing and could perhaps be exposed. That word 'Roman' chimed a note that was personal but was also, I realized, quite detached. Romans were to do with me because I had heard of them, but they were also to do with the significant and hitherto impenetrable mystique of grown-up preoccupations. It was as though the exposure of that chunk of wall had also shown up concealed possibilities. I sniffed the liberations of maturity and grew up a little more, there amid the wreckage of London and the seething spires of willow herb.

Anita Desai

[1937–]

Anita Desai was born Anita Mazumdar in Mussoorie, India. Her father was Bengali and her mother German, and Desai grew up speaking English, German and Hindi. English was, however, the first language in which she learned to write. In 1957 Desai received a BA in English literature from Miranda House, an élite college of Delhi University. After graduating, she spent a year working in Calcutta and then in 1958 she married Ashvin Desai, with whom she has four children.

Desai's first published work was a short story that appeared in an American children's magazine. Her first novel, *Cry, the Peacock* (1963), was praised by critics as lyrical and poetic. Desai's employment of stream-of-consciousness and the way she uses physical landscapes to reflect the psychic landscape of a tortured mind, invited comparisons with Virginia Woolf. In this novel, as in later works, Desai explores the psyche of an 'outsider' – someone who is ensnared by a society in which he or she does not belong. Desai's characters, both male and female, are often victims of their cultural environment, as in *Voices in the City* (1965), *Where Shall We Go This Summer?* (1975) and *In Custody* (1984). Both *In Custody* and *Clear Light of Day* (1980) were short-listed for the Booker Prize.

The themes of alienation and 'foreignness' figure strongly in *Bye-Bye, Blackbird* (1971), which tells of two Indian immigrants living in Britain. By creating one character who decides to remain in Britain and one who decides to return to India, Desai captures the ambiguity of being caught between two cultures. Indeed, Desai herself maintains a certain distance from India in her writing: 'I feel about India as an Indian,' she says, 'but I suppose I think about it as an outsider.' In 1988 she published *Baumgartner's Bombay*, which is written from the point of view of a German in India. He, like the majority of Desai's protagonists, suffers from a sense of alienation, and in this novel, as in her other works, Desai's prose skilfully maintains the tension of his unhappy and ultimately violent life.

In 1986 Desai was a visiting fellow at Girton College, Cambridge. Since then she has remained active in the academic world, dividing her time between Massachusetts, England and India. From 1987 to 1989 she taught at Smith College, and she later became a Purington Professor of English at Mount Holyoke College, Massachusetts. She is currently teaching in the creative writing programme at the Massachusetts Institute of Technology. Desai has published numerous essays, reviews and articles, and her latest novel is *Journey to Ithaca* (1995). She is the author of three children's books, one of which won the Guardian Award for children's fiction in 1982, and she has also published a short story collection, *Games at Twilight* (1978).

In the following section from Desai's novel Bye-Bye, Blackbird *we witness the two protagonists undergoing their comic and slightly surreal encounter with a hitherto imagined London. Desai explores the persistent and undeniably powerful mythology that a colonial centre imposes upon its 'peripheral' subjects.*

From *Bye-Bye, Blackbird*

Riding on the top of the 139, right up in front with only a sheet of glass to separate them from the blue-grey waves of London, they rode, they swam, like porpoises, through the city between banks of clay-red brick walls. Adit, assuming familiarity with it all, assuming the disinterest of a native of the city, lowered his head into the Country Properties column of *The Times*, but Dev, his head aggressively uptilted, stared ahead, turned this way and that and confronted the Battersea power station with the eyes of a conquering soldier marching into Egypt. He had determined to be *blasé*, even contemptuous, for he had early found cynicism to be the easiest and safest of postures, but there were things in London – and the Battersea power station was the first of them– that threw him off his guard, shook him out of his normal attitude of cynical coolness and now, like an idolator catching sight of a renowned shrine, he raised his arms in an unconscious frenzy of excitement at the vision of the four great pillars, one at each corner of the massive grey temple of power, pouring vast billows of dark smoke into an empty, breathless sky.

Battersea, Battersea, Battersea power station! Words of worship roared inside his throat and when he opened his mouth a strangled sound came out to make Adit look up in amazement.

'What's the matter with you, *yar*?' he whispered, fiercely annoyed at such unsophisticated, such outrageous behaviour which so brazenly marked them as strangers, visitors, bumpkins even.

'What's the matter with *me*? Look there, *yar*, look at that – that building.'

'That's the Battersea power station,' Adit hissed.

'Ah, it must be the most magnificent sight in London! God, I'm sure the pyramids have nothing on it. Look at its bulk, look at the way it squats, square and weighty and unremovable on the ground. Look at those vast blank walls – like those of a secret vault of mighty emperors. Look at those towering chimney-stacks sending out the smoke of sacrificial fires. Can't you see the *puja* being conducted in its locked chambers, by priests in saffron robes and vestal maidens in white? Can't you see the great bonfire they've built inside and the herbs, the spices and magic potions they hurl into it? Can't you hear the clanging of great gongs and the blowing of long horns and singing of sweet hymns? I believe the electricity of London is generated by that sacrificial bonfire, right in the innermost heart of that temple. We ought to stand up and bow, Adit. We ought to kneel down and pray. We ought to sing out a hymn – the Vedic hymn to fire –' and, to Adit's agony, Dev began to intone, shrilly, in Sanskrit:

'*Produce thy streams of flames like a broad onslaught,*
Go forth impetuous like a king with his elephant.
Thou art an archer.
Shoot thy sorcerers with thy hottest arrows, O Agni, send forth
  thy heat, thy winged flames . . .'

'Chelsea Bridge!' sang out the conductor. 'Chelsea Bridge!'
Rain on Sunday. Damp raincoats swinging from the gallows in the

corner, wet umbrellas bleeding into a bucket. Electric heaters glaring red like inflamed eyes. Sunday papers littering the floor. Sarah expressionlessly following the thundering vacuum cleaner about. Adit sitting immobile in front of the television screen. Smell of rain, fish, mildew and mud.

'You must be masochists to live in this climate,' declares Dev, for his eyes are burning, his head exploding after an endless morning of reading close print on thin paper and seeing the shadows flicker across the shivering screen. 'Masochists. What a climate, what a stinking climate.'

Adit suddenly jerked into life, joyfully suggests, 'Make a bonfire to the great god Agni. Go on, go to Battersea power station and offer up your flannel underwear, your knitted socks. Ask Agni to send us heat.'

Laurel Lane. To begin with this is Dev's London – the small side lane banked with its brick-walled houses, partly obscured by privet hedges, by lines of washing and, now and then, a creeper of crimson roses or a bush of azaleas as delicate, as fine and airy as a host of pink and white butterflies hovering over a garden gate. In the small pebbly gardens and on narrow pavements, an occasional abandoned toy wagon or garden rake, but rarely an owner of these objects, rarely any human attachment. Lives lived in Laurel Lane are indoor lives. Occasionally a door opens, a stout and chinless matron in a flowered dress and an old cardigan appears with a tub of washing under one arm and clothes pegs stuck in her mouth like outsize teeth, or a younger woman comes out to wheel a sleeping child in its pram. There is a certain hour every afternoon – so Dev has noticed on his indoor days – when Mr Yogi's ice-cream van drives up, playing a gay little tune to summon the children of Laurel Lane. Then, even in wet and freezing weather, an astonishing number of junior citizens explode into the lane, clutching their pennies, to buy ices of great variety in colour. Rough children they look, with patched clothes and dirty boots, but with what fresh faces, what achingly red cheeks and bright, alive eyes – National Health Service children, brought up on free orange juice and good milk, and with money to spare for Mr Yogi's ices.

But Dev is rarely there to watch the appearance and disappearance of this Pied Piper of ices and Laurel Lane remains, to him, a place of shut doors and curtained windows. Spidery aerials perched on rooftops like ritual totem poles are evidence of television sets by the dozen, but never a sound does he hear from them. He does not hear his neighbours – their radios, their quarrels, their children are all kept behind closed doors.

'Now if this were India,' he explodes one dull day, standing at the window, 'I would by now know all my neighbours – even if I had never spoken to them. I'd know their taste in music by the sound of their radios. I'd know the age of their child by the sound of its howling. I'd know if the older children were studying for exams by the sound of lessons being recited. I'd know what food they ate by the smells of their cooking. I'd know which men quarrelled with their wives, which mothers-in-law beat their daughters-in-law – everything. If I lived on a road like this in Calcutta, I would be aware – as aware as can be – of everyone around me. But not here. Here everyone is a stranger and lives in hiding. They live silently and invisibly. It would happen nowhere in India.'

'That must be nice,' said Sarah wistfully, strangely for she had never struck Adit or Dev as being a neighbourly or even curious person. But somehow the picture Dev has coloured for her – bright, verbal crayons sweeping across the black-and-white of the well-known page – appeals to her.

'It isn't,' growled Adit. 'It's bloody noisy and dirty and smelly.'

'But alive,' Sarah protests.

'And this isn't. Or it wouldn't be if it weren't for the pets. There are always the pets,' Dev muses at the window.

The canary in the brightest window, its brass cage sparkling with the freshest polish. Even the most nondescript dog has the brisk air of confidence which is born of the certainty of a good dinner at home, and almost always there is a concerned and affectionate human being at the other end of the leash, sometimes even making human noises at it. But the ones that really captivate Dev – although he will not admit it – are the cats, larger than any he has seen before, fluffed out in billows of fine hair, stalking sedately, royally down the garden paths to settle in a patch of sun on the walls, and serenely – with only the faintest expression of curiosity, subtly dissembled – watch the world go by. They are Bustopher Jones, Deuteronomy and Jennyanydots in person. They do not dart away at his approach, as he is used to having cats do, nor do they glare discouragingly down their noses at his overtures, but look up inquisitively, almost inviting a pat and a bit of conversation about the fine weather, unalarmed and comfortable in the eiderdown furriness. Nothing lean or scarred mars this golden landscape and so captivated is Dev that he cannot bear to speak of it – at least no more than to admit grudgingly, 'Of course they do keep pets. I know which houses keep what pets.'

Dev ventures into the city. He descends, deeper and deeper, into the white-tiled bowels of Clapham tube station. Down into the stark caverns artificially lit, by way of long, ringing staircases where draughts sweep icily up and down and yet leave the underground airless, suffocating. The menacing slither of escalators strikes panic into a speechless Dev as he is swept down with an awful sensation of being taken where he does not want to go. Down, down and farther down – like Alice falling, falling down the rabbit hole, like a Kafka stranger wandering through the dark labyrinth of a prison. On the platform, with blank lights glaring at the cold white tiles all around he stands fearfully with his fellow travellers and darts horrified glances at the strange look these people, who had seemed natural enough in the sunlight of High Street, have acquired in these subterranean depths. Here in the underground their faces have become withdrawn, preoccupied, and are tinged with an unearthly, martian green, their movements are grown furtive and their voices – on the few occasions when they do speak out – chill him with their hollow, clanging harshness. In a panic he throws himself into the tube that has come slipping in like a long worm, and is carried off by it, hurtling through black tunnels in which the air is choked with soot and cinders and the very air is black as in a tomb. Dev is swamped inkily, with a great dread of being caught, stuck in the underground by some accident, some collapse, and being slowly suffocated to a worm's death, never to emerge into freshness and light.

He does emerge, to his amazement, into the most natural freshness and light of Leicester Square – its little park ringed with tulips and green benches on which old men sit, under early summer foliage, reading their papers and scattering crumbs to fat, overfed pigeons. Exhilarated as a man snatched back from the tomb, he walks off, staring at the posters over the theatre doors, advertising plays he has so far only read of but now can actually walk in and see – a miracle that quite unsettles him.

But twice that day he is to relive the experience of delving into the tunnels of London's grim earth and of emerging into the radiance of natural light. In the galleries of the Tate he stumbles upon his own horror of the underground in Sutherland's crazed, dark, blood-stained visions. In considerable agitation, he tries to keep his voice down as he falters, 'Look. Look, Sen, that is what I mean, that is what I was talking about.'

Adit, fearing another pagan outburst as he had suffered on the bus, tells him sternly, 'Those were drawn in wartime, don't you know, when the tubes were used as bomb shelters.'

Stammering with the effort of maintaining his dignity, Dev insists, 'They are no different now,' and he is able to breathe only when Adit leads him into a gallery illuminated with the rosy, noontime visions of the Impressionists.

Similarly, at the National Gallery after walking, awed and subdued past the sombre and gigantic Tintorettos, El Grecos and Titians – all so mighty, so perfect and immense as to seem to be the handiwork not of human beings but of great, solemn gods – he stumbles, once more, upon the Impressionists. Adit watches uneasily as his face is illuminated by reflection. Taking care to speak only in a curt, almost grudging tone which will not betray his perfectly childish sense of joy and liberty, he says it as though a window of a medieval castle has been flung wide open all at once and, in a flash, the grey dawn is over and it is high noon!

'Don't make so much noise,' Adit hisses, 'the attendant is looking at us.'

Giving him a furious look, Dev is happy to walk off alone and revel, without any fear of betraying himself, in the delight of seeing the originals of what he has so far only seen reproductions. He is not so much discovering those well-known South of France landscapes, the greens and oranges of Cézanne, the corn fields and olive trees of Van Gogh, and the muscular ballet girls of Degas in their ethereal tutus, as recognising them. He stands comparing the yellows of the original sunflowers to those in the print hanging on his wall at home when Adit comes up, a little reassured by his quiet behaviour.

'That Renoir,' begins Dev.

'Pronounced Ren-wah, old boy.'

'Renoir,' insists Dev, 'I've seen his pictures in books and they only looked like chocolate box-tops to me. But those ones, they're not, they're not at all –'

'I should think not,' cries Adit indignantly, hastily glancing over his shoulder to see if anyone has overheard this piece of heresy, and then they both gaze in silence at the rays that dripped from Renoir's brush as from the crystals of a chandelier. The dancers are as rosy as he had known they would be but not, he is joyful to see, with paint but with rich blood and good health and he believes he can almost hear their castanets and their tambourines. He has been reading *Renoir My Father* on the boat to England and he is able to inform Adit, proudly, that she is Gabrielle the maid, in one of the many costumes the painter kept for his models. 'She used to cook and wash and mind the babies in his house,' he is able to inform Adit. Now he has met her, the original, and she is smiling and blushing and he can hear the silks of her skirts rustle. Everywhere there is this joyful, magnificent light, like the first advent of light upon earth.

As they go out, reluctantly, Dev allows himself a groan. 'How will I ever go back to looking at prints after this?'

'There's always Shantiniketan,' says Adit, making Dev growl with discontent.

Out in grey-blue Trafalgar Square, they stand at the foot of Nelson's column amongst the fountains. Everything about them is in the colours of a gay-necked pigeon's feathers. The buildings are slate grey, the sky blue-grey, the shadows deep and violet. The fountains spout and sparkle about the grey column and the grey lions, and the spoilt, overfed pigeons tumble above the welter of red umbrellas and blue mackintoshes. Red buses rumble down grey streets and, here and there, at the foot of tall grey pillars or on quiet grey window-sills, stand tubs of pink and blue hydrangeas. At the corners are stands where Dev buys bright postcards with pictures in red and blue.

By the time they find their way to Lyons Corner House for lunch, it is drizzling. In the rain the smile of da Vinci's St Anne lingers, lingers like a wisp of mist, grey-blue and tender.

Suddenly Adit said, 'Why go home already? Let's be devils and do the Victoria and Albert as well, Dev. I want to show you the best collection of Moghul and Rajasthan miniatures there is. And the Kangras –'

'Don't be funny. Do you think I've come to London to see Indian paintings?' snaps Dev, and looks out of the window where St Anne's smile wavers in the rain.

Adit sighs and helps himself to more potatoes.

Christopher Hope
[1944–]

Christopher Hope was born in Johannesburg, South Africa, and was educated at the universities of Witwatersrand and Natal. He worked as a journalist in Durban before leaving for London in 1975. In 1971 he and Mike Kirkwood had privately printed their collection *Whitewashes*, but Hope's first major publication of poetry was *Cape Drives* (1974). This volume focuses on the ambiguous position of the white, English-speaking minority in South Africa and includes 'The Flight of the White South Africans', an elegy to Hope's native land and to the people he would be leaving behind. Hope received the Thomas Pringle Prize in 1972 and the Cholmondeley Award for Poetry in 1974.

Cape Drives was followed by *In the Country of the Black Pig* (1981) and the long poem *Englishmen* (1985). By this time, Hope had developed a reputation for his deft mixture of the comic and tragic, and for his ability to expose the absurdity of the South African racial system without trivializing it. His first novel, *A Separate Development* (1980), received the David Higham Prize for Fiction and was temporarily banned in South Africa. In 1985 Hope won the Whitbread Prize for Fiction for *Kruger's Alp* (1984), a darkly humorous allegory that parodies Bunyan's *Pilgrim's Progress* to examine the abuses of power in South Africa. His 1986 novel, *The Hottentot Room*, provides a bleak vision of exile, as South African expatriates and a German-Jewish refugee whose former husband was a Nazi face corruption and moral dilemmas in a London club. Hope's last work to directly address South African issues is the autobiographical *White Boy Running* (1988), in which he acknowledges that the concept of going 'overseas' was preferable to his growing disenchantment, 'akin to losing a form of religious faith', with South Africa. His novel *Serenity House* (1992) is a satire of modern life in England and the United States, merging the unlikely settings of Florida's Magic Kingdom, Poland's Auschwitz and a home for the elderly in London's Highgate. It was short-listed for the Booker Prize in 1992. Hope is also the author of *My Chocolate*

Redeemer (1989) and the travel commentary *Moscow! Moscow!* (1990),
which won a PEN Award.

Hope's work has been included in a number of anthologies and he has
been published in many magazines and journals, among them the *New
York Times*, the *Times Literary Supplement*, and *London Magazine*. In
addition to his novels and poems, he has written travel commentary,
children's books and plays for radio and television. Hope is a regular
reviewer for the BBC and various newspapers and periodicals, and he
lectures and reads internationally for the British Council. His latest
novel, *Darkest England*, was published in 1996.

In the following extract from Hope's comic novel Darkest England,
*David Mungo Booi, a native of black Africa, is chosen by a conclave of
elders to explore England as a site suitable for settlement and to assess if
the natives are friendly and agreeable. In this satire of the literature of
exploration, the violence of modern British life, as well as the absurdity
of its many rituals, is seen through the eyes of Hope's fictional hero.*

From *Darkest England*

It was an awesome journey, that expedition into the heart of London.
As you travel you might be like the even tinier creatures who live on
a water-spider, floating haphazardly down a stream. You feel you are
in the world as it was in its primeval beginnings. Every so often we
would stop at stations and a group of young warriors, male and
female, would board in a kind of explosion, a whirl of white limbs, a
mass of hands clapping, of feet stamping, of bodies swaying, of eyes
rolling.

I was delighted to have a chance to note the peculiar characteristics of the natives as we rolled slowly southward. The females are
notable for the small development of the mammary organs. Few
have small waists. Both sexes pierce their ears. Some of the young
warriors cut their hair, as do those of the peace tribe, so that it
commands their heads like an axe-blade, which they colour with a
variety of strong hues. Often they employ scarification, and amongst

the most popular of the clan-marks is a stippled line along the temporal lobes from the external edges of the eyebrows to the middle of the cheeks or the lower jaws.

With each stop, a fresh invasion. The chants went up anew, and I felt as if prehistoric man was cursing us, praying to us, welcoming us – who could tell? Their cries were incomprehensible. My friend interpreted for me, saying that some commented on the failures of the French, or the deformities of foreigners generally.

I should not be in the least bit afeared, as this was a perfectly normal practice – bands of sport lovers travelling abroad to support their country.

Love of country among these young men was unashamed, as they repeatedly chanted the beloved name of their sceptred isle, which they pronounced with a curious double beat, accentuating both syllables, ENG-LAND! ENG-LAND! Many carried flags. Not only was the proud standard waved at every opportunity, but many of them had made clothes of the national emblem and wore it as a shirt, or as a scarf or even as trousers. Some flew the flag on the tips of their stout black boots, or had tattooed tiny flaglets on each knuckle. One fine young buck, clearly a super-patriot, had emblazoned the beloved red, white and blue on his shaven skull, and the precious emblem flew wonderfully against the granite gleam of bone. Another had taken matters a step further and, perhaps because he was a great singer, he bellowed out 'God Save the Queen' in a rough baritone, showing, as he did so, that each of his teeth had been stained red, white and blue. This display of what we might call dental patriotism impressed me deeply.

None the less, I had to confide in my mentor that the sight left me secretly appalled, as a sane man would be before an enthusiastic outbreak in the madhouse.

On catching sight of me, they became very excited. Some leaped from their seats, lifting their arms and scratching in their armpits as if troubled by furious itching; some threw monkey nuts in an artillery barrage of shells, ending with a large banana which struck me on the forehead to the accompaniment of loud cheers. They howled, they leapt and spun and made horrid faces. Ugly? Yes, it was ugly enough, but I felt in me a faint response to the terrible frankness of that noise. It was something that we, so far from the night of the First Ages, find so hard to comprehend, that someone from another part of the world should be traditionally saluted with fruit and nuts.

Good Farebrother, seeing my perplexity, assured me that it was all quite normal, really, a regular occurrence, I should not mistake ceremonial displays of aggression for anything more than healthy high spirits. It was not a war they were preparing for, but a sporting ritual. Certainly I need have no fear for myself, since bloodshed was something they generally preferred to pursue abroad, and, wishing to reassure me of this, he now waved and smiled at the young people.

Perhaps this was not helpful, for the crowd began to take a closer interest in my episcopal companion. One young brave, his hair closely shaved, who had until then been preoccupied with the task of carving his name, DARREN, into the seats with a sharpened screwdriver, now tapped the ex-Bishop on the chest and, indicating his lovely purple frock, demanded to know if he were the Pope. The question accompanied by a large wink at his mates, indicating, I felt sure, that here was a sign of that fabled English humour.

The good Farebrother responded equally gaily with a gentle smile that he was Not Guilty! That, to the contrary, he was Church of England, Eng-Land!, giving to the name of his country just the same double emphasis as the young warriors had done, showing that he was emphatically of their kind.

Unfortunately, the joke did not now, as I had expected, lead to general laughter and good humour all round. Not at all. Hearing the word 'Pope', the others began chorusing their desire to perform sexual intercourse with the Pope, whom I took to be some person who inspired deep physical desire in Englishmen. That the young fellows were aroused seemed clear. Calling repeatedly for carnal relations with this Pope person, they grunted, whistled, stamped their feet and brandished their colours; I saw flags in the air, flags in their hair, flags on their fingers and flags on their toes. In this way they arrived at such a state of sexual excitation that some began tearing up the seats and throwing them across the carriage; others began pelting us with coins, and all the time they gave out this curious greeting or salute, perhaps an unconscious expression of their physical erections; that is to say, they lifted stiff arms before their chests and pointed their fingers into the air, as if to suggest the direction from which they expected this longed-for Pope to appear.

I was fascinated. Why, I asked my friend, were these people so filled with desire for the Pope? Did they love him?

On the contrary, came the astonishing reply. They hated him.

Then why did they wish to lie with him?

I had misunderstood the subtleties of the language, said the Bishop, rising from his seat as the missiles rained down on us, and urging me towards the door. The good old Anglo-Saxon expression used did, indeed, refer to coitus, but it was also synonymous with the desire to destroy.

Alas, we were forced to abandon this fascinating etymological discussion, for several coins had struck the Bishop about the head and he was bleeding into his white collar. Seizing my hand, he pulled me into the safety of the corridor, and we beat a retreat to the far end of the train, and locked ourselves in a lavatory.

It was later – oh, so much later – that I remembered, too late, my suitcase and its gifts for the Sovereign. I comforted myself a little with the hope that they might at least be bestowed, by these seeming admirers, on His Majesty the Pope.

And very much later, when I told the good Bishop of my loss, he consoled me by saying that the star-stones at least were safe in his keeping.

We spent the rest of the journey to the capital in the lavatory. I did my best to staunch his bleeding, while he told me how very shocked he had been by such behaviour on what he called his home turf. Sad was a word he used. As well as setback. And scandal. It was also really most unusual. Normally these young people reserved that sort of behaviour for trips abroad.

But they had seemed to be enjoying themselves, I suggested.

This saddened him further. I must be careful not to give way to unwarranted cynicism. We had been exposed to the hooligan element, a tiny hard core of thugs, who were not representative of the great mass of ordinary, decent sports lovers. These sorts of people not only brought the national pastime into disrepute but dragged the country down to a level one was more accustomed to expecting from less civilized people. Still, we must look on the bright side. I had been taught several useful lessons about the patriotism of the young. Having seen what fate awaited the Pope, I could imagine the treatment I would receive if these young patriots took against me. My training in Little Musing had given me the outlines of the camouflage needed if ever I was to travel safely in England. Now the time had come to put a London gloss on the good work.

Shiva Naipaul
[1945–85]

Shiva Naipaul was born in Port of Spain, Trinidad. His childhood was spent with his mother and five sisters, as his father died when he was seven years old and his older brother, the writer V. S. Naipaul, was living in London. Like his brother before him, Shiva Naipaul won a scholarship to Oxford. The journey to England marked Naipaul's first experience of physical dislocation. Later, he would call all travel 'a form of gradual self-extinction'.

Naipaul studied Chinese at Oxford. In 1967 he married Jenny Stuart, with whom he later had a son, Tarun. He began to write his first novel in 1968, his final year at university. Three years later, his completed manuscript was published as *Fireflies* (1971), an accomplished debut that won the John Llewellyn Rhys Memorial Prize, the Winifred Holtby Memorial Prize and the Jock Campbell New Statesman Award. *Fireflies* explores the plight of second- and third-generation Indian immigrants, and the loss of ethnic and cultural identity that characterizes their changing relationship with the Indian communities. Like his second novel, *The Chip-Chip Gatherers* (1973), for which Naipaul won the Whitbread Literary Award, *Fireflies* is set in Trinidad. In both works, Naipaul expresses ambivalent feelings towards his country of birth and the often rigid structure of the Indian family.

The books that followed cover similar themes of class structure, racial tension and physical and emotional dislocation. Both *North of South: An African Journey* (1978) and *Black and White* (1980; later published as *Journey to Nowhere: A New World Tragedy*) investigate the social and political situation of post-colonial Africa and Guyana. In the novel *A Hot Country* (1983; later published as *Love and Death in a Hot Country*) Naipaul creates the country of Cuyama, a fictional amalgam of his observations of Africa and Guyana.

In 1984 he published *Beyond the Dragon's Mouth*. This book, like the posthumously published *An Unfinished Journey* (1986), is a collection of short stories and essays that reflects Naipaul's career as a writer of fiction and a traveller. His career was cut tragically short when Naipaul died of a heart attack in 1985.

A generation after his brother's arrival in London, Shiva Naipaul describes in the following extract from Beyond the Dragon's Mouth *the same district of London, Earls Court, this time through avowedly 'post-colonial' eyes. Unlike his older brother, who still clung to many of the romantic visions that condition the colonial's point of view, Shiva Naipaul sees little beyond the filth and grime, and has a thinly disguised contempt for the multicultural plurality of London.*

Living in Earls Court

I have had the dubious distinction of having lived in Earls Court twice: once (for which I should be excused) right at the beginning when I had only just arrived in England; then again right at the end (when I should have known better) just before I left for India. On both occasions departure was a cause for celebration. I was never happy in Earls Court. The account I shall give of it, therefore, cannot be free from the bias that unhappiness necessarily entails. I view Earls Court through the jaundiced eyes of an ingrained dislike; and where others might see a raffish charm I see only a kind of horror. However, my prejudice should not be interpreted as an implied distaste for London as a whole. That is not the case. I have also lived in Notting Hill Gate, Stockwell, Fulham and Ladbroke Grove. In none of these areas – including Earls Court – did I stay longer than a year. Thus the experience derived from each tend to fuse into a single, indivisible history. On their own they are disjointed fragments. Earls Court is merely an episode – or rather, two episodes.

I was nineteen years old when I left Trinidad to come as a student to England. Coming as I did from the far outside, it was natural that I should think of London as existing in the round. Discrimination did of course develop later on. Ladbroke Grove, Notting Hill Gate, Earls

Court . . . I began to appreciate that they all harboured their own peculiar vibrations. But, at the time, London was simply London: the Big City of which I had always dreamt.

For a few days immediately after I arrived I stayed with my brother in a hotel in Blackheath. The hotel was inhabited chiefly by the middle-aged and solitary. Memories of Blackheath are tinged with the semi-magical quality which invests the week of my arrival: the impression of fantasy – of unreal things happening in an unreal world – was strong. There was a visit to the Observatory at Greenwich. A white line painted on the floor of a light-washed room: the meridian. I remember standing on a grassy hill and looking down at the silver sweep of the Thames knitted with a spidery fretwork of cranes and ships' masts. In a restaurant I ate my first rum-baba.

But the magic soon faded. The polite rituals of the hotel functioned in a void. I began to feel isolated in Blackheath. It seemed an infinity away from what I fondly imagined to be the centre of things. Where that was I had no clear idea. Neither could I say with any certainty what I expected to find when I got there. The pink glow kindling the sky nightly promised adventure. I wished to draw closer to the fiery source producing it. The Big City was beckoning.

Finally I saw a room advertised at a price I could just afford. I rang the number supplied. It turned out to be an Accommodation Agency. Was the room they had advertised still available? Unfortunately no. However – the lady's voice tinkled encouragingly at the other end of the line – they had several like it on their books. Why did I not come to their office?

The office, a cramped cubicle approached up a tortuous flight of stairs, was on the Earls Court Road. A wiry woman in a luminously red cardigan was in charge. I introduced myself.

'Ah! So you are the foreign gentleman who rang earlier.' Her voice had shed its telephonic twinkle. But it was not unfriendly. 'Come in and have a seat and we shall see what we can do for you. We have managed to fix up quite a few coloured people in our time.' She moved briskly to a paper-cluttered desk and sat down. 'Now you say you can't afford more than five pounds a week . . .'

'Maximum,' I said quickly.

'Quite, quite . . . mmm . . .' She thumbed through a box of index cards. 'Student?' she enquired absently after a while.

'Yes.'

'Studying what?'

I told her. The words sounded impossibly big and foolish.

'Really!' Extracting an index card she frowned thoughtfully at it. She reached for the telephone and dialled. 'Some of these landladies are a bit fussy when it comes to . . .' She reverted to her telephonic twinkle. 'Hello. Is that Mrs—? This is the — Accommodation Agency here. I've got a young foreign student who is looking for a room. He seems a nice quiet fellow. What's that? Yes, I'm afraid he is. But . . . no, no. Not at all. Of course I understand.' The receiver clicked down. She considered me. 'Next time I think we'll say straight off that you come from India. It's better not to beat around the bush, don't you agree? Anyway some of them don't mind Indians so much.'

'But I don't come from India.'

'You don't?' She stared at me. 'But you look Indian.'

'Well, I am Indian. But I was born in the West Indies.'

'The West Indies!' She seemed vaguely aghast.

I understood. Sufficient unto any man the handicap of being straightforwardly Indian or straightforwardly West Indian. But to contrive somehow to combine the two was a challenge to reason. An Indian from the West Indies! I was guilty of a compound sin.

'We'll say you are Indian,' she said firmly. 'It's better not to confuse the issue. Don't you agree?' She beamed at me.

'Perhaps we'd better forget the whole thing,' I said.

'Don't give up so easily. We have fixed up a lot of coloured people in our time. Why not you?' She gazed defiantly at the box of index cards.

This was my initiation in the sub-world of 'racial prejudice'. I had read and heard about it at home: nearly everyone who had been to England had his own cautionary tale to tell. Now it was happening to me and I could not quite bring myself to believe in it. Of course I had noticed the slogans daubed on the walls of the tube stations, and morbidly deciphered the illiteracies displayed in the windows of newsagents. 'Room to Let: Regret no Kolored.' 'Room to Let: European Gent. Only.' 'Room to let: Kolored Pipple Need Not Apply.' These signs depressed and amused. It seemed incredible that they should refer to me.

I was surprised to find myself categorized as 'coloured': in Trinidad the term is applied to people of mixed blood – usually black diluted with a dash of 'European'. I have always thought it a detestable euphemism. Nevertheless, since it was one of the basic words in the vocabulary of the boarding-house culture, I had (albeit under protest) to learn to live with it.

I waited while the lady dialled number after number. '. . . I've got a young Indian student here who is looking for a room . . .' Her eyes were clouding with exhaustion. I stopped listening. Then, out of the blue: 'Yes. Yes. As I said, he seems a nice, quiet type. I shall send him around straight away. He's right here with me in the office.' She put the receiver down and regarded me with an air of triumph. 'I told you we could fix you up. Didn't I?'

The house to which I was directed was on one of those streets that lead off the Earls Court Road and blossom into the sudden respectability of a tree-shaded garden square. A roster of names, each with its attendant buzzer, festooned the door. This was bedsitter land with a vengeance. The entrance hall smelled dismally of a mixture of disinfectant and polish. Keys jangling from a giant ring at her waist, the housekeeper led me up several curving flights of red-carpeted stairs towards the twilit region of the top floor. With jailer-like neutrality, she ushered me into a charmless cell, obviously the product of sub-division of what must once have been an average-sized room. An insubstantial hardboard partition, plastered over with a flowery wallpaper, rose with grim commercial finality to the ceiling. The furnishing was spartan: a narrow bed; a dresser with a mirror; a solitary, soiled armchair; a coffee table emblematically ringed with the marks of countless hot cups. The floor was covered by a strip of grey, threadbare carpet. Daylight filtered through a small sash window. A gas fire, inserted into a scorched recess, completed the desolation. This was not how I imagined it would be. The harshness of that room repelled me. Was this the romance of the city? What kind of adventure could spring from a cell such as this? At five guineas a week (without breakfast) it was more than I could really afford. But the prospect of starting from scratch ('. . . I've got a young Indian student here . . .') was equally intimidating. Despairingly, I said I would take it. The Accommodation Agency duly extorted its tribute of a week's rent, and I moved in.

It was an introduction – which could have been gentler – into a new mode of existence. Since then I have lost count of the number of rooms in which I have slept. In Trinidad my geography was stable: I can recall no more than two or three rooms in the course of my nineteen years there. That cell in Earls Court initiated a nomadism which has persisted into the present and which shows no signs of abating. It has become second nature to me. Today, my attachment to Trinidad is sentimental; a child's attachment to the place where he grew up. It does not go beyond that because my real life lies elsewhere – though precisely where it is difficult to say. In London, the vestigial Trinidadian 'roots' I had arrived with underwent a gradual petrification. But the city, while exacting its price, did not confer a new identity: I do not consider myself a Londoner. On a conventional assessment this must be counted as a loss. Yet, on the other hand, it ought to be added that I am not bothered by it. I have no desire either to fabricate new 'roots' or rediscover old ones. Lack of acquaintance has diminished to vanishing point my knowledge of what it means and feels like to 'belong' to a community. This is why I regard with nervous suspicion all those who proclaim its virtues in poetry, prose and politics.

The three weeks I spent in that room are among the unhappiest I can remember. A dreadful anonymity descended. In the mornings I went to the nearby Wimpy Bar where I drank several cups of coffee and pretended to be absorbed in the newspaper. At midday I went to a dark, dingy pub frequented by elderly charladies who drank bottled Guinness. I would buy a pint of bitter and a plate of cheese

and tomato sandwiches. In the evening I went to a coffee bar manned
by Italians, where I bought more sandwiches and drank more coffee.
Through the plate-glass windows I would watch the life of Earls
Court stream past. Then I would return to my cell and crawl into my
narrow bed. I hardly ever saw my fellow inmates whose names
decorated the front door. Two girls shared the room across the
corridor. They would come in late, creaking furtively up the stairs
and laughing softly. As they prepared for bed I could hear the
surreptitious sounds of pop music from their record player – the
house forbade anything of the sort after eleven o'clock. Next door –
behind the partition – was a man who coughed terribly. Some nights,
when he was especially racked, he would get up and pace the room,
muttering to himself in between his spasms. Once I met the girls in
the corridor but we passed without acknowledgement. Amazingly
enough, I never set eyes on my cough-stricken neighbour.

The days slipped by in a haze of coffee, stale sandwiches and sickly
beer. The visits I had planned – to palaces, museums, art galleries –
were never made. I had become frightened of the city and my fright
expressed itself in dulled curiosity and inertia. The glow lighting the
sky nightly was transformed from a promise into a threat. I lost the
desire to seek out its hidden source. My family to whom I had bid
goodbye not that long ago seemed to belong to another life which
had been snatched away from me. Hourly, Trinidad receded. I was
being emptied; reduced to nothing in that room. How easy it is to be
swallowed by the city! The legacy left by that time has not entirely
vanished. Even now, I occasionally experience a thrill of fear when I
suddenly come upon one of the dizzying vistas of anonymous urban
housing and have to walk along streets that are like mirror
reflections of each other. Though it was not what my innocence had
envisaged, those three weeks were an adventure. But the adventure
exists only in retrospect: at the time I was not even fully conscious of
my misery.

Six years later – and under very different circumstances – I returned
to Earls Court. Much had happened to me in the intervening period:

I had completed an undistinguished four years at Oxford; I had acquired a wife; I had written my first novel. My boyhood was over. Something else had happened: my attitude to the city had altered. I had lost the desire to lay bare its secrets. Perhaps I had stopped believing there were any secrets to be laid bare. When I arrived in Earls Court for the second time it was my fourth change of address in two years. By then nomadism had become a habit. Shifting restlessly from one set of furnished rooms to another, I was living, in a sense, like a vagrant. The city was merely a convenient backdrop for my activities. While being in it I was not truly of it. No doubt writing and the private world it entails assisted in the process of withdrawal and detachment. I was leading an artificial and protected existence. Matters might have been difficult if I had been forced to earn my living in the ordinary way. As it was, I had little direct contact with the life lived around me. I observed, as it were, through glass.

Whether by day or by night, Earls Court knows no stillness; no moments of tranquillity. The big lorries thunder ceaselessly. On the Earls Court Road noise acquires a demonic quality, endowing the constant flow with an autonomous, impersonal character. Step out of your front door and the reverberating thunder breaks loose like a dammed wall of water obtaining release. The air is a soup of diesel oil and petrol fumes, rank and acrid to the taste. Have a window cleaned and within hours a mildewed sediment will spread like mould across the glass. It is the industrial equivalent of the encroaching jungle. Puny men, trapped in this tide, can meet sudden death. The drama unfolds with the rigidity of a sacrificial ritual: a screech of brakes; the peculiar thud of unyielding metal on soft human flesh; a pool of blood staining the asphalt; the chorus wail of a police siren. Early the next morning a truck of the Royal borough will arrive and wash away the lingering traces of the sacrifice into the gutter. The God has been appeased.

The tube station is the soul of the place made visible. Around and about it Earls Court anchors itself. Out of it is disgorged and into it is ingested a steady stream of humanity. A multi-hued, multi-lingual crowd is always gathered near its entrance. Earls Court is nothing if not cosmopolitan. Long-haired students from the Continent weighted under rucksacks studded with the flags of their countries pore over street maps. Bearded Australians study the poster that invites them to join the Zambesi Club – Rhodesians, South Africans, New Zealanders and Canadians also welcome. West Indians – lithe black bucks dressed in the height of fashion – parade aimlessly. A shrunken veteran of the First World War, a hat upturned at his feet, scrapes at a violin. Another ferrety old man, half-asleep on a box, clutches in his lap a stack of weeklies from the 'underground' press. Waking with a start, he holds aloft *The Red Mole*; and then, just as abruptly, his hand falls and he relapses back into slumber. The flower sellers (who would buy flowers in Earls Court?) sprinkle water on their wilting exhibits. From the hamburger joint not many yards away throbs a delirium of pop music. Hippie-clad young men and women swagger in and out. Those of the tribe who congregate in Earls Court have a tough vacancy of expression: they represent the fag end of that particular dream of gentleness.

The elemental necessities are available in abundance. The Accommodation Agencies and the proliferating cheap hotels will always be able to provide you with a roof above your head; the gaudy constellation of cheap eating places will always provide you with food to fill your stomach; and, satisfying another need, the army of prostitutes – male as well as female – will always provide you with the cheap solace of their bodies. Watch the group of men, not all of whom are old and mackintoshed, assembled round the window of the newsagent and intently perusing the quaintly worded cards which are mixed in with blandishments to join overland trips to Australia and South Africa. 'Grounded Air Hostess Seeks New Position.' 'Chocolate Baby Teaches French. Very Strict.' 'Handsome Young Man Willing to Walk Dog.' Numbers are hastily jotted down on scraps of paper and the prospective client slips discreetly away in search of a telephone booth. With a quiet shuffle those at the rear shoulder forward. These havens of sexual delight are usually on the Warwick Road. I have often wandered along that bleak strip where, behind the drawn curtains of dank basements, passion is so easily bought and expended.

At dusk, on certain evenings, a fresh performer joins the circus. The hoarse orator of the World Socialist Party exhorts his handful of listeners to overthrow the exploiters and establish the universal brotherhood of man. In Earls Court his message falls on stony ground. In that chaos there are no allegiances. A man leans against a lamppost being sick. No one pays him any attention. Two women stagger along the pavement in the middle of the afternoon. One of them lies on the pavement and, lifting up her skirt, kicks her legs up in the air. Her companion, laughing uproariously, picks her up. They drift on and repeat the exhibition further down the road. No one pays them any attention. Late one evening I see a drunk approach the display window of the shop downstairs. He is carrying a brick in each hand. Calmly, deliberately, he takes aim. There is an explosion of shattering glass. The passers-by, their faces averted, hurry on. Like the appeal to universal brotherhood, the act of violence falls on stony ground.

Earls Court offers to its denizens the life of the city at its rawest and purest. It is uncompromisingly urban; a conglomeration of solitary individuals. Relinquishing responsibility, it offers frenzy. Therein lies its attraction. Nothing is permanent in Earls Court. The restaurants come and go with bewildering rapidity; the bedsitter population is notoriously ephemeral. Yet, the transience is superficial: it is the transience of a purgatorial clearing-house. The actors change but the play, revolving on its febrile treadmill, remains much the same.

One lunch time I went to the pub where six years before I used to sit and look at the charladies sipping their bottled Guinness. It had undergone a metamorphosis. Carpeted steps led to an upper bar where girls in hot-pants doled out the drinks. Sliding glass panels opened on to a terrace set out with tables shaded by colourful umbrellas. The charladies had disappeared tracelessly. I descended to the gloomy cavern of the lower bar. Strobe lights coruscated like demented fireflies in the interior recesses of the gloom. There was the heavy pound of rhythm and blues from scattered speakers. Groups

of men, their faces indistinct, lowered their heads over glasses of beer.
The garish designs of a watered-down pop art decorated the walls. I
bought my drink and settled in a corner. It was a weird, timeless
world. The music stopped and the strobe lights were extinguished.
Out of the hush drooled the West Indian voice of a disc jockey.

'And now specially for you cool cats out there something real hip.
The beautiful Cheryl is gonna dance just for you.'

The groups of men surged forward into a solid phalanx and fenced
in the wooden-floored circle where the beautiful Cheryl would
perform. A spotlight was switched on. Then Cheryl herself appeared,
a slight, pretty girl with protruding collar-bones. She was dressed in a
shimmering bikini hung with silvery tassels and a pair of white boots
that reached up above her knees. Moving awkwardly in her boots
she came and stood limply, head bowed, in the middle of the circle: a
drowned mermaid in the glare of the spotlight.

The voice of the disc jockey drooled again. 'Ready, Cheryl baby?
Then let's swing it. Shake it up! Hey! Hey!'

An ear-splitting volley of music crashed forth and Cheryl, roused
from her hibernatory stillness, pitched into her gyrations. She
bobbed and weaved; she brandished her pale arms; she rotated her
hips. The strobe lights flashed. A shine of sweat overspread her
cheeks. She quivered orgasmically as the music climbed to a
crescendo and, when it had passed, she rippled with the tremors of
post-coital exhaustion and sank, eyes closed, on to the wooden
boards of the arena. It had been a fine performance but she was not
applauded. She rose to her feet and was once again a drowned
mermaid in the glare of the spotlight. Ploughing a passage through
her impassive masculine audience, she disappeared behind a door
marked 'Staff Only'.

'That was way out, Cheryl baby. Thank you. And now we're
gonna groove some more with the dynamic Shirley. She's gonna get
you cats out there real hot under the collar. Hey! Hey!'

I did not wait to see the dynamic Shirley. Outside a fine rain was
falling. The big lorries roared, tyres squelching on the wet roadway. I
breathed in the soupy air blowing in chill gusts. In its metamorphosis

that pub had conformed to the underlying spirit of Earls Court. A further revolution of the febrile treadmill: it was no more than that. Beautiful Cheryl and dynamic Shirley were part of the quick, passionate flux; souls resting a while in the clearing-house. Eventually, they too would be swept away as the charladies had been swept away, leaving no trace. That was the iron law of Earls Court.

The usual crowd was gathered outside the tube station. His unfilled hat dampening in the rain, the veteran of the First World War scraped undaunted at his violin. Behind him, the collar of his donkey-jacket raised protectively, the agent of the underground press slept fitfully on his box.

Some months later I too was swept away. I could not work in Earls Court. Already I had fled once to a cottage in Suffolk where I stayed for six months. There I finished my second novel. On my return I found Earls Court even more intolerable. There being little to keep me, my urge to vagrancy reasserted itself. I obeyed the iron law and left. I write this in an Indian hill station. From the balcony of the hotel I can see the snow peaks of the Himalayas on clear days. Then the mists descend and they vanish completely. It is as if they had never been there; as if I were the victim of an illusion. At this distance, Earls Court too seems illusory. It is as if I had never been there; as if it had never existed. Alas, I know that that is not so.

Salman Rushdie

[1947–]

Salman Rushdie was born in Bombay, India, the oldest child and only son in an affluent Muslim family. At the age of fourteen, he left India to study at Rugby in England. Rushdie eventually took a history degree at King's College, Cambridge. Meanwhile, in 1967 his parents moved to Pakistan.

Surrounded by books and story-tellers in his youth, Rushdie knew that he wanted to become a writer from an early age. After graduating from King's College, he stayed in England, where he worked in the theatre and as a copywriter in an advertising agency. His first novel, *Grimus* (1979), was met with negative reviews. Undaunted by the setback, he wrote *Midnight's Children* (1981), an innovative blend of fantasy and reality. Ambitiously conceived and widely praised, this novel was born of Rushdie's desire to write an 'epic' about India, and was begun when he revisited Bombay after a ten-year absence. *Midnight's Children* won the Booker Prize in 1981, ushering Rushdie into the literary spotlight and enabling him to begin writing full-time.

The next novel, *Shame* (1983), is set in Pakistan, where it was banned upon publication. In 1986 Rushdie travelled to Nicaragua as a guest of the Sandinista Association of Cultural Workers. The result of his visit was *The Jaguar Smile: A Nicaraguan Journey* (1987). In 1989 Rushdie published *The Satanic Verses*. Set in Margaret Thatcher's Britain, the novel contains what Rushdie calls the 'most spectacular act of immigration' that he could imagine, when his two Indian protagonists fall out of the sky and into the English Channel. Both an attempt to 'give voice and fictional flesh to the immigrant culture' and an exploration of religious faith, *The Satanic Verses* was banned in India a week after its British publication. Several countries with large Muslim populations soon followed suit.

In 1991 Rushdie published *Haroun and the Sea of Stories* and *Imaginary Homelands: Essays and Criticism, 1981–1991*. In 1994 he published a collection of short stories, *East, West*, and in 1995 his first major novel in six years, *The Moor's Last Sigh*, appeared. It was short-listed for the Booker Prize and won the Whitbread Prize for best novel of the year.

Rushdie's 'post-colonial' essay 'A General Election' (1983) tackles British society with the kind of unsheathed vigour that a 'colonial' writer might well have shied away from. Here is the fully developed voice of the British writer who was not born in Britain but who fearlessly dares to criticize. This is no Equiano, learning the language and the customs, nor a C. L. R. James, anxious to impress. The ramparts have been breached, neither by stealth nor by bluster. The force of confident and elegant argument challenges the reader's understanding of what constitutes a 'British' writer.

A General Election

I returned to England only recently, after spending two months in India, and was feeling pretty disorientated even before the general election was called. Now, as successive opinion polls inform us of the near-inevitability of a more or less enormous Tory victory, my sense of alienation has blossomed into something close to full-scale culture shock. ' 'Tis a mad world you have here, my masters.'

Have they been putting something in the drinking water while I've been away? I had always thought that the British prided themselves on their common sense, on good old-fashioned down-to-earth realism. But the election of 1983 is beginning to look more and more like a dark fantasy, a fiction so outrageously improbable that any novelist would be ridiculed if he dreamed it up.

Consider this fiction. A Tory Prime Minister, Maggie May, gets elected on the basis of her promises to cut direct taxation and to get the country back to work ('Labour isn't working'). During the next four years she increases direct taxation and contrives to add almost two million people to the dole queues. And she throws in all sorts of extra goodies: a fifth of the country's manufacturing industry lies in ruins, and (although she claims repeatedly to have vanquished the monster Inflation) she presides over the largest increase in prices of any British Prime Minister. The country's housing programme grinds to a halt; schools and hospitals are closed; the Nationality Act robs Britons of their 900-year-old right to citizenship by virtue of birth; and the great windfall of North Sea oil money is squandered on financing unemployment. Money is poured into the police force, and as a result notifiable crimes rise by twenty-eight per cent.

She constantly tells the nation that cash limits are tight, but finds untold billions to spend on a crazy war whose legacy includes the export of drinking water to the South Atlantic at a cost to the British taxpayer of five pence a pint; and, speaking of peace, she earmarks further untold billions for the purchase of the latest weapons of death, although common sense, not to mention history, clearly indicates that the more such weapons exist, the more likely they are to be used.

So far, the story of Prime Minister May is almost credible. The fictional character does come across as unusually cruel, incompetent, unscrupulous and violent, but there have just occasionally been Tory politicians of whom such a description would not be wholly inaccurate. No, the story only falls apart when it gets to the end: Maggie May decides to go to the country, and instead of being hounded into the outer darkness, or at least Tasmania, like her namesake, it seems that she is to receive a vote of confidence; that five more years of cruelty, incompetence, etc., is what the electorate wants.

The hapless novelist submits his story, and is immediately submerged in a flood of rejection slips. Desperately, he tries to make his narrative more convincing. Maggie May's political opponents are presented as hopelessly divided. The presence of alleged 'full-time socialists' amongst her foes alarms the people. The leader of the Labour Party wears a crumpled donkey-jacket at the Cenotaph and keeps falling over his dog. But still (the rejection slips point out) the fact remains that for Mrs May to hold anything like the lead that the polls say she holds, the unemployed – or some of them, anyway –

must be planning to vote for her; and so must some of the homeless, some of the businessmen whose businesses she has destroyed, some of the women who will be worse off when (for instance) her proposal to means-test child benefits becomes law, and many of the trade unionists whose rights she proposes so severely to erode.

At this point, our imaginary novelist (compromising the integrity of his vision for the sake of publication) would, in all probability, agree to rewrite his ending. The trumpets sound, the sleeping citizenry awakes, *le jour de gloire* arrives, and Maggie May gets, in 1983, the same sort of bum's rush given to her hero Winston Churchill in 1945.

Is it not passing strange that this, the plausible and happy ending, is the one that looks, in the cold light of real-life Britain, like the one in which it's almost impossible to believe?

I find myself entertaining Spenglerian thoughts about how there can be times when all that is worst in a people rises to the surface and expresses itself in its government. There are, of course, many Britains, and many of them – the sceptical, questioning, radical, reformist, libertarian, non-conformist Britains – I have always admired greatly. But these Britains are presently in retreat, even in disarray; while nanny-Britain, strait-laced Victoria-reborn Britain, class-ridden know-your-place Britain, thin-lipped, jingoist Britain, is in charge. Dark goddesses rule; brightness falls from the air. 'The Ancient Britons,' says the best of history books, *1066 and All That*, 'painted themselves true blue, or woad, and fought heroically under their dashing queen, Woadicea.' The Britons are even more Ancient now, but they have been fighting once again, and that blue dye takes a long time to wear off. Woadicea rides again.

What an achievement is hers! She has persuaded the nation that everything that goes wrong, from unemployment to the crime rate, is an Act of God or someone else's fault, that the forces of organized labour are actually the enemies of organized labour; that we can only defend ourselves by giving the United States the power of life and death over us; that to be an 'activist' is somehow far worse than being an inactivist, and that the left must once more be thought of in

Latin, as sinister. She propounds what is in fact an ideology of impotence masquerading as resolution, a con-trick, and it looks as though it's going to work: Maggie's sting.

And it was as recently as 1945 that the British people, politicized by their wartime experiences, threw off the yoke of the true-blue ruling class . . . How quickly the wheel has turned, how quickly faith has been lost in the party they forged as their weapon, how depressingly willing the nation seems to be to start touching forelocks once again. The worst thing about this election is that nobody seems really angry about what has happened, is happening, and is sure to go on happening if Mrs Thatcher is standing on the steps of No. 10 on the morning of 10 June. (What will she quote from this time? St Francis of Assisi again? St Joan? The Hitler Diaries?)

I believe the absence of widespread anger matters enormously, for this reason: that democracy can only thrive in a turbulent climate. Where there is acquiescence, cynicism, passivity, resignation, 'inactivism', the road is clear for those who would rob us of our rights.

So, finally, and in spite of all the predictions and probabilities, I refuse to accept that the cause is lost. Despair brings comfort to one's enemies. And elections are not, at bottom, about reasoned arguments; they are about passions. It is just conceivable that even now, in this eleventh hour, a rage can be kindled in the people, rage against the dying of the light that Thatcherism represents. The electorate, we are told, has never been so volatile; so maybe the miracle can still be worked. Maybe, on the day, real life will turn out to obey the same laws of probability as fiction, and sanity will return.

If not, we can look forward to five more years of going to the dogs. *Guardian* readers will no doubt remember these unappealing canines; a few years ago, they used to be known as the running dogs of capitalism.

Abdulrazak Gurnah

[1948–]

Abdulrazak Gurnah was born in Zanzibar, Tanzania. He left Africa in 1967, at the age of eighteen. The young African boy Hassan in his first novel, *Memory of Departure* (1987), also leaves home at an early age. In a letter to his loved one, nineteen-year-old Hassan explains the reason for his emigration: 'Perhaps because I saw nothing but the misery and defeat of my people. I saw nothing but a clinging to old habits.' Trying to come to terms with his identity, Hassan refers to himself as an 'exile': 'It makes it easier to bear this feeling because I can give it a name that does not shame me.' Praised by critics as a poetic and compassionate debut, *Memory of Departure* prompted comparisons with James Joyce's *Portrait of the Artist as a Young Man*. It was followed in 1988 by *Pilgrim's Way*, a novel in which the main character, Daud, is a self-described 'alienated creature' – an African in England whose life becomes increasingly complicated when he falls in love with a white woman. In 1990 Gurnah published *Dottie*, which touches upon similar themes of displacement and interracial relations.

In 1993 Gurnah edited *Essays on African Writing: A Re-evaluation*. In his introduction, he reiterates the ambivalent feelings of post-colonial African writers towards European intervention in their country of birth. Gurnah currently lives in Canterbury, England, where he teaches literature at the University of Kent. He is also associate editor of the journal *Wasafiri*. In 1994 Gurnah published a fourth novel, *Paradise*, which was short-listed for that year's Booker Prize. *Paradise* is set in German East Africa during the First World War and explores the reactions of the locals as their homeland is torn by conflict and colonial rule. His latest novel, *Admiring Silence*, was published in the autumn of 1996.

The central character in Gurnah's novel Pilgrim's Way *is sadly aware that the English perceive him to be little more than the flotsam of empire. He is trying to understand why England is not the place that he expected it to be. This England of cathedrals and spires, to his eyes, is far from 'civilized'.*

From *Pilgrim's Way*

It was just after seven and the pub was almost empty. The only other customer apart from Daud was a thin, old man leaning over his drink at a corner of the bar. The barman was talking to him, and nodded at Daud to show that he had seen him and would presently attend to him. It was getting towards the end of the week and money was short, so Daud bought himself the cheapest half-pint of beer and sat in the alcove by the window. The beer tasted watery and sour, but he shut his eyes and gulped it.

He heard the barman chuckling softly at something that the old man had said. They both turned to look at him. The old man grinned as he leant back to stare at Daud over an angle of his shoulder, nodding as if he intended to reassure and calm him. Daud made his face as lugubrious as he could and his eyes glassy and blank, blind to the old man's antics. He thought of the grin as the one that won an empire. It was the pick-pocket's smile, given tongue in cheek and intended to distract and soothe the innocent prey while the thief helped himself to the valuables. It had travelled the seven seas, flashing at unsuspecting wogs the world over. Millions of them succumbed to it, laughing at its transparently conniving intention, and assuming that the mind behind such a ridiculous face must be as idiotic. Daud imagined how embarrassing the sight would have been: half-naked men, skins baked red by the sun, smiling with such complete insincerity. By the time the victims discovered that those bared fangs had every intention of chomping through their comic and woggish world, there was little for them to do but watch with terror as the monsters devoured them. *Never again*, Daud vowed. *Go find yourself another comedy act, you old fool.*

He felt exposed when he sat in a pub alone, and worried that somebody would come to speak to him, and flash yellow teeth at him. When he was new in England, and innocent of the profound antagonism he aroused by his mere presence, he had gone into pubs he should not have gone into. At one he was refused the cigarettes and matches he had gone in to buy. To begin with, he thought that the barman was mad, a *character* who was going to shame him by some act of perversity. Then he saw the grins all around the pub and understood. He had wanted to protest, to make a scene and perhaps hurl a curse on the inn-keeper. Afterwards he had replayed the scene in every detail, except that in these latter versions he was not flustered with surprise and had the perfect riposte to their abuse. He imagined and rehearsed in front of a mirror how he thought his father might protest at such a public indignity. But that first time he had simply stood in the pub, unable to summon the words in the stranger's language, and watched the grins turn him into a clown.

At another pub, the Seven Compasses, he was told that the spaghetti advertised on the menu was finished, when he could see hot, steaming plates being passed over the counter. He had asked to see the landlord, sniffing his pound note ostentatiously to indicate the drift of his case, but he had noticed a few of the beefier patrons getting interested. *No need for alarm. God save the Queen*, he said and ran.

A group of burghers had chased him out of another pub with their stares and angry comments, incensed that he had invaded their gathering and ruined their pleasure. *This could have happened to you*, he cried as he stood at the door. *Fate could have dealt you such a body blow too, and you might have found yourself as unfortunately miscast as I, chased from one haven to another, wretched and despised.* They had turned round and barked their hearty burgher guffaws, their breaths smelling of the burnt fats of animals. *Oh my goodness*, they said. *Oh goodness gracious me.*

The most poignant exclusion was from The Cricketers, where he had gone two or three times and had begun to feel safe. The photographs on the walls were a disappointment, honouring only English and Australian players. There were no Sir Garys and no Three Ws, but he found the cricket paraphernalia on the walls soothing. In the end the landlady had asked him to leave. She told him she could not be sure of restraining her husband from jumping over the bar and cracking him one. So he had gone, saddened and shaken that it was a lover of that noble game who had so misused him.

Daud took as long as he could over his half-pint, but nobody turned up to buy him another one. It was still light outside when he left. He turned into one of the lanes by the cathedral and headed towards the hospital. The route he followed was the same as the one he took in the morning when he went to work. It occurred to him that he could have found something more interesting to do in the evening than that. Had his life become so empty? How would he feel if anyone found out that this was how he spent his hours? He shrugged off the intimations of inadequacy, tossed his head at them, and walked on.

It was a warm June evening, and Daud would not have been surprised to see pavements teeming with frisky teenagers and cocky young men, with a sprinkling of responsible adults taking a stroll and shooting the breeze. Instead the streets were empty and afflicted with gloom. He hurried now, made uncomfortable by the silence and the expectancy of the streets. It was as if the town had been abandoned, its purpose fulfilled, and its inhabitants engaged elsewhere in other pursuits. He avoided the darkest alleys. Who knew what might jump out of them? Who would hear his screams for help?

He imagined a recently returned representative of the greatest empire the world had ever seen walking these streets, after what had seemed like centuries of absence, when the thought of the conviviality of his people would have sustained him while he tortured the silent, sullen peoples under his charge. He would surely have screamed with anguish as he strolled the soulless streets of the evangelical heartland of the old country, and saw the self-deception he had practised in the isolation of his imperial outpost. With what relish he would then recall the hypnotic throbbing of the jungle drums and the scratchings of the shrill cicadas in the tropical night.

How fulfilling would seem those endless, dreary afternoons in the tropical hell-hole, where men were still men and knew the potency of rank and power. Surely, surely! But there was very little for him to feel smug about, Daud reminded himself. Shrill cicadas or no, at least the streets were paved and clean, and no scavenging dogs roamed the streets at night, looking for carrion. When he arrives at his house and runs the shower, water will sprinkle out of the rose, instead of dust and the whine of rusted cogs and nuts. His lights worked, his toilet flushed and there were always onions in the shops. He admired the organization that could make all that function, and pave the paths and make the trains run.

The clock on St George's Tower said twenty minutes past eight. It was always seven minutes slow. He knew this from long experience, but felt it was a small and bearable eccentricity. The tower was the only thing within a radius of hundreds of yards to have survived the wartime bombing. Perhaps, he thought, its heart had stopped for seven minutes. It survived and now stood squat on its arches and colonnades like an old molar. The bombs had been meant for the cathedral, but it had escaped almost untouched, its precious glass long since secreted away, and its granite walls and spires secure from all but the most direct of hits. Almost by a miracle, the little streets leading to the cathedral had also survived, leaving the monument to Norman piety nestling in its medieval inaccessibility, buffered by a warren of winding alleys.

He looked through the open gate to the cathedral into the floodlit maw of its precincts. He caught a glimpse of the stone massif, with its elegant spires looking even more like fairy-tale towers in the unreal light. For all the years he had lived in the town, he had never been inside the cathedral. He had walked through the grounds hundreds of times, taking a short-cut through the Queens Gate. He had been chased through the cloisters by a group of skinheads: *Gi' us a kiss, nigger*. He gave them a good view of his right royal arse and shouted abuse as he ran. *Go suck a dodo, you fucking pricks*. But he had never been inside the cathedral; which those skinheads probably had.

He took the path across the common to Bishop Street. Most

people called it the rec, which had disconcerted him at first. He had thought it was *wreck*, the site of some immemorial foundering. The rec was in a sunken piece of ground surrounded by high banks overgrown with bushes and trees. One path ran alongside the road just below the bank. The one he took cut across the playing pitches and would bring him out by the disused water mill near Bishop Street. He knew it was a mistake as soon as he had gone far enough to be unable to withdraw without looking scared. He saw a man scrambling down the bank from the road, watched him bend down to take his dog off the lead. He was always wary of dogs, and this one was large and sleek, with a drooling lower jaw that made it look hungry. He glanced away quickly so as not to attract its attention, the way a child might shut its eyes tight to rid itself of a monster that was threatening it. He kept to the path and stretched his legs, aware that with every step he was moving farther from the road and the street-lights, and deeper into the darkness. After a while it became obvious that the couple were after him. From a dozen yards, Daud saw the man start to grin. He threw dignity to the winds and fled, the dog panting and leaping behind him. He heard the man laugh and then whistle for the dog to come back. When he reached the little bridge that straddled the stream, which was the boundary of the rec, Daud stopped and called down a round of curses and plagues on the man. He had not seen him properly, only a glimpse of a skinny figure in an overcoat, with greying hair slicked back like an unfunny parody of a silent-movie star, but he was sure God would have no difficulty identifying him. He had probably come across him before.

He heard the cathedral bells tolling nine as he reached his door. He let himself in, holding his breath and then allowing the air to enter his lungs in small pockets. The landlord believed in piano keys but was very reluctant to have the rotten floor-boards seen to. Daud had even openly questioned his belief: *How can you say you believe in the co-existence of the races, like the black and white keys on a piano, and then exploit me and my people in this way?* He had especially enjoyed that *my people*, and had watched the man squirm with shame and anguish, confident that his floor-boards would be fixed. But the landlord had controlled his pain in some way, and confessed to Daud that he could not get the repairs done unless he received a little more rent.

Daud switched the television on and sat down in front of it. It was more for the noise and distraction that he put it on, to dispel the grip of misery that the silent house had on him. It did not work; and he heard through the strident music on the television the angry grumbles of his mind as it refused to be silenced so easily.

The thought of the letters he needed to write reproached him with its habitual and irresistible force. With it came the memory of what he had left behind, and he felt resolve wobbling, and wondered if the habit of endurance had made him uncritical and self-deluding. Flashes of warm golden beaches appeared in his mind, although he was often unsure if the image were not one he had culled from brochures of other lands. He could not resist the romance and drama of his isolation, and he felt himself giving way. He remembered the walk to school and felt himself straining for every step, for a picture of the shops and the people he would have passed. Then he knew he had gone too far as the faces of old friends came to chide him with his neglect.

He rarely heard from anybody, and he was happy with that. Letters from old friends were always full of an optimism about England that he found embarrassing. They were so far removed from the humiliating truth of his life that they could be taken for mockery, although he knew that was not so. For they had done a good job, he thought, those who had gone to take the torch of wisdom and learning to the benighted millions of Africa. They had left a whole age group hankering for the land that had produced their teachers. Poor Rabearivelo, the Malagasy poet, had committed suicide when he failed to get to France. *It was enough to make you laugh*, Daud thought, *until you read his poems. And then you wondered how a mind like that could be so easily eaten*. He hated getting letters from his friends, and dreaded having to reply. He found himself cultivating an eccentric style when he wrote to them, in the hope that they would be too embarrassed about his decline to be able to reply. His father's generation was safe. They had been born while the memory of a time without Europeans was still fresh in people's minds, before the grin of empire had filled the rest with the self-despising anxiety of frightened men.

George Szirtes

[1948–]

George Szirtes was born in Budapest, Hungary. In 1956, following the
uprising in Budapest, he and his parents left for England. In 1970, while
at Leeds College of Art, Szirtes married Clarissa Upchurch, with whom
he has two children. He received a BA in fine art in 1972. Leeds was also
where he met the poet Martin Bell, who, impressed by the younger poet's
combination of 'English individualism and European culture', encouraged Szirtes's writing. Szirtes himself recognizes the dualism that inhabits
his work, although he has referred to it more bluntly as 'a conflict
between two states of mind'.

From 1972 to 1973 Szirtes studied at Goldsmiths' College in London,
and in 1973 he began to teach part-time. Between 1975 and 1987 he
worked as the head of art at various schools in Hertfordshire. Szirtes's
art education has had a subtle yet profound influence on his poetry, as is
evident from his first collection, *The Slant Door* (1979). In 1980 he
received the Geoffrey Faber Memorial Prize and in 1981 he published his
second volume of poetry, *November and May*. *Short Wave* (1983) soon
followed, as did an Arts Council grant in 1984. In the mid-1980s, Szirtes
made a series of return journeys to Hungary, some of which were
supported by the British Council. His first visit rejuvenated his sense of
his native language – a language that he'd nearly forgotten after many
years of speaking and writing in English. He began to translate poetry
and prose, and published *The Photographer in Winter* (1986), which, he
says, is an attempt to understand his own 'dual heritage'. Szirtes received
the Cholmondeley Award in 1987 and in 1988 he wrote *Metro*, a highly
personal volume of poetry. *Metro* explores the period of time from 1944
to 1945 when his father was held in a labour camp and his mother was
imprisoned in Ravensbruck. Several of the poems are written as
imagined letters from his mother to her brother. In 1991 Szirtes
published *Bridge Passages*.

Since 1987 Szirtes has worked as a part-time staff member at St
Christopher School in Letchworth, Hertfordshire and is a proprietor of

Starwheel Press in Hitchin. He continues to publish work in which he utilizes history and myth, as well as certain English sensibilities and literary traditions, to evoke Central European events.

Szirtes's poetry explores the interface between 'this' England and a 'remembered' other, all the while gently probing the past in an attempt to make sense of both a personal and a public history. 'The Child I Never Was' (1986) and 'Assassins' (1983) are meditations upon England, whoever or whatever she may be.

THE CHILD I NEVER WAS

The child I never was could show you bones
that are pure England. All his metaphors
are drawn from water. His ears admit the sea
even to locked rooms with massive doors.

Look, let me make him for you: comb his hair
with venus comb, a wicked drupe for mouth,
twin abalones for ears, sharp auger teeth,
an open scalloped lung, a nautilus
for codpiece, cowrie knuckles, nacreous.
Let him shiver for you in the air.

The English schoolboy cannot understand
a country that is set in seas of land.

The child I never was makes poetry
of memories of landscape haunted by sea.
He stands in an attic and shows you his collection
of huge shells, and with an air of introspection
cracks his knuckle bones.

ASSASSINS

My people, by whom I mean those curious sets
Of non-relations in provincial towns,

Sit ripening brightly in the *Weltanschauung*
Of other poets. Here is one who follows
A second-hand pair of shoes into the Courts
Of Social History. Another ransacks
His late unlettered father's bedside drawer
And finds dead ukuleles littered there.
What heraldic yet surreal landscapes!
To lie in the bed of your ancestors
And feel the fit. To hear the neighbourhood
Stirring in its ancient sleep and rhyme
The dead into their regiments of pain.
The poverty of old shoes runs away
With its own eloquence. And yet they write good books.

But I think of an England where the ghosts
Are restless solitaries or assassins.
They cannot speak but run about in sunlight
Demanding restoration of the birch
And death as public as the crime is private.
They have lost time. The Russians on Burns night
Celebrate their history of combustions.
Their people lie in complete unity
In graves as large as Europe and as lonely.

Timothy Mo

[1950-]

Timothy Mo was born in Hong Kong. At the age of ten he left for England, where he has lived ever since. He was educated at St John's College, Oxford, and then began working as a journalist in London for the *Times Educational Supplement*, the *New Statesman* and *Boxing News*. In 1980 he published his first novel, *The Monkey King*, which was heralded by critics as a mature and exciting debut. It received the Geoffrey Faber Memorial Prize. Mo's next publication was *Sour Sweet* (1982), which was short-listed for the Whitbread Award and the Booker Prize, and won the Hawthornden Prize. Set in England, from its opening sentence Mo's novel explores the plight of a Chinese immigrant family: 'The Chens had been living in the UK for four years, which was long enough to have lost their place in the society from which they had emigrated but not long enough to feel comfortable in the new.'

An Insular Possession (1986), set during the Opium Wars, is a complicated novel that fuses history and fiction by using postmodernist multiplicities of perspective and technique. With *The Redundancy of Courage* (1991), Mo further established his reputation as a darkly comic satirist whose characters, while driven by selfish desires, are ultimately controlled by the relentless – and often humorous – power of fate. He published his fifth novel, *Brownout on Breadfruit Boulevard*, in 1995.

The Chen family in Mo's extraordinary novel Sour Sweet *live in London, but do so without any sense of expectation or any real desire to 'negotiate' with England. In the following extract from the novel, the family have to move out from behind the façade of their home and attempt to interact with English society. They do so while forcefully maintaining their view of the English as 'the other', which provides us with a unique perspective on English life.*

From *Sour Sweet*

Before they knew what was happening, Mui had copies of the evening newspapers covering the floor. Random triangles of purple and orange carpet showed through gaps in the pages.

Such and such a place looked promising, Mui would announce from her knees. Then Chen or Lily would do their best to find disadvantages: this place was too far out or the rent of that place was too high. This other place was a district of Indians who wouldn't eat their food (Chen knew quite well they would).

Finally, though, they had to do something. Chen arranged to see premises in south London, currently being converted to commercial use, which he had not been able to discredit from information in the newspaper.

They travelled in a family group, Man Kee in a cloth sling on his aunt's back. It was the first time Chen had been on public transport with Lily in over two years and the first time ever with his son. He had, of course, brought Mui from the airport to the flat. Remembering Mui's first difficulties in adjusting to her new life, he wondered whether the initial shock of descending into an Underground station and boarding one of the thundering, segmented, silver and red serpents might have been responsible for the dazed state of her first months. 'Perhaps I was miserly not to take a taxi?'

Looking at Mui now as she confidently pulled the bell cord of the 113 over her head and as she insouciantly (rather saucily, Chen thought) stared back at the burly West Indian bus conductor (it was a mandatory stop and fare stage, not a request, a distinction Mui had yet to learn and one unexplicated by the TV serial), Chen was unable to connect this young woman with the shrinking creature who had sat next to him all those months ago. As they congregated on the open platform of the bus, Mui pressed the red button causing the bell to ting again, more faintly. Just to make sure, she gave it three more rings. The conductor at the other end of the bus leant over a seat to shake a finger at them. Chen could see his black face contorting in the frame formed by the window. Getting in on the act, not to be outdone, Lily rang once as well, then lifted Man Kee in his sling on Mui's back and, holding his dimpled fist, helped *him* to ring lightly, four times in rapid succession. *Ping! Ping! Ping! Ping!* Chen shook his head vigorously at his wife.

The bus jerked to a halt, though fortunately Lily, who had an excellent sense of balance anyway, had been sensibly holding with her free hand the white pole bisecting the entrance to the bus. Chen bundled the women off into the empty road.

'Husband, the stop is a hundred yards away!'

'Do what I tell you!'

But he was not quick enough to be out of earshot of the conductor. As the vehicle moved off again the conductor was still on the platform looking back at them, no longer hurling abuse now he knew who the culprits were but shaking his capped head at the antics of the lunatic Chinese who smiled serenely, bafflingly, maddeningly at him as they disappeared into the specks far down the road.

And indeed there was an impression of invincible eccentricity about the little group now re-forming on the pavement for the next stage of its journey. Chen appeared unremarkable enough in his black trousers and brown padded jacket; although his trilby hat was a bit odd as accessory to these. The girls, however, having no uniform to provide them with an approximate sartorial guideline, nor a job to get them out of the house, had become rather disorganized about their clothing. One relaxation of convention had led to another. Both were wearing thin tunic suits in a tiny floral pattern (unfortunately no longer interchangeable as Mui was getting quite comfortable in her figure). Over these summery suits each was wearing a baggy cardigan of Chen's. Lily's was grey with walnut leather buttons, Mui's olive-green in a chunky knit with transparent plastic toggles. Mui almost filled her woollen but, having shorter arms than her brother-in-law, had been forced to roll the sleeves back several times. Lily, on the other hand, found Chen's sleeves too short, uncomfortably so, even with the cuffs rolled down, so that the top part of the garment acted as a strait-jacket, riding up under the armpits and exposing her wrists and a substantial length of her shapely forearm, while around her slender waist the cardigan's elasticated bottom had concertinaed in a thick roll rather like the domed edge of a toadstool. Lily's flat shoes – the ones she wore to the shops – were being repaired, which had left her with the choice of house-slippers or a pair of slightly longer than ankle-length well-ington boots (in the vernacular 'larbah boot'), relic of typhoon seasons on the flooded barrack roof in Hong Kong, into which she had finally thrust her narrow, sockless feet. Mui had commandeered a pair of Chen's size 7 shoes, laceless unhappily, in which her own size 3 feet floundered like landed fish. She proceeded with a circular, scuffling motion, reminding Lily of the way Father had advanced on his opponents in order simultaneously to hook their leading leg and protect his own groin from counter flick-kicks. Despite the three pairs of her sister's socks she was wearing (which was why Lily's bare feet were now rapidly blistering) every now and then a shoe would detach itself from Mui's foot and Lily would fear for Man Kee in his sling on his aunt's back – though Lily had no doubts Mui would fall heroically *forward* on her face if the need arose.

Now they set off to the Underground station from which they would take a train to the railway station from which they would take a final bus to their destination. Man Kee dozed placidly in Mui's back, waking briefly as the train clattered through an eerie, spark-lit crossroad of tunnels and regarding his father with a large, incurious and unblinking eye before falling asleep again. Chen was grateful for this. The boy seemed quieter these days, or was it just that he was seeing him in the day?

On the BR train, where they had an entire compartment to themselves, Chen positioned himself near the window, ready to spring tiger-like on Mui should she succumb to temptation in the shape of the alarm cord. Irresponsible of the English authorities to put it so conveniently at hand; it was far too easy to pull. Also, it bore great resemblance to the bus cord which one might legitimately, under certain circumstances, pull. The red handle on the Under-ground was far less ambiguous, especially as this train kept stopping and starting at a variety of small stations in response to a pinging clearly audible in the compartment. But Mui, hunched forwards with Man Kee on her back, chin cupped in hands, was looking eagerly out of the streaky window. Chen began to relax. The girls woke him at the station. He pretended he had just closed his eyes.

The premises, directly opposite the bus stop, were being gutted. Shattered glass lay perilously on the pavement. Two windows had been knocked into one. The new front had been daubed with smears of white paint to prevent people accidentally sticking their arms through it. Through a clear square of glass they could see snakes of bunched electrical coils dropping from the ceiling.

Workmen came out, scraping their heavy boots on the plank floor. Chen was wary of this class of Englishman, crossing to the other side of the road on his way home from work as they spilled out of the pubs long after their statutory closing time, he used to think with fear and resentment. Mui and Lily stared at them with a blatant curiosity which, Chen knew, could offend. The English were peppery, often manufacturing pretexts for anger where none reasonably existed: a stare held too long, failure to meet their round eye at all. The girls' exposure to this kind of thing had not been as thoroughgoing as his, he thought protectively. He waved them away. 'Let's go.' The workmen seemed, fortunately, to be ignoring them so far. Mui had poked her head through the door and was inspecting the interior. Curls of wood-shavings covered the wood floor. There was a smell of fresh putty.

'Brother-in-law, this is too big for us. We are small people only.'

Chen, too, had been taken aback by the properness of the place, the presence of the workmen and the wholesale repairs they were making. This was not what he had been looking for. He wanted a more cautious, less obtrusive start. A place like this could be unlucky; it was arrogant, defying fate. This could be a large restaurant. Mui, although over-awed, was still curious. Chen took her by the arm and drew her outside. The workmen were brewing tea over a primus, stirring gobs of condensed milk into the pan which contained the boiling tea. When the Chens were twenty yards down the street the workmen began to whoop and stamp. Chen hurried his women on.

'What do the *gwai lo* sing, Brother-in-law?'

'They are singing songs, Mui.'

'What songs, Brother-in-law?'

'Their own songs, Mui.'

'Ah.'

'Don't look back, Lily.'

Lily, however, was not to be so easily denied. She turned round and with an arm through Mui's so she would not crash into a lamp post began to walk with short steps in the same direction as the others facing backwards (one of the exercises she had performed with Father in the courtyard).

'Lily!' Chen whirled round, scandalised. But now he was also able to see that the noise the workmen were making had nothing to do with them at all but involved one of their own number who had met with an accident (Chen thought it likely from his behaviour) involving the upsetting of hot liquid, in all likelihood tea, on to a sensitive part of his anatomy. Lily tittered. Chen found nothing amusing about the man's mishap, *faan gwai* or not. In fact he felt distinct masculine solidarity with him. Did the girls realize how painful this could be? Perhaps they knew and didn't care? Knew and gloated? Chen glanced at the nape of Lily's graceful neck, one of the few parts of her body that had up till now always pleased him. He must spend more time with Man Kee, he decided, staring into that infant's open, phlegmatic eye. He couldn't approve of all this female influence.

They had reached the end of the road. Chen did not want to retrace their steps and took them down a smaller street on the right. From here they reached the main road again which, on a whim, Chen crossed. Loyally, the girls followed, though Lily's feet were by now really quite painful in her wellingtons and Mui's back was aching from the weight of Man Kee's sling.

It became apparent that the main road formed an unofficial kind of boundary. The side they were now on was older, more dilapidated than the north side, a change which took place with startling swiftness. They had been walking for three minutes and already the houses were visibly decayed. They passed a derelict terrace, the doors and windows covered with corrugated-tin sheets; through rusted holes in the crinkled metal they could see grass growing in the roofless rooms. There was still a sofa in one of the ruined houses and its springs had burst out of the rotten cloth like a robot's innards. This was more like it, Chen thought with satisfaction; they would start here. It was ideal. *Hardly anyone would come to the shop!* Stray business, that was. Obviously one needed a modicum of local custom to survive. He had a little money left. Lily had also surprised him by revealing the existence of a fragrant hoard in the tea tin. At first pleased, he had later been unsettled by this evidence of his wife's capacity to sacrifice immediate gratification and defer it for future providential uses, and even more upsetting, to carry it out secretly without his discovering. Not that there was anything sneaky or reprehensible about it. Nevertheless, he could hardly believe Lily had found a margin on the house-keeping. Whole new regions of the female psyche, not only unexplored but their existence hitherto unsuspected, opened before him. Chen did his best to put the whole thing out of his mind as quickly as possible. If there was more to Lily than he had ever imagined he did not, at this comparatively late stage of things, want to know. Could she, for instance, have manipulated *him* into directly raising the question of a move? When all along it had been she who wanted it? Had she known all the time and been laughing at him? Chen looked at her talking innocently with Mui (why were they both limping?) and frowned. What deceptions and secrets lay behind the childishly smooth skin of those faces? Chen decided to give Lily enough room to manoeuvre in future – for both their sakes.

They had now arrived at an open space, a demolition site, bounded by tall, braced buildings on two sides. In the middle there was an untended fire blazing. Chen led his party across the scattered bricks and tins. Lily deliberately walked through the large puddles, pleased with this chance to turn her boots to use. There had been, she now remembered, a small leak in the left boot at ankle height but time seemed to have plugged it. Fearing for Man Kee on such treacherous terrain, she took him from Mui and slung him on her own back. Mui, who was, indeed, experiencing some difficulties keeping her shoes on, fell behind the others. Lily and Chen approached the fire, which was much larger than appeared from a distance and was composed of rags, planks, straw packing, and half a car tyre which was giving off fumes and black smoke. There was no indication who had built it unless it was the English boys, throwing green bottles against the buttresses at the far end of the site. They had been hidden by smoke. But wouldn't they have been poking the fire with sticks? Lily turned to Mui to share a Kwangsi memory but she had vanished. A moment later Mui materialized through a pall of smoke, coughing and red-eyed. The wind had changed! 'It's not good to rub your eyes, Mui. Let them water.'

This piece of well-meant advice did not seem to be at all appreciated.

Mui scuffed resentfully after Chen, ploughing straight through a pile of beer tins and sending them clattering against fallen masonry and into puddles, just like a *gwai lo* hooligan. By the time she had rejoined Chen on the road her shoes were white with the ash from previous fires which lay thickly on this side of the site. As they turned the corner Lily took a last look at the fire, still burning in isolation, with nobody so much as throwing one extra plank on it or even enjoying its heat. How strange the English were, how indifferent, how careless of the consequences of their own deeds! And as for their attitude to their old people it was nothing less than shameful neglect, a national disgrace. With the image of the fire and the plight of the English aged now inextricably merged in her mind – both to do somehow with loneliness and a shirking of responsibilities as well as inevitable physical extinction – Lily wandered abstractedly down the road, barely listening to Chen. (Perhaps the fumes of the fire had poisoned her without her being aware of it.)

Each of the party was now locked into his or her own thoughts, no longer functioning as a single unit with a common purpose, the girls' sense of their own individuality reinforced by nagging little corporal pains: Lily vicariously indignant on behalf of others less fortunate than herself, dimly conscious of pinched, raw toes; Mui regretting having ever implanted the idea of a move into her sister's and brother-in-law's heads, sidling along like a crippled land-crab and wishing she was in front of her television. Only Chen was happy, walking on a cushion of air in this suburban wilderness where one street led into its twin, the whole area having the effect of a maze through its uniformity. Chen chattered excitedly to Lily. Here was where they should settle; this was perfect. Lily wasn't altogether happy but she didn't want to curb Husband's enthusiasm at this stage. 'You know best, Husband,' and she left the decision in his hands.

When they got home Lily levered her wellingtons off with difficulty and – a stroke of inspiration – soaked her sore feet in what was left of the mixture she had bottled for Husband's flu. So eager to dose others, it was the first time she had tried her own medicine. Of course, it was the least objectionable way of taking it. As it turned out, the mixture, at first astringently refreshing on hot blistered skin, then warming and soothing, proved a panacea. Or (Lily pondered later) had her memory failed her? Had she been, in fact, administering to Husband not Father's patented internal draught but the liniment he had used to toughen the calluses on his already formidably armoured knuckles? At any rate her feet gave her no trouble the next day, while Mui was still limping. Rather ostentatiously, Lily thought.

Two days later Chen went to reconnoitre the area again. He insisted on going solo and was surprised at the lack of resistance from the girls, contradictory creatures that they were. The workmen were having another tea-break when he passed them. What incorrigible idlers! Crossing the main road into the ruined district but going in another direction this time, he found what he wanted. Within the week he was able to present the girls with the accomplished fact: premises vacant and ready for occupation in two weeks.

William Boyd

[1952–]

William Boyd was born in Accra, Ghana. The son of a physician and a
schoolteacher, he spent his early years in Ghana and Nigeria before
leaving, in 1961, for a boarding school in Scotland. Boyd later attended
the University of Nice and the University of Glasgow. In 1975 he married
Susan Wilson, a publishing company publicity director, and in that same
year he began a postgraduate programme at Jesus College in Oxford. In
1981 Boyd became a television critic for the *New Statesman*. He also
worked as a fiction reviewer for the London *Sunday Times* and as a
lecturer in English at St Hilda's College, Oxford, before turning to
writing full-time.

Boyd's first novel was the widely praised *A Good Man in Africa*
(1981), a comic romp that depicts the sex and alcohol-soaked mishaps of
British diplomat Morgan Leafy. The novel earned Boyd comparisons
with Evelyn Waugh and Kingsley Amis, and received the Whitbread
Literary Award for best first novel and the 1982 Somerset Maugham
Award. In 1981 Boyd also published a collection of stories called *On the
Yankee Station*. In the following year his second novel, *An Ice-Cream
War*, won the John Llewelyn Rhys Memorial Prize and was short-listed
for the Booker Prize. The novel is set in East Africa during the First
World War and uses interweaving narratives to expose the senselessness
of combat. 1984 saw the publication of *Stars and Bars*, a novel which
follows the misadventures of a displaced Englishman as he bumbles
through New York City and America's Deep South.

The New Confessions (1987) tells of a Scottish film-maker who, while
a prisoner of war during the First World War, decides to adapt French
philosopher Jean Jacques Rousseau's *Confessions* to the silent screen.
Brazzaville Beach (1990), which won the 1990 James Tait Black
Memorial Prize and the McVitie Award, is a structurally complex novel
narrated by a young English primatologist working in Africa in the early
1970s. In addition to several screenplays, adaptations, short stories and
reviews, Boyd has recently published *The Blue Afternoon* (1993), a

mystery and a love story that spans several decades and countries. It won the 1993 Sunday Express Book of the Year Award. His latest published work is *The Destiny of Nathalie 'X'* (1995), a collection of short stories. Boyd currently lives in London and France.

In this autobiographical essay, 'Fly Away Home' (1997), Boyd captures the ambivalence of a childhood characterized by arrival and departure. Recalling his experiences as a young boy travelling between England and Africa, he is moved to question his place in both worlds and to examine the true nature of 'home'.

Fly Away Home

York, Hermes, Argonaut, Stratocruiser, Superconstellation, Britannia, Boeing 707, VC 10 . . . The story of my early encounters with England is a small history of aviation. I do not remember the York, a development of the Lancaster bomber, I believe, but in 1952 – the year I was born – my flying life began, in a Hermes. I was born in March in a military hospital in Accra, the capital of the Gold Coast. Four months later I was carried up the steps to the waiting Hermes to begin my first flight from my native land back to the place my parents came from. The Hermes followed the York on the first passenger services from Gold Coast to London, making a series of short hops across the great protruding bulge of western Africa – Accra, Lagos, Kano, Tripoli – before crossing the Mediterranean to Madrid, Rome or Frankfurt and then on to London. The whole journey took seventeen hours.

I do remember the Argonaut quite well, however, a British version of the DC6, a four-engined prop plane that did not owe anything to Second World War precursors and was the first to make the trans-Sahara overfly routine (if one discounts the truly terrifying turbulence), and was thus able to cut the time of the West Africa to London trip substantially. We would land in Kano in northern Nigeria to refuel before setting off on the long leg over the desert to Tripoli. Kano airport was so fly-infested that the airport buildings were proofed with mosquito wire. Vultures perched on the control tower. We always crossed the Sahara at night (perhaps at the level the planes flew in those days the turbulence made it impassable when the sun was up) and we would arrive at Tripoli as dawn broke. For this reason Tripoli airport always seemed dramatic and somewhat disturbing to me, as I recall: its hangars were colandered from Second World War shrapnel and in the pale light you could see cannibalised hulks of Italian bombers of the same era rusting mysteriously in the thin blond grass that fringed the runways. Beyond the perimeter fence camels grazed . . . There was still one more stop to be made in mainland Europe before we cruised over the English Channel to land at London airport – as Heathrow was always quaintly referred to in those days.

The Stratocruiser represented the ultimate in luxury. Twin-decked, with a glassy, round, bulbous nose, the plane tried to simulate the elegance of the Pullman cars in transcontinental express trains. Seats were arranged in fours, pairs facing each other. Above our heads was a reach-me-down bunk bed for children. On the lower deck was a small bar accessed by a tight spiral staircase, which I remember my parents descending for a cocktail before the meal was served – a side of roast beef on a silver trolley, the steward carving slices off it as if he were for all the world in the Savoy Grill and not 20,000 feet above the dark wadis and sand seas of the endless Sahara.

All these aeroplanes and their successors – the Britannia, the VC10 and so on – were in the livery of BOAC – the British Overseas Airways Corporation – crisp white and navy blue and badged with the famous speedbird logo (now long vanished). As I grew older and became conscious of our annual trips back to Britain on leave, the planes, and by extension the company, came to represent the country by proxy, as if a little segment of Britain had been sent out to the colonies to fetch us back to the motherland. It was a kind of idealized metaphor, I suppose – the smart modern planes and their smart modern crew luring us on board with their smiles and their trays of boiled sweets – showing us what we had left behind, reminding us of our good fortune in being able to return.

My early experience of air travel instilled in me a love of flying, of airports and all the accoutrements of aviation which has not left me to this day. How could such an introduction to flight, at such an impressionable age, and with such magnificent ambassadors, not fail to entrance? As children our idea of a treat was to be driven from home to Accra airport to look at the BOAC plane. One runway, one uneven expanse of tarmac apron, a control tower, a few hangars, some low sheds doubling as immigration and customs, arrival and departure halls, Accra airport was modest and unassuming in the extreme. Across the road from the airport was the airport hotel, called The Lisbon for some forgotten reason, a single-storied wooden building with a wide veranda. On Saturday nights a highlife band would play and the more daring young expatriate couples would come there to dance. Like all airport hotels in Africa, it effortlessly maintained a louche and faintly racy ambience. We children would take our drinks – our Fanta and Cokes – and go and stand at the wood paling fence and stare at the silver giant, propellers stilled, parked on the tarmac. Fuel bowsers and generators hummed, linked trolleys bouncing with luggage trundled from the departure lounge, engineers and cleaners ran up and down the wheeled steps set against the doorways. Then came the crew, then came the long lines of passengers. Doors were closed, propellers turned, the plane was freed from its various appurtenances and it taxied to the end of the runway.

To see it lift off and climb into the dusty evening air was both exhilarating and melancholy, emotions perhaps not fully compre-hended then but more easily analysed now. It has to be understood that in the 1950s, certainly from an African perspective, these tremendous aeroplanes, and the world they both encompassed and conjured up, were for us a vision of immense and modern glamour and at the same time, like all people being left behind, we felt a sense of flatness and disappointment lingering as we returned to the car and were driven home, counting the weeks and months until it would be our turn to cross that cracked, uneven piste towards the blue and white flying machine and be carried away by it also, cosseted and nourished, across the desert to Europe, to England, homeward.

As you mounted the steps towards the door, almost swooning with excitement, the first impression, aside from the stewardess (a figure of unearthly exoticism), was olfactory. The smell of the fly spray that was liberally pumped throughout the plane's interior prior to take-off was both sweet and oddly choking. It was a smell replicated nowhere else in my range of nasal memory – part marzipan, part cough medicine, part liqueur, part candy, part liniment . . . I could not place it: our fly sprays at home did not smell remotely the same. But whatever it was, whatever brand it was or compound of chemical meeting unnatural fabric in a confined space, the BOAC version was potent and palpable. It was always, for me at least, the first smell of England. It was a kind of Rubicon; as you stepped over the threshold and were directed down the aisle, your lungs were filled with this curious reek. You soon became used to it but it signalled that your journey home had truly begun.

And yet my real home was in West Africa, in the Gold Coast – which in 1957 became Ghana. Until my tenth year I spent only summers in Britain, almost always in Scotland. But my parental home was in Ghana, and so were my bedroom, my things, my school, my friends. Scotland was where my relatives lived, where we rented a house and my parents caught up with their families. We were always in transit, welcomed but always 'just visiting'. The real business of my life lay at the end of another plane journey in the reverse direction. And the comparative brevity of the annual leave never allowed us fully to integrate, to take things for granted, to become *au fait* with the latest fads and fashions. Little details remind me now of that sense of apartness. I felt ill at ease walking past school playgrounds, always stared at. Why wasn't this boy (me) at school? (One could sense the unspoken question.) How were my sullenly curious coevals to know that African school holidays did not coincide with the British? If I had not detoured, I crossed the street, head down. I never felt comfortable with children of my age group *en masse*. I remember my father too, a man of status and real importance on the university campus, where he ran a hospital and health clinics responsible for 20,000 people, fumbling like a new immigrant with his unfamiliar change as he tried to buy a newspaper in Edinburgh. You could sense the newsagent's impatience building as my father picked and prodded hesitantly at a palmful of coins. I possessed also a vague embarrassment about my clothes. The shorts and sandals and shirts made from local tie-dyed cloth – which were wholly unexceptional in Ghana – seemed eccentric, not to say bizarre, in breezy St Andrews or the High Street in Peebles. I had no long trousers at all, and how I coveted my first pair of jeans – finally bought at the age of nine with an aunt in a department store in Birmingham – at last, knees covered, I might not stand out from the crowd. Needless to say, I never felt like this in Africa, where I roamed about the countryside, cycled through the streets and boulevards of the enormous, sprawling campus, possessing the place so thoroughly, so intimately, that such unreflecting familiarity has never been reproduced, no matter where I have subsequently lived. I knew paths through the bush, short cuts through servants' quarters. I knew where the biggest mangoes grew, the best spot to catch pythons, what pie dogs to avoid, how to eat fufu, who would sell you a single stick of chewing gum, what were the rules and penalties of a complicated game involving the spinning of hollow snail shells . . . My life in Africa up until the age of ten was a modest but genuine idyll and its basic elements will be familiar to anyone who has grown up in the tropics – the child, the white child, still possessed a form of tolerant *laissez-passer* denied the adult. We were unnoticed, or barely noticed, everywhere – which, when freedom to come and go is all you ask, is the best and most sincere form of welcome.

And then June came round and the rainy season threatened and it was time to go on leave. BOAC would send one of its planes to fetch us and the strange and exciting process that led to our landfall in England would begin. Sunset in Kano, the lurching roller-coaster of the night flight across the Sahara, dawn in Tripoli, morning in Madrid or Rome – finally peering through clearing clouds at the green patchwork of English fields and the occasional wink of sunburst from a car's windscreen. London airport. More low wooden buildings. Lino and Formica. Tall blue policemen. Pale pasty faces. Strange accents . . . And somewhere, deep inside me, the private hollow of fear and insecurity that all aliens (however legal) carry within them. My passport was British, so why was I uneasy?

It all changed when I was sent to boarding school (in Scotland), something that happened to all expatriate children, as inevitable as puberty. However, my routine was turned on its head, everything was reversed: now I flew to Africa in the holidays. My family, my home, my room, my things, my friends were all as they had always been but now I saw them for only two months of the year. But back in Britain I was beginning to understand the place; I was beginning to be assimilated; I had started to fit in.

I was barely four months old when I made that first flight in the Hermes from Africa to England in 1952. My parents took me up to Scotland to present me to my grandmothers and the rest of the family. For some reason my father went back early and my mother and I joined him some weeks later at the end of our leave. By curious chance, as we were waiting in London airport for our plane to be called, there was a photographer from the *Evening Standard* patrolling the departure lounge looking for a light-hearted filler, I suppose, a bit of human interest for a corner of a page, snapping babes in arms about to go on a long plane journey, still a rarish event in those days, no doubt. My mother has kept the cutting. In the picture one glum and tearful toddler sits morosely on her mother's knee. Opposite, is me, aged six months, fizzing with energy, bald and beefy as a Buddha, beaming hugely, my mother's arm clamped around my middle trying to stop the thrashing and the squirming. 'Why is master William Andrew Murray Boyd so happy?' the caption asks. I could not answer then, but I can now – I was flying home.

Linton Kwesi Johnson

[1952–]

Linton Kwesi Johnson was born in Chapelton, a small rural town in Jamaica. In 1963 he left Jamaica to join his mother in London, where she lived in the largely West Indian-inhabited Brixton. Johnson was educated in Brixton and later received a BA in sociology from Goldsmiths' College, London. When he was about seventeen years old, he began to write. He later described his work as 'a result of the tension between Jamaican Creole and Jamaican English and between those and English English'.

While he was still at school, Johnson became involved with the political activist group the Black Panthers, and later he became a founder member of the Brixton-based Race Today collective. It was in the journal *Race Today* that Johnson's poems were first printed, and it was under the collective's guidance that he published his first volume of poetry, *Voices of the Living and the Dead* (1974). His second collection, *Dread Beat An' Blood* (1975), includes 'Yout Scene', the first poem that Johnson wrote in the Jamaican language. At the point that he began to write in dialect, Johnson says, music entered his poetry as well. The music is both figurative and literal, for in 1978 Johnson released *Dread Beat An' Blood* on vinyl. It was the first LP recording of his 'reggae poetry' or, to use a term that Johnson coined himself, 'dub poetry'. Subsequent albums include *Forces of Victory* (1979), *Bass Culture* (1980) and *Making History* (1984). In 1980, he started his own record label, LKJ. Johnson has continued to publish his poetry in book form, writing 'Inglan is a Bitch' in 1980, and publishing *Tings and Times: Selected Poems* (also released as an album) in 1991.

Nearly all of Johnson's poems are political in nature. In a broad sense, they are responses to the state of the world, urgent illustrations of the violence of both the oppressors and the oppressed. Often written in the language of England's black urban youth – a group 'new in age / but not in rage' – Johnson's poems have an oral quality that lends them a sense of vitality and relevance.

In addition to his writing and political work, Johnson has worked as a
library resources and education officer at Keskidee Arts Centre, in
London. In 1977 he received a C. Day Lewis Fellowship and taught as
writer-in-residence in the London Borough of Lambeth. He is an associate
fellow of Warwick University and an honorary fellow of Wolverhampton
Polytechnic, and in 1990 he received an award at the XIII Premo
Internazionale Ultimo Novecento from the city of Pisa for his musical and
poetic accomplishments. Johnson has performed his work throughout the
world.

*Johnson's poetry articulates the fears and concerns of both the
generation of West Indians who arrived in Britain in the 1950s to work
in factories and the generation of non-white Britons who were born in
Britain and have no memories of life in another place. There is little
romance in either generation's view of Britain. The following poem,
'Inglan is a Bitch', is an apt summary of the feelings of many in Britain,
both young and old, both then and now.*

INGLAN IS A BITCH

w'en mi jus' come to Landan toun
mi use to work pan di andahgroun
but workin' pan di andahgroun
y'u don't get fi know your way aroun'

Inglan is a bitch
dere's no escapin' it
Inglan is a bitch
dere's no runnin' whey fram it

mi get a lickle jab in a big 'otell
an awftah a while, mi woz doin' quite well
dem staat mi aaf as a dish-washah
but w'en mi tek a stack, mi noh tun clack – watchah!

Inglan is a bitch
dere's no escapin' it

Inglan is a bitch
noh baddah try fi hide fram it

w'en dem gi' you di lickle wage packit
fus dem rab it wid dem big tax rackit
y'u haffi struggle fi mek en's meet
an' w'en y'u goh a y'u bed y'u jus' cant sleep

Inglan is a bitch
dere's no escapin' it
Inglan is a bitch
a noh lie mi a tell, a true

mi use to work dig ditch w'en it cowl noh bitch
mi did strang like a mule, but, bwoy, mi did fool
den awftah a while mi jus' stap dhu ovahtime
den awftah a while mi jus' phu dung mi tool

Inglan is a bitch
dere's no escapin' it
Inglan is a bitch
y'u haffi know how fi suvvive in it

well mi dhu day wok an' mi dhu nite wok
mi dhu clean wok an' mi dhu dutty wok
dem seh dat black man is very lazy
but if y'u si how mi wok y'u woulda sey mi crazy

Inglan is a bitch
dere's no escapin' it
Inglan is a bitch
y'u bettah face up to it

dem have a lickle facktri up inna Brackly
inna disya facktri all dem dhu is pack crackry
fi di laas fifteen years dem get mi laybah
now awftah fifteen years mi fall out a fayvah

Inglan is a bitch

dere's no escapin' it
Inglan is a bitch
dere's no runnin' whey fram it

mi know dem have work, work in abundant
yet still, dem mek mi redundant
now, at fifty-five mi gettin' quite ol'
yet still, dem sen' mi fi goh draw dole

Inglan is a bitch
dere's no escapin' it
Inglan is a bitch fi true
is whey wi a goh dhu 'bout it?

Romesh Gunesekera

[1954–]

Romesh Gunesekera was born into a distinguished family in Sri Lanka. When he was twelve years old, he left for the Philippines and four years later moved to Liverpool to board at a small public school. He later attended Liverpool University, where he studied English and philosophy. In 1993 he published a collection of stories entitled *Monkfish Moon*. Like Gunesekera himself, the characters in these stories are caught between the worlds of their colonial homelands and England.

Gunesekera's first novel, *Reef* (1994), written with a Writer's Bursary from the Arts Council of Great Britain, is the moving tale of a young boy named Triton who works for a marine biologist in Colombo, Sri Lanka. Triton begins as an innocent, impressionable servant, but by the end of the book Sri Lanka is in the midst of political upheaval and Triton and his master have moved to London, where Triton eventually establishes his own restaurant. Through a rich, sensuous and often humorous narrative, Gunesekera depicts Triton's emotional growth and disillusionment. *Reef* won the *Yorkshire Post*'s Best First Work Award, and was short-listed for the 1994 Booker Prize.

Gunesekera has two daughters and currently works in the London headquarters of the British Council.

The following extract from Reef addresses the step-by-step method by which assimilation into English society takes place. Gunesekera wishes us to understand that the process of becoming English is one fraught with danger. The slow inevitability of accepting that one stands at the head of a 'line of bedraggled, cosmopolitan itinerants' is lyrically evoked.

Strandline

In London, Mister Salgado settled us into an apartment near Gloucester Road and immediately started work at his institute. It rained continuously in those first months, dribbling down the sides of the building and darkening the wintry sky. The rain seemed to denude the trees and shrink the earth outside our window. I stayed indoors most of the time with the television on. Mister Salgado didn't have much time to show me anything. We didn't go anywhere until the following spring, when he arranged a visit to Wales where a colleague of his had a cottage to rent.

There was a pebble beach at the bottom of the cliff near the cottage. When the tide retreated, the shingle gave way to muddy sand and revealed the debris of a whole new world to me: Irish moss, moon jelly, sea kelp, razor-clams and cockle-shells, sand dollars and frisbees, blue nylon rope and dead sea urchins. In the evenings, when I walked along the path of crushed, purple-ringed mussel-shells and grey whelks, I would hear the sea birds cry, plaintive calls of cormorants and black-tipped herring-gulls as sad as our uprooted, overshadowed lives. Then the northern sun would find its prism and the sky would flare into an incandescent sunset above the oil refinery on the other side of the estuary; petrochemicals stained the air in mauve and pink as deliciously as the Tropic of Capricorn off our coral-spangled south coast back home. The sea shimmering between the black humps of barnacled rocks, mullioned with gold bladder-wrack like beached whales, thickened into a great beast reaching landward, snuffling and gurgling. The sky would redden, the earth redden, the sea redden. In pockmarked, marooned rock pools speckled hermit-crabs and rubbery, red sea anemones dug in; limpets and periwinkles and bubble weed held fast waiting for the tide. Thin, furry tongues flickered out of their lidded shells, casting for the slightest light in the eddies of cool water.

I asked Mister Salgado, 'Do all the oceans flow one into the other? Is it the same sea here as back home?'

'Maybe.' He shrugged. 'The earth has spun with its real stars under a beautiful blue robe ever since the beginning of time. Now as the coral disappears, there will be nothing but sea and we will all return to it.'

The sea in our loins. A tear-drop for an island. A spinning blue globule for a planet. Salt. A wound.

Back home that April, in 1971, the first of the insurgencies erupted in a frenzy of gunfire and small explosions. Bands of zealous young guerrillas roamed the villages and townships staking out their place in a crude unending cortège. Thousands were killed in the reprisals. The earth of a generation was forever cauterized. 'Our civilizations are so frail,' Mister Salgado said, reading the news reports of ghastly beheadings on the beach. But these were only precursors of the staggering brutality that came, wave after wave, in the decades that followed: the suffocating infernos, the burning necklaces, flaming molten rings of fire; the Reign of Terror, abductions, disappearances and the crimes of ideology; this suppurating ethnic war. The bodies would roll again and again in the surf, they would be washed in by the tide and be beached by the dozen. The lives of brothers, sisters, men and women, lovers, fathers and mothers and children would be blighted time and again, unremembered.

But as we walked up the sheep-hill together he would only say, 'She could have been here, you know. Plucking mushrooms out of the earth, or tying a knot in the long grass.' He would hold my arm and step over the puddles on the pewter rocks. 'Look at the bracken rippling between the heather. Here even the wind weeps.'

In our Victorian London home, I would simmer a packet of green flageolets soaked in cold water for six hours; I would wait for him to spill another sentence or two from his head and mark one day from the next.

His job at the institute proved short-lived. 'Another country running out of money,' he said, nurturing his own tight-lipped regression. Back home when he had told his assistants that the south-coast project had been suspended, Wijetunga had gone crazy. He had threatened to blow up the bungalow. 'We can do it,' he had shrieked, shaking a clenched fist. *No messing, boyo.* But here, when it came to his turn, Mister Salgado took the news as another simple fact of life.

He found another, more modest job with a local education authority. 'It's not what you do every day, but the thoughts that you live with that matter,' he would tell me, tapping his head with his finger. 'That, after all, is the sum total of your life in the end.' I would light the gas fire in the sitting-room and bring out the beer.

'So, why did we come here then?' I asked. 'Like refugees?'

'We came to see and learn,' he said, parting the net curtains and staring out at a line of closely pollarded trees. 'Remember?'

But are we not all refugees from something? Whether we stay or go or return, we all need refuge from the world beyond our fingertips at some time. When I was asked by a woman at the pub, 'Have you come from Africa, away from that wicked Amin?' I said, 'No, I am an explorer on a voyage of discovery,' as I imagined my Mister Salgado would have replied. The smoke was thick and heavy like a cloud of yeast spread everywhere. She laughed, touching my arm and moving closer in the dark. A warm Shetland jumper. A slack but yielding skin with patchouli behind her ears. I was learning that human history is always a story of somebody's diaspora: a struggle between those who expel, repel or curtail – possess, divide and rule – and those who keep the flame alive from night to night, mouth to mouth, enlarging the world with each flick of a tongue.

Every May I brought out our summer clothes with their bygone labels – *Batik Boutique*, *CoolMan of Colpetty* – and replenished the spice-racks in the larder. I would try to imagine where I would be, and he, the coming winter when the snow might fall for Christmas and Norfolk turkeys would brown in native kitchens: we would move to yet another short-let property. Mister Salgado's hair turned grey from the temples upward and he began to wear tinted spectacles. Finally, in '76, he said it was time to settle down. He bought a maisonette in Earls Court. There was a magnolia tree in the garden. We learned to sit silently in big, brown chairs and watch the creamy flowers peel, petal by petal, under a red sun sinking somewhere in Wiltshire.

I read all Mister Salgado's books, one by one, over the years. There must have been a thousand books in the sitting-room by the end, each a doorway leading somewhere I had never been before. And even after I had read all of them, each time I looked I would find something new. A play of light and shadow; something flitting in and out of a story I knew by heart. New books came every week. After years of tracking his books and after thousands of pages read and reread, I knew instinctively where he would put the newcomers, as if we had both attuned our own inner shelving to a common frame out of the things we read, separately, in our time together. We never spoke about it, but I am sure he also constructed a kind of syllabus for me to follow. He would leave particular books in particular places: on the toilet roll or on top of a pile of his clothes or balanced precariously on the edge of a table with a teacup on top, knowing I would tidy them away and, as I did so, would dip in and be captivated: *The Wishing Well*, *Ginipettiya*, *The Island*. I am sure he wanted me to read these books, but I don't know whether he knew that I read all his other books as well; all his boxed but boundless realities.

I went to classes and other libraries, night and day, for almost all the years we spent in London together; broke all the old taboos and slowly freed myself from the demons of our past: what is over is over forever, I thought.

'Why is it so much less frightening here,' I asked him, 'even on the darkest night?'

'It's your imagination,' he said. 'It is not yet poisoned in this place.' As if we each had an inner threshold that had to be breached before our surroundings could torment us.

One day I showed him a newspaper report about a symposium on Man and Coral that had taken place. 'You should have been there,' I said. 'Presiding over it all.'

He looked wistful. 'It was a kind of obsession before, you know.'

'But other people now, at last, all over the world seem to share that obsession . . .'

'You remember, all one ocean, no? The debris of one mind floats to another. The same little polyp grows the idea in another head.' He smiled and touched my head. 'But these gatherings are full of people who see the world in a different way now. They carry a lot of heavy equipment, you know. Suntan oil. Scuba tanks. They are only concerned with the how, not the why. I belong to another world. Even Darwin searched his desk for a pen, more than the seabed, you know. He relied on reports, talk, gossip. A tallowline. He looked into himself. In our minds we have swum in the same sea. Do you understand? An imagined world.'

The one time I did swim out to Mister Salgado's real reef, back home, I was frightened by its exuberance. The shallow water seethed with creatures. Flickering eyes, whirling tails, fish of a hundred colours darting and digging, sea snakes, sea-slugs, tentacles sprouting and grasping everywhere. It was a jungle of writhing shapes, magnified and distorted, growing at every move, looming out of the unknown, startling in its hidden brilliance. Suspended in the most primal of sensations, I slowly began to see that everything was perpetually devouring its surroundings. I swam into a sea of sound; my hoarse breathing suddenly punctuated by clicking and clattering, the crunching of fish feeding on the white tips of golden staghorn. My own fingertips seemed to whiten before me as trigger-fish, angel-fish, tiger-fish, tetrons, electrons and sandstone puffer-fish swirled around me, ever hungry.

Mister Salgado shook his head. 'I should have done something of my own with that bay. I used to think that in a month or two, the next year, I would have a chance to turn the whole bay into a sanctuary. A marine park. I used to plan it in my head: how I'd build a jetty, a safe marina for little blue glass-bottomed boats, some outriggers with red sails, and then a sort of floating restaurant at one end. You could have produced your finest chilli crab there, you know, and the best stuffed sea-cucumbers. Just think of it: a row of silver tureens with red crab-claws in black bean sauce, yellow rice and squid in red wine, a roasted red snapper as big as your arm, shark fin and fried seaweed. It would have been a temple to your gastronomic god, no? I thought of it like a ring, a circular platform with the sea in the middle. We could have farmed for the table and nurtured rare breeds for the wild. A centre to study our prehistory.

We could have shown the world something then, something really fabulous. What a waste.'

'Let's do it here,' I said. 'Let's open a restaurant here, in London.'

'That's for you to do,' he said. 'Some day, for yourself.'

He bought the red Volkswagen about that time and taught me to drive. We motored all over the country. We would fill up the tank on a Sunday morning, and drive for miles visiting every historic house, garden, park and museum within a day's circuit. 'The Cook's Tour' he called it with a happy smile, and everywhere explained to me the origins of each artefact we came across. 'The urge to build, to transform nature, to make something out of nothing is universal. But to conserve, to protect, to care for the past is something we have to learn,' he would say.

One cold, wet afternoon we came back to discover a small snack-bar at the end of our road up for sale. Mister Salgado said, 'Here's your chance. Make it come true.' He invested the last of his savings in it. I painted it the colours of our tropical sea. Bought some wicker chairs and a blackboard for the menu. I put coloured lights outside and bucket lanterns inside. It was ready to grow. Mister Salgado beamed.

Then, in the summer of 1983, mobs went on the rampage in Colombo. We saw pictures of young men, who looked no different from me, going berserk on what could have been our main road. The rampant violence made the television news night after night for weeks. There had been nothing like it when trouble had broken out before, when books had been burned and the first skirmishes had started. Even during the insurgency of '71, the news had come only in drifts, distanced. But this time images of cruelty, the birth of a war, flickered on the screens across the world as it happened. I remembered my fervent schoolmaster: his wobbly, black bicycle with its rust-eaten chain-guard, the schoolbook he always carried with him and the black umbrella that would bloom in the warm rain. I had found him in a ditch on the edge of our rice-field, that unsettled month which ended with me coming to Mister Salgado's house. His legs had been broken by a bunch of older boys who used to huddle in a hut in the schoolyard and chant the slogans of a shrinking world.

At the end of the summer, out of the blue one day, Tippy telephoned Mister Salgado. He was changing planes at Heathrow, heading for New York to do some deal. He said he got our number from Directory Enquiries; Tippy knew how things worked all over the world. He said it was wartime now, back home. 'Buggers are playing hell.' He talked about the political shenanigans, the posturing and the big money that was there to be made as always out of big trouble. 'Big bucks, boy,' he said. 'Big bloody bucks.' Right at the end he mentioned Nili. He said she was in a sanatorium off the Galle Road. She was on her own. The business with Robert had ended soon after we had left. He had gone back to the States. Eventually she had started a venture of her own: a guest house for tourists. It had done well. But then during the violence of the summer, a mob had been tipped off that Danton Chidambaram and another Tamil family had been given shelter there by Nili. Their own homes had been gutted. She had hidden the two families upstairs and scolded the louts who came after them. The next night a mob had come with cans of kerosene and set fire to the place. There had been wild dancing in the street. She went to pieces. 'In a mess, *men*. Hopeless. You know how it is, *machang* . . . killing herself now. She has no one, really.'

Mister Salgado put the phone down and pressed his fingers to his temples. He repeated what Tippy had said to him. He told me he had to go and see her. 'I must go back.'

I had once asked her advice about a dish I was making. She had shrugged her shoulders and said, 'You are the master now, the master of cooking!' I didn't tell my Mister Salgado that. Instead I said, 'It's been too many years. So much has happened.' I modelled my voice on his as I had always wanted to, but I knew I could not stop him. I should not.

'You know, Triton,' he said at the end, 'we are only what we remember, nothing more . . . all we have is the memory of what we have done or not done; whom we might have touched, even for a moment . . .' His eyes were swollen with folds of dark skin under and over each eye. I knew he was going to leave me and he would never come back. I would remain and finally have to learn to live on my own. Only then did it dawn on me that this might be what I wanted deep down inside. What perhaps I had always wanted. The nights would be long at the Earls Court snack shop with its line of bedraggled, cosmopolitan itinerants. But they were the people I had to attend to: my future. My life would become a dream of musky hair, smoky bars and garish neon eyes. I would learn to talk and joke and entertain, to perfect the swagger of one who has found his vocation and, at last, a place to call his own. The snack shop would one day turn into a restaurant and I into a restaurateur. It was the only way I could succeed: without a past, without a name, without Ranjan Salgado standing by my side.

On a crisp cloudless Sunday morning, I drove him to the airport. At the check-in counter, while searching for his ticket, he came across his spare keys. 'Here, you'd better have these,' he said and handed them to me. A couple of hours later he flew out, after a glimmer of hope in a faraway house of sorrow.

Kazuo Ishiguro

[1954–]

Kazuo Ishiguro was born in Nagasaki, Japan. He left in 1960, when his father, a scientist working for the British government, was transferred to England. The move was meant to be temporary, but the family never returned to Japan. Ishiguro's formal education took place in Britain, where he attended a boys' grammar school in Surrey and then the University of Kent at Canterbury, from where he received a BA in English and philosophy in 1978. Ishiguro was a community worker for the Renfrew Social Work Department before taking an MA in creative writing at the University of East Anglia in Norwich. Thereafter, he was employed as a social worker for one year.

Ishiguro's first novel, *A Pale View of Hills*, was published in 1982. Set in present-day rural England, it is the haunting story of a Japanese widow whose oldest daughter has just committed suicide. A year after the book was published, Ishiguro received the Winifred Holtby Prize. In 1986 he published *An Artist of the Floating World*, for which he won the Whitbread Award for book of the year. As in his first novel, the narrator is Japanese by birth and struggles to reconcile the past and present.

In 1989 *The Remains of the Day* was published. In this novel, the protagonist is a traditional English butler who faces disillusionment on a personal and national level in post-war England. With his sympathetic portrayals of human characters through first-person narratives, Ishiguro explores the difficult balance between personal and public morality. *The Remains of the Day* won the Booker Prize in 1989, and was later filmed, with a screenplay by Ruth Prawer Jhabvala.

Ishiguro is a Fellow of the Royal Society of Literature. He lives in north London with his wife and daughter. His latest novel is *The Unconsoled* (1995).

The Remains of the Day *is set in 1956, as Britain is passing through the Suez Crisis and coming to terms with the changes associated with losing an empire. The novel suggests a national nostalgia for the past, as*

questions of class and nationality are suddenly vitally important.
Stevens, the butler-narrator, clings desperately to redundant notions of
'rank and order' as embodied in his profession, while the malaise in
society becomes increasingly pervasive.

From *The Remains of the Day*

Tonight, I find myself here in a guest house in the city of Salisbury.
The first day of my trip is now completed, and all in all, I must say I
am quite satisfied. This expedition began this morning almost an
hour later than I had planned, despite my having completed my
packing and loaded the Ford with all necessary items well before
eight o'clock. What with Mrs Clements and the girls also gone for
the week, I suppose I was very conscious of the fact that once I
departed, Darlington Hall would stand empty for probably the first
time this century – perhaps for the first time since the day it was built.
It was an odd feeling and perhaps accounts for why I delayed my
departure so long, wandering around the house many times over,
checking one last time that all was in order.

It is hard to explain my feelings once I did finally set off. For the
first twenty minutes or so of motoring, I cannot say I was seized by
any excitement or anticipation at all. This was due, no doubt, to the
fact that though I motored further and further from the house, I
continued to find myself in surroundings with which I had at least a
passing acquaintance. Now I had always supposed I had travelled
very little, restricted as I am by my responsibilities in the house, but
of course, over time, one does make various excursions for one
professional reason or another, and it would seem I have become
much more acquainted with those neighbouring districts than I had
realized. For as I say, as I motored on in the sunshine towards the
Berkshire border, I continued to be surprised by the familiarity of the
country around me.

But then eventually the surroundings grew unrecognizable and I
knew I had gone beyond all previous boundaries. I have heard

people describe the moment, when setting sail in a ship, when one finally loses sight of the land. I imagine the experience of unease mixed with exhilaration often described in connection with this moment is very similar to what I felt in the Ford as the surroundings grew strange around me. This occurred just after I took a turning and found myself on a road curving around the edge of a hill. I could sense the steep drop to my left, though I could not see it due to the trees and thick foliage that lined the roadside. The feeling swept over me that I had truly left Darlington Hall behind, and I must confess I did feel a slight sense of alarm – a sense aggravated by the feeling that I was perhaps not on the correct road at all, but speeding off in totally the wrong direction into a wilderness. It was only the feeling of a moment, but it caused me to slow down. And even when I had assured myself I was on the right road, I felt compelled to stop the car a moment to take stock, as it were.

I decided to step out and stretch my legs a little and when I did so, I received a stronger impression than ever of being perched on the side of a hill. On one side of the road, thickets and small trees rose steeply, while on the other I could now glimpse through the foliage the distant countryside.

I believe I had walked a little way along the roadside, peering through the foliage hoping to get a better view, when I heard a voice behind me. Until this point, of course, I had believed myself quite alone and I turned in some surprise. A little way further up the road on the opposite side, I could see the start of a footpath, which disappeared steeply up into the thickets. Sitting on the large stone that marked this spot was a thin, white-haired man in a cloth cap, smoking his pipe. He called to me again and though I could not quite make out his words, I could see him gesturing for me to join him. For a moment, I took him for a vagrant, but then I saw he was just some local fellow enjoying the fresh air and summer sunshine, and saw no reason not to comply.

'Just wondering, sir,' he said, as I approached, 'how your legs were.'

'I beg your pardon?'

The fellow gestured up the footpath. 'You got to have a good pair of legs and a good pair of lungs to go up there. Me, I haven't got neither, so I stay down here. But if I was in better shape, I'd be sitting up there. There's a nice little spot up there, a bench and everything. And you won't get a better view anywhere in the whole of England.'

'If what you say is true,' I said, 'I think I'd rather stay here. I happen to be embarking on a motoring trip during the course of which I hope to see many splendid views. To see the best before I have properly begun would be somewhat premature.'

The fellow did not seem to understand me, for he simply said again: 'You won't see a better view in the whole of England. But I tell you, you need a good pair of legs and a good pair of lungs.' Then he added: 'I can see you're in good shape for your age, sir. I'd say you could make your way up there, no trouble. I mean, even I can manage on a good day.'

I glanced up the path, which did look steep and rather rough.

'I'm telling you, sir, you'll be sorry if you don't take a walk up there. And you never know. A couple more years and it might be too late' – he gave a rather vulgar laugh – 'Better go on up while you still can.'

It occurs to me now that the man might just possibly have meant this in a humorous sort of way; that is to say, he intended it as a bantering remark. But this morning, I must say, I found it quite offensive and it may well have been the urge to demonstrate just how foolish his insinuation had been that caused me to set off up the footpath.

In any case, I am very glad I did so. Certainly, it was quite a strenuous walk – though I can say it failed to cause me any real difficulty – the path rising in zigzags up the hillside for a hundred yards or so. I then reached a small clearing, undoubtedly the spot the man had referred to. Here one was met by a bench – and indeed, by a most marvellous view over miles of the surrounding countryside.

What I saw was principally field upon field rolling off into the far distance. The land rose and fell gently, and the fields were bordered by hedges and trees. There were dots in some of the distant fields which I assumed to be sheep. To my right, almost on the horizon, I thought I could see the square tower of a church.

It was a fine feeling indeed to be standing up there like that, with the sound of summer all around one and a light breeze on one's face. And I believe it was then, looking on that view, that I began for the first time to adopt a frame of mind appropriate for the journey before me. For it was then that I felt the first healthy flush of anticipation for the many interesting experiences I know these days ahead hold in store for me. And indeed, it was then that I felt a new resolve not to be daunted in respect to the one professional task I have entrusted myself with on this trip; that is to say, regarding Miss Kenton and our present staffing problems.

But that was this morning. This evening I find myself settled here in this comfortable guest house in a street not far from the centre of Salisbury. It is, I suppose, a relatively modest establishment, but very clean and perfectly adequate for my needs. The landlady, a woman of around forty or so, appears to regard me as a rather grand visitor on account of Mr Farraday's Ford and the high quality of my suit. This afternoon – I arrived in Salisbury at around three thirty – when I entered my address in her register as 'Darlington Hall', I could see her look at me with some trepidation, assuming no doubt that I was some gentleman used to such places as the Ritz or the Dorchester and that I would storm out of her guest house on being shown my room. She informed me that a double room at the front was available, though I was welcome to it for the price of a single.

I was then brought up to this room, in which, at that point of the day, the sun was lighting up the floral patterns of the wallpaper quite agreeably. There were twin beds and a pair of good-sized windows overlooking the street. On inquiring where the bathroom was, the woman told me in a timid voice that although it was the door facing mine, there would be no hot water available until after supper. I asked her to bring me up a pot of tea, and when she had gone, inspected the room further. The beds were perfectly clean and had been well made. The basin in the corner was also very clean. On looking out of the windows, one saw on the opposite side of the street a bakery displaying a variety of pastries, a chemist's shop and a barber's. Further along, one could see where the street passed over a round-backed bridge and on into more rural surroundings. I refreshed my face and hands with cold water at the basin, then seated myself on a hard-backed chair left near one of the windows to await my tea.

I would suppose it was shortly after four o'clock that I left the guest house and ventured out into the streets of Salisbury. The wide, airy nature of the streets here give the city a marvellously spacious feel, so that I found it most easy to spend some hours just strolling in the gently warm sunshine. Moreover, I discovered the city to be one of many charms; time and again, I found myself wandering past delightful rows of old timber-fronted houses, or crossing some little stone footbridge over one of the many streams that flow through the city. And of course, I did not fail to visit the fine cathedral, much praised by Mrs Symons in her volume. This august building was hardly difficult for me to locate, its looming spire being ever-visible wherever one goes in Salisbury. Indeed, as I was making my way back to this guest house this evening, I glanced back over my shoulder on a number of occasions and was met each time by a view of the sun setting behind that great spire.

And yet tonight, in the quiet of this room, I find that what really remains with me from this first day's travel is not Salisbury Cathedral, nor any of the other charming sights of this city, but rather that marvellous view encountered this morning of the rolling English countryside. Now I am quite prepared to believe that other countries can offer more obviously spectacular scenery. Indeed, I have seen in encyclopedias and the *National Geographic Magazine* breathtaking photographs of sights from various corners of the globe; magnificent canyons and waterfalls, raggedly beautiful mountains. It has never, of course, been my privilege to have seen such things at first hand, but I will nevertheless hazard this with some confidence: the English landscape at its finest – such as I saw it this morning – possesses a quality that the landscapes of other nations, however more superficially dramatic, inevitably fail to possess. It is, I believe, a quality that will mark out the English landscape to any objective observer as the most deeply satisfying in the world, and this quality is probably best summed up by the term 'greatness'. For it is true, when I stood on that high ledge this morning and viewed the land before me, I distinctly felt that rare, yet unmistakable feeling – the feeling that one is in the presence of greatness. We call this land of ours *Great* Britain, and there may be those who believe this a somewhat immodest practice. Yet I would venture that the landscape of our country alone would justify the use of this lofty adjective.

And yet what precisely is this 'greatness'? Just where, or in what, does it lie? I am quite aware it would take a far wiser head than mine to answer such a question, but if I were forced to hazard a guess, I would say that it is the very *lack* of obvious drama or spectacle that sets the beauty of our land apart. What is pertinent is the calmness of that beauty, its sense of restraint. It is as though the land knows of its own beauty, of its own greatness, and feels no need to shout it. In comparison, the sorts of sights offered in such places as Africa and America, though undoubtedly very exciting, would, I am sure, strike the objective viewer as inferior on account of their unseemly demonstrativeness.

This whole question is very akin to the question that has caused much debate in our profession over the years: what is a 'great' butler? I can recall many hours of enjoyable discussion on this topic around the fire of the servants' hall at the end of a day. You will notice I say 'what' rather than 'who' is a great butler; for there was actually no serious dispute as to the identity of the men who set the standards amongst our generation. That is to say, I am talking of the likes of Mr Marshall of Charleville House, or Mr Lane of Bridewood. If you have ever had the privilege of meeting such men, you will no doubt know of the quality they possess to which I refer. But you will no doubt also understand what I mean when I say it is not at all easy to define just what this quality is.

Incidentally, now that I come to think further about it, it is not quite true to say there was no dispute as to *who* were the great butlers. What I should have said was that there was no serious dispute among professionals of quality who had any discernment in such matters. Of course, the servants' hall at Darlington Hall, like any servants' hall anywhere, was obliged to receive employees of varying degrees of intellect and perception, and I recall many a time having to bite my lip while some employee – and at times, I regret to say, members of my own staff – excitedly eulogized the likes of, say, Mr Jack Neighbours.

I have nothing against Mr Jack Neighbours, who sadly, I understand, was killed in the war. I mention him simply because his was a typical case. For two or three years in the mid-thirties, Mr Neighbours's name seemed to dominate conversations in every servants' hall in the land. As I say, at Darlington Hall too, many a visiting employee would bring the latest tales of Mr Neighbours's achievements, so that I and the likes of Mr Graham would have to share the frustrating experience of hearing anecdote after anecdote relating to him. And most frustrating of all would be having to witness at the conclusion of each such anecdote otherwise decent employees shaking their heads in wonder and uttering phrases like: 'That Mr Neighbours, he really is the best.'

Now I do not doubt that Mr Neighbours had good organizational skills; he did, I understand, mastermind a number of large occasions with conspicuous style. But at no stage did he ever approach the status of a great butler. I could have told you this at the height of his reputation, just as I could have predicted his downfall after a few short years in the limelight.

How often have you known it for the butler who is on everyone's lips one day as the greatest of his generation to be proved demonstrably within a few years to have been nothing of the sort? And yet those very same employees who once heaped praise on him will be too busy eulogizing some new figure to stop and examine their sense of judgement. The object of this sort of servants' hall talk is invariably some butler who has come to the fore quite suddenly through having been appointed by a prominent house, and who has perhaps managed to pull off two or three large occasions with some success. There will then be all sorts of rumours buzzing through servants' halls up and down the country to the effect that he has been approached by this or that personage or that several of the highest houses are competing for his services with wildly high wages. And what has happened before a few years have passed? This same invincible figure has been held responsible for some blunder, or has for some other reason fallen out of favour with his employers, leaves the house where he came to fame and is never heard of again. Meanwhile, those same gossipers will have found yet some other newcomer about whom to enthuse. Visiting valets, I have found, are often the worst offenders, aspiring as they usually do to the position of butler with some urgency. They it is who tend to be always insisting this or that figure is the one to emulate, or repeating what some particular hero is said to have pronounced upon professional matters.

But then, of course, I hasten to add, there are many valets who would never dream of indulging in this sort of folly – who are, in fact, professionals of the highest discernment. When two or three such persons were gathered together at our servants' hall – I mean of the calibre of, say, Mr Graham, with whom now, sadly, I seem to have lost touch – we would have some of the most stimulating and intelligent debates on every aspect of our vocation. Indeed, today, those evenings rank amongst my fondest memories from those times.

But let me return to the question that is of genuine interest, this question we so enjoyed debating when our evenings were not spoilt by chatter from those who lacked any fundamental understanding of the profession; that is to say, the question '*what* is a great butler?'

David Dabydeen

[1955-]

David Dabydeen was born on a sugar plantation in Berbice, Guyana (formerly British Guiana). His work is greatly influenced by the racial violence of the early 1960s that he observed during his childhood. When he was twelve years old, Dabydeen moved to England, where, after his parents' divorce, he grew up in the care of the local authorities. He attended the universities of Cambridge and London, and received his doctorate in 1982.

Dabydeen's career has effectively been a blend of writing and scholarship. His academic appointments include a research fellowship at Wolfson College, Oxford, and a lectureship at the Centre for Caribbean Studies at the University of Warwick, where he is now the Director of Studies. He remains dedicated to raising political and personal consciousness through his teaching, and his poetry exhibits similar goals. In 1984 he published *Slave Song*, a series of poems narrated by sugar-cane cutters and ironically presented by Dabydeen under a cloak of 'scholarly' translations and notes. Through these dramatic monologues, Dabydeen expresses the 'erotic energies of the colonial experience' and the spiritual and physical suffering of his characters, who long to possess the 'ideal' characteristics they see embodied in whites. *Slave Song* earned Dabydeen the 1984 Commonwealth Poetry Prize and the Quiller-Couch Prize at Cambridge.

In 1985 Dabydeen edited *The Black Presence in English Literature* with Paul Edwards. *Hogarth's Blacks: Images of Blacks in Eighteenth-century English Art* was his second academic publication, a book which can be read in conjunction with his work *Hogarth, Walpole and Commercial Britain* (1987). Both are studies of the painter William Hogarth and the relatively progressive depiction of blacks in his art. In 1988 Dabydeen published his second collection of poetry, *Coolie Odyssey*. In this volume he evokes the experiences of East Indians in both Britain and the Caribbean, and comments on the effects of colonialism.

Dabydeen's first novel, *The Intended*, was published in 1991 and won the Guyana Prize for Literature. It is an autobiographical account of the author's boyhood in Guyana, and subsequent emigration to England, and illustrates Dabydeen's personal struggle to replace feelings of self-loathing and inferiority with a sense of pride. In 1993 Dabydeen published *Disappearance*, which is narrated by a young West Indian engineer who has been employed to rescue a deteriorating village on the Kent coast. *Turner: New and Selected Poems* was published in 1994 and his third novel, *The Counting House*, in 1996.

Memories of colonial exploitation are always close to the surface in Dabydeen's work. His poem 'London Taxi Driver' (1988) is typical of his impatience with the damage that the metropolitan world continues to inflict on the psyche of the immigrant. Without the warm mythological sense of Britain that seemed to form an important backdrop to the work of earlier generations of West Indian-born writers, Dabydeen's juxtaposition of present-day Britain with remembered 'home' is disturbing.

LONDON TAXI DRIVER

From Tooting, where I picked him up, to Waterloo,
He honked, swerved, swore,
Paused at the twin-tubbed buttocks of High Street Wives,
Jerked forward again,
Unwound the window as we sped along,
Hawked and spat.

The talk was mostly solitary,
Of the new single, of missing the pools by bleeding two,
Of some sweet bitch in some soap serial,
How he'd like to mount and stuff her lipsticked mouth,
His eyes suddenly dreamy with designs –
Nearly missing a light he slammed the car stop,
Snatched the hand-brake up.
Wheel throbbed in hand, engine giddy with anticipation.
As we toured the slums of Lambeth the meter ticked greedily.

He has come far and paid much for the journey
From some village in Berbice where mule carts laze
And stumble over broken paths,
Past the women with buckets on their heads puffed
With ghee and pregnancy,
Past the men slowly bent over earth, shovelling,
Past the clutch of mud huts jostling for the shade,
Their Hindu flags of folk defiant rituals
That provoked the Imperial swords of Christendom
Discoloured, hang their heads and rot
On bamboo pikes:
Now he knows more the drama of amber red and green,
Mutinies against double-yellow lines,
His aggression is horned like ancient clarions,
He grunts rebellion
In back seat discount sex
With the night's last whore.

Michael Hofmann

[1957–]

Michael Hofmann was born in Freiburg, Germany. When he was seven years old, he left Germany for Britain. He was educated in Edinburgh, Bristol and Winchester before attending Magdalene College, Cambridge. Hofmann received a BA in English in 1979 and in 1980 he continued his studies at the University of Regensburg and at Trinity College in Cambridge. Upon obtaining his graduate degree in 1983, Hofmann became a freelance writer.

Hofmann's debut volume of poetry, *Nights in the Iron Hotel* (1983), signalled the emergence of an unusual and significant talent. With prosaic rhythms and an offbeat sense of irony, his poems juxtapose familiarity with foreignness. The sense of 'otherness' is continued in his next collection, *Acrimony* (1986), which is divided into two parts. The first deals with a variety of emotional and political issues; the second is an intimate exploration of Hofmann's complex relationship with his father, the novelist Gert Hofmann.

K.S. in Lakeland: New and Selected Poems was published in 1990. Hofmann has also translated several works from German, including Kurt Tucholsky's *Castle Gripsholm* (1985), his father's *The Film Explainer* (1995), and Joseph Roth's *The Legend of the Holy Drinker* (1989). In 1984 he was the recipient of the Cholmondeley Award and in 1988 he won both the Geoffrey Faber Memorial Prize and the Schlegel-Tieck Prize. Since 1990 Hofmann has been teaching creative writing at the University of Florida in Gainesville.

Hofmann's poetry exhibits a private anxiety altogether different from Dabydeen's largely historically conditioned work. 'The Machine That Cried' (1986) depicts the often desperate, and always moving, desire of a young man to understand his dual heritage and then make a choice as to where his future lies.

THE MACHINE THAT CRIED

'Il n'y a pas de détail' – Paul Valéry

When I learned that my parents were returning
to Germany, and that I was to be jettisoned,
I gave a sudden lurch into infancy and Englishness.
Carpets again loomed large in my world: I sought out
their fabric and warmth, where there was nowhere to fall . . .

I took up jigsaw puzzles, read mystical cricket thrillers
passing all understanding, even collected toy soldiers
and killed them with matchsticks fired from the World War One
field-guns I bought from Peter Oborn down the road
– he must have had something German, with that name –

who lived alone with his mother, like a man . . .
My classmates were equipped with sexual insults
for the foaming lace of the English women playing Wimbledon,
but I watched them blandly on our rented set
behind drawn curtains, without ever getting the point.

My building-projects were as ambitious as the Tower of Babel.
Something automotive of my construction limped across the
     floor
to no purpose, only lugging its heavy battery.
Was there perhaps some future for Christiaan Barnard,
or the electric car, a milk-float groaning like a sacred heart?

I imagined Moog as von Moog, a mad German scientist.
His synthesizer was supposed to be the last word in versatility,
but when I first heard it on Chicory Tip's
Son of My Father, it was just a unisono metallic drone,
five notes, as inhibited and pleonastic as the title.

My father bought a gramophone, a black box,
and played late Beethoven on it, which my mother was always
to associate with her miscarriage of that year.

I was forever carrying it up to my room,
and quietly playing through my infant collection of singles,

Led Zeppelin, The Tremeloes, *My Sweet Lord* . . .
The drums cut like a scalpel across the other instruments.
Sometimes the turntable rotated slowly, then everything
went flat, and I thought how with a little more care
it could have been all right. There again, so many things

were undependable . . . My first-ever British accent wavered
between Pakistani and Welsh. I called *Bruce's* record shop
just for someone to talk to. He said, 'Certainly, Madam.'
Weeks later, it was 'Yes sir, you can bring your children.'
It seemed I had engineered my own birth in the new country.

Ben Okri
[1959–]

Ben Okri was born in Minna, Nigeria. He was educated in Nigeria and at the University of Essex in Colchester, where he received a BA in comparative literature. In 1981 he became poetry editor of the journal *West Africa*, a position he held for the next six years. In 1984 he also worked as a broadcaster for the BBC World Service programme *Network Africa*. Okri is a full-time writer and occasional reviewer for the *Guardian*, the *Observer* and the *New Statesman*.

Okri's first novel, *Flowers and Shadows* (1980), is an understated yet emotional portrayal of a young Nigerian boy's journey into adulthood. Published when Okri was twenty-one, the novel adheres to a conventional structure, one which Okri would abandon for a more experimental form in his next book, *The Landscapes Within* (1981). With a precise, compassionate writing style that earned him comparisons with Chinua Achebe and Wole Soyinka, Okri tells the tale of a painter who is confronted with social and political corruption. Okri continued to move away from literary convention with his next two short-story collections, *Incidents at the Shrine* (1986) and *Stars of the New Curfew* (1989). In the former, his settings include Nigeria during the time of the Civil War, the depressed streets of London and a fictional landscape that is a dreamlike amalgam of African sensibilities and Margaret Thatcher's England. In both volumes Okri uses hallucinatory, sometimes nightmarish images. He continued to employ 'magic realism' in his next novel, *Famished Road* (1991), a sensuous tale filled with bizarre characters and narrated by a 'spirit child', it won the 1991 Booker Prize. Two years later Okri published a sequel, *Songs of Enchantment*. His latest novels are *Astonishing the Gods* (1995) and *Dangerous Love* (1996).

Okri's work returns us to the alienation of the British writers of African origin in the eighteenth-century. In his story 'Disparities' (1986) the narrator is at different times at odds with British society in terms of class, race and the 'simple' ability to support himself in a relentlessly hostile

London. This is a terrifying vision of a late-twentieth-century Britain
that is thoroughly unreceptive, a country in which, despite the plurality
of cultures and people, a 'visitor' can become a 'stranger' before he or
she knows quite what has happened.

Disparities

I do not know what season it is. It might be spring, summer or
winter, for all anyone cares. Autumn always misses me for some
reason. It probably is winter. It always seems to be winter in this
damn poxy place. When the sun is up and people make a nuisance of
themselves, revealing flaccid and shapeless bodies, I am always
aware of a chill in my marrow. My fingers tremble. My toes squash
together. And my teeth chatter. That is the worst; there is more. And
when the severity of the grey weather returns, when the seasons run
into one another, and when advertisements everywhere irritate the
eye and spirit – depicting vivid roses, family togetherness and
laughter mouth-deep – I cannot help feeling that civilizations are
based on an uneasy yoking of lies; and that is precisely when the
sight of flowers and pubs and massive white houses and people
depresses me most; when, in fact, I am most nauseated. Then I have
constant fits of puking, nervous tremulation and withdrawal
symptoms so merciless that I cannot separate the world from the
sharp exultant pangs in my chest. My resistance is low. The only
season I know from this side of the battering days is starvation. I
know it is warm when I have filled my stomach with a tin of baked
beans; it is tepid when I must have had a piece of toast; and it is cold
when I have bloated my stomach on a pint of milk some idiot left
standing on a doorstep. When an individual learns to cope with the
absurdity of seasons without changing trivial externalities – *then*, in
my estimation, *they* have acquired the most vital trappings of
culture. All else is just overlaid loneliness and desperation and group
brutality.

The trouble is I lived in a house for a few days. My first house. It was all peaceful and full of dogshit and totally decrepit. The walls had been broken down, cushions torn, the windows fitted with gashed rubbish-bin linings. It was a lovely place; I had never before found such serenity. To have a house, that is the end of the journey of our solitude.

Then, of all the horrible things that can happen to disrupt such a discovery – a bunch of undergraduates moved in upstairs. They made a hell of a lot of noise, had long drinking and smoking parties, talked about books and 1940s clothes and turbans and dope from exotic places and the Vice-Chancellor. They brought with them a large tape-recorder and played reggae and heavy metal music. Then they brought in mattresses, pillows, food, lampshades, silk screens and large lurid posters and *books*. Imagine my revulsion. They talked about Marx and Lévi-Strauss and Sartre and now and then one of the girls would say how easy it was to appreciate those *bastards* (she said this laughingly) when one is stoned.

That was it. Definitely. It was enough that one had to bear oneself in a single frame, but to add to that a bunch of undergraduates who were playing holiday games with broken and empty houses was more than any person could stand without going berserk. A genocidal mood gripped me. I got my bundle together and stormed upstairs. The house was in a far worse state of devastation than I imagined. The banisters had all been knocked down and attempts had been made to wreck the stairs. The rooms were bad. I banged around up into the higher reaches of the house and eventually found the students.

The door to their room had been broken down. There were about six of them. Group desolation. Indeed, they were all variations of a type: their hair dyed red or blue or purple; they wore tight-fitting trousers, the girls wore desperate short dresses, and their eyelids were painted with iridescent sheen. I found it impossible to see one for the other; they seemed so interchangeable. The room had been cleared up, it was almost – a *room*. There were mirrors all over the place and their interchangeability, reflecting back and forth, compounded my confusion. When I banged in they were lying down, coupled, women to women, men to men, women to men. They jerked their heads, responding awkwardly to the reggae music.

For a long moment words escaped me. One of them said something about going home and returning shortly; another replied, saying that this was a good 'scene' and forget home and 'check it out, yeh.' Another said: 'Yeh, pass the joint' – and for some group reason they all *laughed*. Two things happened inside me: I was angry; and I instantly became aware of a low point in my season. I didn't want to eat or anything like that; I was simply possessed with the desire to retch. Instead, I kicked one of their mirrors. They *laughed*. One of them said: 'Hey, man, are you the *landlord*?' And another said: 'Pass the joint.' And another: 'Join the party.' And another one (laughingly): 'I tell you, right: *we are landlords*.' The voices merged and became cluttered: 'We are Communists. Anarcho-Communists.' My toes felt squashed. '*Get it, right: we are Comfemists*.' My throat began a curious process of strangling me and my head grew livid with twitches. 'WE ARE WHITE. BUT WE ARE FUCKTOGETHER-NESS, RIGHT.' There was a diminutive black girl with them. She was cradled by a white girl with a pinched face and elaborate gestures. They were giggling. The music stopped. The girl with the pinched face stood up: 'WE STAND FOR FREEDOM.' I turned around, tripped over some stupid fitting and fumbled my way down the beautiful death trap that was the stairs. When I came out into the street I could still hear them laughing.

Well. So. I was yet again unhoused. Landlords have the queerest ways. Anyway. That was that. And who denies that the system (monster invisible) has the capacity to absorb all its blighted offshoots? And so I took to the streets. The long, endless streets. Plane trees growing from cement. I walked and walked and I inspected the houses as I went along. Houses. I avoided taking in the eye-sores that were human beings and stuck my gaze to the pavement in front of me. This was highly rewarding for I was entertained with the shapes of dogshit. This is the height of civilization. This is what to look out for when everything else seems a nightmare. Following these patterns, and where they seemed to lead, I came to a park.

The park was all right, as parks in this place go. All the usual greenery and undulations and grey statues and rundown cafés and playgrounds. And, of course, there were people. I saw old men and women with dogs. Children playing about in all the sorts of games in which they are for ever trapped as children. They ran about, shouted, cried, called names, laughed, were sweet; they formed little groups and kept the brutality intact; they pretended they were adults, calling the different names of animals and birds and flowers. The older people were no different: they trundled around, looked wistfully at the sky, pretended to enjoy their isolation, called to their dogs, looked on fondly and complacently when their dogs urinated: they smiled at the children, sat stiffly on benches. When the children's football rolled towards them they sometimes kicked it back with a crotchety grace. I saw the young couples nestled together near a tree or in the open fields; they, too, looked complacent – the whole of nature as a lover's dream. They laughed, nice little laughs without any depth and without any pain. Insipid love; cultured laughter. Or they threw balls at one another, stiffly mimicking the children; or they walked slowly along, hair fingered by the wind, their faces pale pink on blue-white. They, too, must enjoy their isolation.

So I followed my compass. Away from the wreckful siege. It pointed north, to the furthest part where there were no landscaped undulations and no lovers and no children of any sort; where only nobbled and ugly trees consorted and where the earth was slashed in the beginnings of some building project recently liberated from red-tape. I first of all eased myself comfortably on one of these trees and then I searched for an area of unattractive grass. Not far from where I was going to sit there was a bird. Maggots crawled out of its beak. I stared at it for a while, all sorts of temptations going through my mind. It was upturned in a grotesque enchantment and for a while I experienced a cluttered remembrance of all those fairy-tales that were bludgeoned into us when young. The memories irritated me. I spat, generously, and then I lay down. There seemed no distance between me and the sky. I hate skies. They seemed to me a sentimental creation. Skies are something else that has been bludgeoned into us. They are everywhere: in adverts, on window-panes, reflected in patches of dog piss. Hardly a conversation takes place without someone mentioning the sky: hardly you open a novel without the author attempting some sort of description. Honestly. Skies are quite boring. Anyway. I entertained the thought, and I am ashamed of it, and my shame is my business, of how it would be like to be able to leave this body and become part of the sky. The relentless visitations! The upending of myths and the tremendous reversals and the creating of new myths to enable people to become complacent again!

I was about to explore the true foulness of the fantasy when, of all visitations, a bunch of children led by a schoolteacher went past. If they had just tramped past and gone on, and on, it would have been fine. But no. Every sweet solitude had to be destroyed. And they lingered. The teacher told them the names of trees (elm, plane, horsechestnut, etc.), asked them the names of the cloud formations, told them not to fight, asked them to pay attention, and so on. If it had been just a little educational trip it would have been fine. Horrors – the children began to prowl around. They brought back mushrooms, worms skewered on twigs, butterflies cupped in hands; they had a *picnic*. Then at one point the most annoying thing happened: they saw *the enchanted bird*. If there is anything more annoying than the self-conscious giggles of lovers it is the sound of inquisitive children. This is what happened. Three of the kids were running about, chasing one another. They saw me and stopped. They looked at me and looked at each other and then they laughed. They whispered among themselves. Their interest soon vanished. They had seen the bird.

'What is it?'

'It's a bird.'

They stood around the bird. One of them kicked it over and ran away. The others ran with her. They soon came back.

'What is it?'

'It's a dead pigeon.'

'It's a dead pigeon – ooooooh.'

They ran away again and came back.

'What is it?'

'I thought it was a dead duck.'

'A dead duck!'

'It's a *dead pigeon*. Can't you see?'

They poked at the bird again. One of them lifted it up delicately with the tip of her fingers as though it were the most diseased thing imaginable. Then she dropped it.

'Uuuuuuhhhh. It's got maggots all over it.'

They regarded the bird for a moment. There was a morbid fascination in their eyes. I had seen adult mutations of that look several times. It is a look that is perched between the power for terror and the possibility of inflicting that terror. I have seen it highly concentrated, and hidden, when a policeman regards me at night, a moment before he grabs me by the collar and shoves me out of the Tube station where he knows I have to spend the night. I have seen it frustrated and sly when I encounter bands of youths. I have seen it in the men when they think I am more than eyeing their women. And when I saw it then in the eyes of those children I could not restrain myself from yelling. They looked at me. Shocked, I looked at them.

Their teacher, eyeing me with metallic severity, said: 'Jane, leave the bird alone. Come on, come along, girls.'

The girls regarded me with utmost suspicion. They stared at me and stared at the bird. I think they must have ascertained the most intriguing relationship between me and that bird. Fear trembled in their eyes. Fear and eternal curiosity. They waited for one of them to make the first movement. One of them did and the next minute they all fled. I watched them. The teacher moved them on. They talked among themselves and kept looking back at me. Maybe they expected me to turn into a huge black bird and take off into the air.

Anyway, I tried to recover my reverie about some sort of room in the sky where lies and illusions and self-deceptions are made naked; and where humanity can recover its very basic sense of terror and compassion. But nothing is allowed me. A dog came towards me from across the fields. It stopped at the tree where I had earlier on eased myself; it raised a hind leg and urinated. Then it too saw me. Sniffed me out. Barked and barked; and then it discovered the bird. It sniffed the bird, carried it off in its mouth, and brought it back again. The dog's owner, an old man with an absurd sense of self-dignity, trundled past me, saw me, but, thanks to decorum, pretended not to see me.

He stopped, whistled, and said as if to a child: 'Come on, Jimmy.' The dog raced off, and the old man followed. Dogs and their owners always make such a pair. That, again, was that. I got up, made my way through the park and hugged the streets again.

It really does pay to avoid the sight of human beings. I had a windfall; I found a pound note. There it was wet and stuck to the ground among the leaves that had fallen from the plane trees. Plane trees grow from cement. That was that. And it called for a celebration of another minor season. I decided to make my way to a favourite pub in town. When I arrived, pushing aggressively through the door, the barman instantly recognized me and that morbid fascination leapt into his eyes. He licked his lips. He had a bullying face with a wild growth of beard. He was tall. He had that angry and grumpy air of one who had kicked himself out of a rebellious and idealistic generation. I suspected that running the pub was for him an act of masochistically gutting the dreams that had abandoned him. The pub stank thoroughly. It had for its clientele the very cream of leftovers, kicked-outs, eternal trendies, hoboes, weirdos, addicts and pedlars. The foulest exhalations of humanity were nowhere so pungent. The pub and its depressing decor, having soaked in the infinitely varied stinks of its customers, recycled its pollutions free of charge with the drinks. And this is precisely what the pub celebrates. I didn't mind: I had been entangled in enough fights and had uttered enough that was blasphemous to enable me to buy drinks on credit. After all, having a credit is one of the finer things of life.

So the barman watched me. His face twitched. He moved towards me: 'What will it be? Paying up? Or more credit?'

Before I could make up my mind, an old man rushed at me. The wheels grind: and one has to take the grindings as they come. The old man offered to buy me a drink. We had an unstated pact that had been going on for weeks. Whenever I came in he would rush to buy me a drink and then I was supposed to listen to the accumulation of his problems. He told me everything. He told me about how he had hated going to the war. He told me of his first wife, who had made several attempts to kill him; and his second wife, who didn't like sex; and how he gave up wives and discovered prostitutes. He told about his overdrafts, how he contracted VD, his suicide attempts, his varicose veins and how they throbbed and about the cat he bought and was forced to kill one wintry night. It was the way it purred, he said, the way it shivered. He simply inundated me with the grimiest details of his condition. I didn't mind; I had my drinks paid for; and besides, his account of his own suffering had a bracing effect on me. Whenever I saw him I knew that my dose of participation in humanity was assured. Then I could go away, search for a place for the night, and dream about varicose veins and strangled kittens.

He was holding a newspaper. He trembled as if in the grip of a curious sexual fever. His fingers twitched. The barman looked on, his mouth twisted in a peculiar dream of sadism. I ordered two drinks: a half for the old man and a pint for me. The barman licked his lips. The old man stuttered and brought out his crinkled wallet. I fingered my windfall; I laughed. Someone put a coin into the jukebox and plunged that human cesspit into perfect unmelodious gloom. The barman plonked the drinks on the counter, and scowled. I plonked my windfall on the counter, hugged the drinks, and edged the old man into one of the grimy seats.

I tasted my drink and then took a mouthful. The old man smiled. He put his newspaper down on the table and then struggled with his pocket. He was always doing things like that. Grey with decrepit mystery, he brought out a packet of razorblades from the side pocket of his coat.

'I am going to have a shave,' he smiled.

'Here?'

'No. Later.'

I drank some more. The bar filled up, became crowded, and all the groups that fought for supremacy made their loud noises in the dull lights of the pub. He drank as well. He looked around, from one group to the next, from one spaced-out hippy to another hash-pedlar. He was uncertain. He struggled with his pockets again and brought out a handkerchief. It was stained beyond description.

'You should be a magician,' I said.

He smiled, but his face made it into a mask of anguish. That bilious face! He coughed, looked at me, coughed again. He scraped his throat with the cough, out flew his phlegm. The phlegm – thick, green and sludgy – was trapped between his mouth and the handkerchief. Then it dribbled down his chin. He rescued it with the handkerchief. I could see how the handkerchief got its colour. He smiled again, a perfect mask. He was not satisfied: with another deep-grinding cough he dragged up more phlegm; the same thing happened. I caught myself watching. I could no longer taste my drink; everything soon seemed to be composed of the old man's phlegm. Then he began to talk. Uncertain. He did not know if the pact was still operative; he rambled. He told me of the foxes he saw along the desolate railway tracks at night. He told me of the old woman who had died downstairs. At some point when my disgust had begun to turn upon itself, I told him to stop.

'What's the matter?'

That bilious face!

'I want you to listen to me.'

He nodded. Then without knowing why I began to talk. That's how we do it sometimes. We talk ourselves into the inescapable heart of our predicament. I told him about the number of times I had been beaten up outside Tube stations at night. I told him where I had to sleep, unmentionable places that leave a dampness in the soul. I told him how I wander around the city inspecting the houses with only a tubful of yoghurt in my stomach. I am on hunger-strike, I said. I can't strike and I'm hungry. When I had a fever, only the streets saw me through it. I just went on and on till I got so confused in the heart of what I was saying that all I wanted to do was fall asleep. I was tired; I had drained myself; I stopped. When I looked up, the old man was crying. He sobbed and puckered his lips and scratched his hands. I was irritated. I picked up the newspaper and read the story of a Nigerian who had left a quarter of a million pounds in the back of a taxi-cab. The old man still wept and kicked on the seat. Everyone looked at us; they didn't really care; it was the common run of the place. The old man suddenly stopped crying. He picked up the packet of razorblades and made for the toilet. It occurred to me, as he stumbled against the table and spilled some of our drink, that I *needed* razorblades. I followed him and after a scuffle disarmed the decrepit magician of the packet. He went back to his chair and I got fed up with the whole farce. I felt dizzy. I recognized the dizziness: it was the mark of a low season. When it first happened to me I thought it was an early sign that I was going mad. Then I learned that all I really needed was a pint of some idiot's milk and a can of baked beans.

I got up; I told the old man to have my drink and asked him for some cigarettes. He threw his well-fingered packet at me. I went out, avoiding the bullying glance of the barman, glad to be rid of that insistent sound of weeping, which is a mark of when people have lost a temporary haven; and glad also to be rid of that whole bunch of depressives and trendies who mistake the fact of their lostness for the attraction of the outsider's confusion.

As I walked down the darkened streets and inspected the curtained windows of the houses, I found that I had discovered something. I had found, in that sweet-tempered solitude of the streets, a huge and wonderfully small room in the sky that is composed of ten thousand taxi-cabs and pasted over with the quarter of a million pounds that belonged to a Nigerian. And in this discovery I dreamed of several silk-yards of myths and realities and enchantments with which to remake the cracked music of all wretched people.

Yes, I dreamed. I had discovered, for example, that there had been a mistake. Everyone had been fooled: I had perpetrated a hoax. Nobody knew it but: I WAS THE TAXI-CAB DRIVER. What a shock it was, coming to myself. Tramping down the grey streets, inspecting the houses, I followed myself, haunted by the desires in that hoax.

This is how it happened, not too long ago. I was a taxi-cab driver, cruising along. This man in a brown suit flagged me. He had a briefcase. The first thought that crossed my mind was that he was a Nigerian. Rich Nigerian. I had picked up several of them before. I stopped and he climbed in. I looked at him in the mirror. He looked respectable and had an air of charismatic indifference. Politician or businessman. He told me where to drop him and before we got there he decided to stop off at Marks & Spencer. He stayed there a long time. He was probably buying up the entire establishment. I had picked up a few of them and had been pretty shocked at the number of stereos, videos and boxes of cereal that they took back home. I waited for the man. Let it be known that I waited. Then I took one look at the briefcase and drove away angrily. When I discovered the quarter of a million pounds in it, the first thing I did was to dump the cab. I caught a plane to America, bummed around for a while, came back, and changed my colour. It seemed to me a simple matter. People have been executed for much less than leaving a quarter of a million pounds in a starving man's cab. People, in fact, should be hanged for carrying that kind of money around. What more could I do to help the starving, the miserable, the drought-ridden bastards of this world than to drive off with such money? That, however, is as far as my solution got. When I came back, and changed my colour, and saw all those stupid television news stories of the anguished Nigerian and the reward he was offering, I simply laughed my head off. I lugged the briefcase with me wherever I went. One day I found myself on a bridge over the Thames. Somehow I trapped myself into one of those moods when you think the whole ineluctable mystery of life is caught in the river's reflections. I saw this white boy on the water flowing beneath the bridge. There was a group of people on the shore; they were shouting. Perfect fool that I was – I allowed a feeling of chivalry to come over me: I jumped into the river. When I splashed into the water I suddenly realized that the briefcase was gone. The boy was nowhere in sight. I swam around and soon saw a body floating, its head beneath the water. I swam after it and several confused thrashings later, the water surging into my mouth, I brought him ashore. The boy was dead and already bloated. The people who were clamouring on the shore, I discovered, had nothing whatever to do with the body. Then I remembered the briefcase. Hungry, wet, haunted by the faces of the anguished Nigerian, I shouted: 'There is a quarter of a million pounds floating on the river.' Before I could dive back in to rescue the briefcase, the inevitable happened. The Thames soon swarmed with a quarter of a million pirates, rogues and hassled people who had long since had enough. They bobbed and kicked, a riot on the waters, for a leather briefcase that would open up a feverish haven of dreams and close up, for ever, the embattled roomful of desires. The police got into it and I slipped away, angry and frustrated and cheated of myself. I hope that they never recovered the money.

That was a dream that drowned.

What a shock it was, coming to myself, when plane trees grown from cement and when the seasons of the streets yielded a dream of wonder. I found a house. I had always wanted to own a house. I inspected it. Bats flew out of the windows. I went up the creaking stairs and peeked around the eerie rooms. There was excreta all over the place, but that was of no serious consequence. I lit a match and found one of the rooms more tolerable than the others. I sat down and took in the smells of rubble and suicides and the decaying of human structures. I looked outside the window and found that it was morning.

Acknowledgements

The editor and publishers wish to thank the following who have kindly given permission to print extracts and copyright material in this anthology:

J. G. BALLARD: 'First Impressions of London' from *A User's Guide to the Millennium* by J. G. Ballard, HarperCollins, 1996. © J. G. Ballard, 1993. Reproduced by permission of the author c/o Margaret Hanbury, 27 Walcot Square, London SE11 4UB.

JAMES BERRY: 'From Lucy: Englan' Lady' and 'From Lucy: Carnival Wedd'n', 1981' from *Lucy's Letters and Loving*, by James Berry, New Beacon Books Ltd, 1982.

WILLIAM BOYD: 'Fly Away Home' © William Boyd, 1997. Reproduced by permission of the author.

E. R. BRAITHWAITE: From *Choice of Straws* by E. R. Braithwaite, The Bodley Head, London, 1965. Reproduced by permission of Random House UK Ltd.

DAVID DABYDEEN: 'London Taxi Driver' from *Coolie Odyssey* by David Dabydeen, Hansib Publishing Ltd and Dangaroo Press, 1988. Reproduced by permission of Curtis Brown Ltd, London, on behalf of David Dabydeen.

ANITA DESAI: From *Bye-Bye Blackbird* by Anita Desai, Vision Books Private Ltd., 1985. © Anita Desai, 1985. Reproduced by permission of the author, c/o Rogers, Coleridge & White Ltd, London.

LAWRENCE DURRELL: From *Spirit of Place* by Lawrence Durrell, Faber and Faber Ltd, London, and E. P. Dutton & Co., Inc., 1969. Reproduced by permission of Curtis Brown Ltd., London, on behalf of The Estate of Lawrence Durrell. © The Estate of Lawrence Durrell, 1969.

T. S. ELIOT: Letter to Henry Eliot and letter to Eleanor Hinkley from
The Letters of T. S. Eliot 1898–1922, edited by Valerie Eliot, Faber and
Faber Ltd, 1988.

EVA FIGES: From *Little Eden: a Child at War* by Eva Figes, Persea
Books, 1978. © Eva Figes, 1978. Reproduced by permission of the
author c/o Rogers, Coleridge & White Ltd, London.

ROMESH GUNESEKERA: From *Reef* by Romesh Gunesekera, Granta
Books, London, 1994. © Romesh Gunesekera, 1994. US rights granted
by The New Press.

ABDULRAZAK GURNAH: From *Pilgrims Way* by Abdulrazak Gurnah,
Jonathan Cape, 1988. © Abdulrazak Gurnah, 1988. Reproduced by
permission of the author, c/o Rogers, Coleridge & White Ltd, London.

WILSON HARRIS: From *The Angel at the Gate* by Wilson Harris, Faber
and Faber Ltd, London, 1982. © Wilson Harris, 1982. Reproduced by
permission of Faber and Faber Ltd.

MICHAEL HOFMANN: 'The Machine that Cried' from *Acrimony* by
Michael Hofmann, Faber and Faber, London, 1986. Reproduced by
permission of the author.

CHRISTOPHER HOPE: From *Darkest England* by Christopher Hope,
Macmillan/Picador (UK) and W. W. Norton (USA), 1996.
© Christopher Hope, 1986. Reproduced by permission of the author,
c/o Rogers, Coleridge & White Ltd, London.

KAZUO ISHIGURO: From *Remains of the Day*, Faber and Faber Ltd,
1989. © Kazuo Ishiguro, 1989. Reprinted by permission of Alfred A.
Knopf Inc., Faber and Faber Ltd and Rogers, Coleridge & White Ltd,
London.

C. L. R. JAMES: 'Bloomsbury: An Encounter with Edith Sitwell' from
The C. L. R. James Reader, Blackwell Publishers, London, 1992. ©
C. L. R. James, 1992. Reproduced by permission of Curtis Brown
Group Ltd, London.

RUTH PRAWER JHABVALA: From *Three Continents* by Ruth Prawer
Jhabvala, William Morrow and Company, Inc., 1987. Reproduced by
permission of John Murray (Publishers) Ltd. and Harriet Wasserman
Literary Agency, Inc.

LINTON KWESI JOHNSON: 'Inglan is a bitch' from *Inglan Is a Bitch*,
Race Today Publications, 1980. Reproduced by permission of the author.

RUDYARD KIPLING: 'The English Flag' from *Rudyard Kipling's Verse: Definitive Edition*, 1885–1932, by Rudyard Kipling, Doubleday, Doran & Company (USA), 1934. Reproduced by permission of A. P. Watt Ltd. on behalf of The National Trust for Places of Historic Interest or National Beauty.

GEORGE LAMMING: From *The Emigrants* by George Lamming, Michael Joseph, London, 1954. Reproduced by permission of the author.

WYNDHAM LEWIS: From *The Letters of Wyndham Lewis*, Methuen & Co. Ltd, London, 1963. © Wyndham Lewis Memorial Trust, London, England, 1963.

DORIS LESSING: 'In Defence of the Underground' from *London Observed* by Doris Lessing, HarperCollins Publishers, 1992. © 1992, Doris Lessing. Reprinted by kind permission of Jonathan Clowes Ltd., London, on behalf of Doris Lessing.

PENELOPE LIVELY: From *Oleander, Jacaranda* by Penelope Lively, HarperCollins Publishers, 1994. © Penelope Lively, 1994. Reprinted by permission of HarperCollins Publishers, Inc. and Penguin Books Ltd.

TIMOTHY MO: From *Sour Sweet* by Timothy Mo, Vintage Books, 1985. Reproduced by permission of André Deutsch Ltd.

SHIVA NAIPAUL: From *Beyond the Dragon's Mouth* by Shiva Naipaul, Viking Penguin Inc., 1984. Reproduced by permission of Aitken & Stone Ltd.

V. S. NAIPAUL: From *The Enigma of Arrival* by V. S. Naipaul, Alfred A. Knopf, 1987. Reproduced by permission of Aitken & Stone Ltd.

BEN OKRI: 'Disparities' from *Incidents at the Shrine* by Ben Okri, Heinemann, London, 1986. Reproduced by permission of David Godwin Associates.

GEORGE ORWELL: From *Down and Out in Paris and London*, Harper & Brothers Publishers, 1933. © The Estate of the late Sonia Brownell Orwell and Martin Secker and Warburg Ltd. Excerpt from *Down and Out in Paris and London*, © George Orwell, 1933 and renewed 1961 by Sonia Pitt-Rivers, reprinted by permission of Harcourt Brace & Company.

PETER PORTER: 'An Ingrate's England' from *Possible Worlds* by Peter

Index